Pitt Latin American Series

Revolution and the Multiclass Coalition in Nicaragua

Mark Everingham

University of Pittsburgh Press

Pittsburgh and London

Published by the University of Pittsburgh Press, Pittsburgh, Pa. 15260
Copyright © 1996, University of Pittsburgh Press
All rights reserved
Manufactured in the United States of America
Printed on acid-free paper

Designed by Jane Tenenbaum

Library of Congress Cataloging-in-Publication Data
Everingham, Mark, 1962–
 Revolution and the multiclass coalition in Nicaragua / Mark Everingham.
   p.   cm. — (Pitt Latin American series)
 Includes bibliographical references and index.
 ISBN 0-8229-3933-9 (alk. paper). — ISBN 0-8229-5590-3 (pbk. : alk. paper)
 1. Nicaragua—Politics and government—1937–1979. 2. Nicaragua—Social conditions. 3. Nicaragua—Economic conditions—1918–1979. 4. Coalition governments—Nicaragua. 5. Elite (Social sciences)—Nicaragua. 6. Social classes—Nicaragua. I. Title. II. Series.
JL1616.E94   1996
320.97285'09'045—dc20   95-46278
                                                                CIP
A CIP catalogue record for this book is available from the British Library.
Eurospan, London

Go south to the place
where oceans close in tight;
When in the summertime
the sun parches by night;
Now less must be enough
for those who stayed behind;
Why have they come here?
where were they last year?
So much like before,
their lands burn once more.

M.E.

CONTENTS

	List of Tables and Figures	ix
	List of Acronyms	xi
	Acknowledgments	xv
1	Introduction: The Nicaraguan Revolution in Perspective	3
2	Theories of Revolution and Revolutionary Coalitions	14
3	Defining the Dynasty and Changing Elite Relations, 1950–1962	44
4	Business, Politics, and Agro-Industrialization, 1963–1972	59
5	Class Structure and Political Organization: Land, Labor, and Opposition	86
6	The Political Roots of Cross-Class Cooperation, 1973–1977	110
7	The Alliance of Convenience and Necessity, 1978–1980	138
8	Conclusions and Reflections	177
	Notes	191
	References	197
	Index	213

TABLES AND FIGURES

Tables

1	Bank Credit for Major Export Crops, 1953–1960	52
2	Loans from Development Institutions, 1961–1970	64
3	Share of Export Crop of Total Exports, 1960–1979 (Nicaragua)	66
4	Cotton Export Production, 1962–1970	67
5	The Beef Export Sector, 1950–1970	70
6	Share of Export Crop of Total Exports, 1960–1979 (El Salvador)	75
7	Rural Economic Change, 1960–1979	89
8	Land-Use Area, 1970	89
9	Cotton and Beef Exports, 1973–1978	121
10	Official Lending, 1973–1978	123

Figures

1	Nicaraguan Agricultural Exports and Related Industry	73
2	"Somoza Incorporated" (circa 1970)	81
3	Financial Portfolio of Banco de América (BANAMER)	82
4	Financial Portfolio of Banco Nicaragüense (BANIC)	84

LIST OF ACRONYMS

AID	Agency for International Development
ANC	Conservative National Action Party
ANDEN	National Association of Nicaraguan Educators
ANEP	National Association of Private Enterprise
APP	Area of People's Property
ASGANIC	Association of Nicaraguan Cattle Ranchers
ATC	Association of Rural Workers
BANAMER	Banco de América
BANIC	Banco Nicaragüense
BCN	Central Bank of Nicaragua
BND	National Development Bank
BNN	National Bank of Nicaragua
BPR	Popular Revolutionary Bloc
CABEI	Central American Bank of Economic Integration
CACM	Central American Common Market
CADIN	Chamber of Industry
CAPSA	Savings and Loan Corporation
CDS	Sandinista Defense Committees
CEB	Ecclesial Base Community
CGT	General Confederation of Workers
CGTi	Independent General Confederation of Workers
CONAL	National Cotton Commission of Nicaragua
COSEP	Superior Council of Private Enterprise
COSIP	Superior Council of Private Initiative
CST	Confederation of Sandinista Workers
CTN	Confederation of Nicaraguan Workers

LIST OF ACRONYMS

CUS	Council of Union Unity
CUTS	United Confederation of Salvadoran Workers
DFI	Direct Foreign Investment
ECLA	Economic Commission on Latin America
EDUCREDITO	Educational Credit System
EXIMBANK	Export-Import Bank
FAGANIC	Federation of Nicaraguan Cattle Ranchers
FALANGE	Armed Forces of National Liberation for the War of Extermination
FAO	Broad Opposition Front
FARO	Front of Agriculturalists of the Eastern Region
FAPU	United Popular Action Front
FECCAS	Christian Federation of Salvadoran Rural Workers
FER	Revolutionary Students Front
FETSALUD	Federation of Health Workers
FMLN	Farabundo Martí National Liberation Front
FPN	National Patriotic Front
FPL	Popular Forces of Liberation
FSLN	Sandinista National Liberation Front
FTM	Federation of Workers of Managua
FUNDE	Nicaraguan Development Foundation
GDP	gross domestic product
GPP	Prolonged Popular War
IAN	Nicaraguan Agricultural Institute
IBRD	International Bank of Reconstruction and Development
IDB	Inter-American Development Bank
IFAGAN	Institute of Cattle Development
IMF	International Monetary Fund
INCAE	Central American Institute of Business Administration
INDE	Nicaraguan Institute of Development
INFONAC	National Development Institute
ISA	Ingenio San Antonio
ISTA	Salvadoran Institute of Agrarian Transformation
JRN	Governing Junta of National Reconstruction
JS-19	Sandinista Youth Organization (19 July)
LAAD	Latin American Agribusiness Development Corporation

LIST OF ACRONYMS

MDN	Nicaraguan Democratic Movement
MIDINRA	Ministry of Agricultural Development and Agrarian Reform
MLC	Liberal Constitutionalist Movement
MNC	multinational corporation
MNR	National Revolutionary Movement
MPDC	Christian Democratic Popular Movement
MPU	United People's Movement
OAS	Organization of American States
ORDEN	National Democratic Organization
PADF	Pan-American Development Fund
PCN	National Conservative Party (Nicaragua)
PCN	National Conciliation Party (El Salvador)
PDC	Christian Democratic Party
PLI	Independent Liberal Party
PLN	National Liberal Party
PPSC	People's Social Christian Party
PSCN	Nicaraguan Social Christian Party
PSN	Nicaraguan Socialist Party
RN	National Resistance
SEAAS	Syndicate of Carpenters, Bricklayers, and Masons
SIECA	Secretariat of Central American Economic Integration
TP	Proletarian Tendency
UCA	University of Central America
UDEL	Democratic Union of Liberation
UDN	National Democratic Union
UNAM	National Autonomous University of Mexico
UNAN	National Autonomous University of Nicaragua
UNAP	National Union of Popular Action
UNE	Union of Nicaraguan Employees
UNO	National Opposition Union
UNOC	Union of Catholic Workers
UPANIC	Union of Nicaraguan Agricultural Producers
UTC	Union of Rural Workers

ACKNOWLEDGMENTS

I must first express my deepest gratitude to my mentor and friend, Cynthia McClintock, who supported my original research interest in the impetus behind revolutionary collective action in Latin America and the developing world. During my doctoral program at George Washington University, she encouraged me to challenge some of the conventional theoretical wisdom regarding the comparative study of revolution and demonstrated to me what being a first-rate scholar is all about. Her intellect and character inspire this book. In addition to Professor McClintock's guidance at George Washington, the perspectives of Harvey Feigenbaum and Peter Klarén on how societies develop and change required me to refine my thinking about Central America. William LeoGrande of the American University read the original manuscript and generously suggested inventive ways to improve its exposition.

The Organization of American States granted me a fellowship to conduct field research in Nicaragua and Central America in 1991 and 1992. Dr. Domingo Acevedo of the Inter-American Commission on Human Rights offered his invaluable assistance before, during, and after the fellowship period. Miriam Tunnerman of the OAS national office in Managua also deserves my sincere appreciation for her logistical support along the way. I could not have completed my work in Nicaragua without the help of Mary Lou González, Edgard Parrales, Roland Membreño, Francisco López, and María Aminta Díaz. They offered me their friendship and a profound understanding of Nicaraguan politics and society.

I also benefited from the advice of top scholars on the Central American crisis: Thomas Walker, Harvey Williams, and Rose Spalding provided critical feedback while I was developing the initial research plan in 1989 and 1990. Jeff Goodwin contributed his important critique of my theoretical argument during the review process by the University of Pittsburgh Press. His serious and constructive participation made a positive impact on the final version of the manuscript. Finally, I must thank Lilya Lorrin, formerly of the University of Pittsburgh Press, for her patience and good-natured demeanor during the review process, and Elizabeth Detwiler for copyediting and preparing my work for publication.

Revolution and the Multiclass Coalition in Nicaragua

1

Introduction: The Nicaraguan Revolution in Perspective

The Nicaraguan revolution was not peasant, proletarian, or bourgeois. People of almost every social stratum actively participated in the overthrow of the Somoza dictatorship by contributing his or her might, mind, or money to collective action. On 19 July 1979, it was difficult to find a citizen in the country who did not talk like a revolutionary and claim the vindication of national hero and martyr, Augusto César Sandino. Therefore, a clear understanding of the significance of the Nicaraguan experience partially rests on how and why disparate social groups formed a revolutionary alliance in the late 1970s. "The whole world was Sandinista"[1] when Anastasio Somoza Debayle fled his bunker after the National Guard disintegrated at the hands of the Sandinista National Liberation Front (FSLN). Yet, the euphoria of the victory of Sandinismo would prove incapable of reconciling severe contradictions between genuine social revolution and the expectations of elite groups with more limited views about the prospect of political change.

Deep-rooted social tensions were exacerbated once revolution occurred in Nicaragua. The elimination of the Somoza regime forced a sudden confrontation between political and economic elites and mobilized masses. But, the pervasive influence of a neopatrimonial dictatorship for more than forty years did not wholly determine the process and outcome of the revolutionary situation. In 1990, Nicaragua entered a period of new government in which political conflict and negotiation include some of the same Sandinistas and "progressive" elites who conspired against Somoza between 1977 and 1979. Reviving broad social cooperation will help

Nicaragua to achieve the common goals of sustained economic development and democracy over the long term.

The central question of this study is what characteristics of Nicaragua's political and economic development after World War II explain a revolutionary pattern featuring cross-class collective action. More specifically, how and why did some economic elites become collaborators with the Sandinistas in toppling the Somoza dynasty? A significant part of the theoretical literature has emphasized the crucial role of broad opposition coalitions in recent episodes of revolution in the developing world. By early 1979, students, urban industrial and rural agricultural workers, peasants, professionals, and some businessmen supported the FSLN. The fact that some leaders of elite political and economic organizations chose to align with a guerrilla movement has been a rare phenomenon. Wealth and radical intellectuals have been antagonistic forces in Latin America.

Therefore, special attention will be devoted to the origin and development of new capitalist interests in agriculture, industry, and commerce during the export-led industrialization between 1950 and 1970. The focus will be on the specific circumstances that gave rise to a large, but politically weak, business and professional community tied to export agriculture and the national banking system. Many exporters, industrialists, merchants, lawyers, economists, and engineers were the younger generations of old landed families from Granada or the Occident. Their livelihoods depended on new industrial, commercial, and financial opportunities inherent in the favorable investment climate cultivated by the Alliance for Progress and the Central American Common Market in the 1960s. This new layer of elites deferred to the Somozas' personal hand in the bureaucratic apparatus while benefiting from state economic policies. New sectors of the upper class did not become part of a power monopoly between the oligarchy, the military, and the bourgeoisie that can be found in other Latin American countries.

Elite alienation occurred simultaneously with mass mobilization as the national crisis mounted in the 1970s. There were sincere efforts on the part of some elites to solidify a centrist reform movement beginning in 1974. Businessmen and professionals did not protest the dictatorship for the same reasons as working-class groups. It is necessary to examine how economic and social development under dictatorial rule after 1950 affected overall class relations and political arrangements between elites inside and outside the Somocista machine. The impetus for a cross-class revolutionary alliance emerged from these circumstances.

The Analytical Frame of Inquiry

Several themes of the study of development recur in the detailed historical analysis of the Nicaraguan revolution in subsequent chapters. One is modernization. Under what conditions does rapid economic and social metamorphosis lead to political instability? When do fundamental structural changes, such as rural dislocation, urbanization, and industrialization, facilitate the onset of a revolutionary situation? The impact these phenomena have on the existing institutional structure underlies modernization theory. A basic assumption of this study is that the potential for revolutionary pressure in most developing societies can be traced to exclusionary forms of government. However, the failure of the "political system" to address demands for political participation explains little about how social alliances take shape.

Modernization in small agrarian societies has meant fundamental change in the countryside. The transformation of rural class relationships and the introduction of complex industrial processes were especially integral to Nicaragua's development after 1950. Access to land and sources of employment are often unavailable to the poor rural population in the transition to a more market-oriented economy. Then, is there a relationship between the degree of rural social inequality that results from the deepening of capitalist production and the potential for class-based revolution? Does the condition of the peasantry and rural labor affect the political disposition of elites toward revolutionary activity?

Recent comparative research has investigated how regime type and the nature of dictatorship affect patterns of revolution and when social groups may act collectively. Do the characteristics of certain regimes facilitate or militate against the formation of broad revolutionary coalitions? More specifically, can the presence or absence of a broad social alliance be accounted for by examining the strategies and policies of dictatorship? This question requires consideration of state autonomy and strength as independent variables. A prominent argument is that neopatrimonial dictatorships, like the Somoza dynasty, are more susceptible to elite desertion to a radical guerrilla vanguard than "impersonal" bureaucratic authoritarian regimes, like in El Salvador. In other words, the structure of authoritarian rule has influenced the path of social conflict and the potential for cross-class cooperation in Central America.

The last point calls for a discussion of the impact of class structures and elite interests and capacities on coalition-building. The "social-structural" method of analysis that links the behavior of social groups to their relative positions in the political and economic order, and to the historical development of the class configuration around the state, is useful here. This study will examine the organization and exercise of political power in Nicaragua after 1950. The Somoza regime served to reconcile competing elite factions of the upper social strata while dominating institutions that governed agro-industrialization. A clear understanding of institutionalized class relations is essential to explain the origins of political instability. Class conflict is often a central feature of revolutionary situations. However, a coalition between economic elites and a guerrilla movement, acting on behalf of the poor, indicates that revolutionary patterns are not always completely defined by interclass hostilities.

The upper class can consist of more than one unified exploitive core of capitalists acting solely against workers and peasants. Competition among capital fragments accounts for pressure from within the upper class to change relations of production. Wealthy sectors have encouraged popular uprisings to gain political power and reshape the economic order to favor their capitalist enterprises. However, the willingness of landowners, businessmen, and professionals to participate in revolution is not always determined by economic interests alone. When do elite groups mobilize not to change relations of production, but rather only to seize power from those who rule the state? Conflict in the upper class can be the result of a disruption of political arrangements among elites supporting and influencing the existing regime.

Clearly, economic elites share the objective of extracting resources from the producing classes and often converge politically to maintain control over the means of production. A deterioration of elite relations can ensue from disputes over the allocation of resources and control of decision-making processes rather than from contradictions between parochial economic interests. Analyses of revolution in the Third World have emphasized elite relations on the national level rather than just conflict between exploiters and the exploited to explain processes of change. When elite groups try and fail to alter the political and social landscape peacefully, they may seek accommodation with a coherent popular revolutionary movement. Then, one task is to identify elite segments of the capitalist class in Nicaragua and evaluate their political relationships with each other and their relative influence over the state. The existence of multiple elite groups with unequal levels of discretionary power implies the potential for elite rivalry. The main contention of this study is that emphases on structural change, regime type, and class relations must be enhanced by a theory of elite conflict to comprehend fully the advent of a broad alliance that includes landowners and entrepreneurs.

Another variable that has not received enough attention is the ideological flexibility of revolutionaries and elites in times of crisis. Especially when open civil war is imminent, insurrectionary momentum can lead to the gravitation of the rich to the radical. Cross-class cooperation rests on deliberate efforts by alienated elites and guerrillas to cultivate mutual trust and establish communication between interests which would find little common ground under peaceful or less threatening political conditions. Thus, it is important to explore the development of coordination between elites and revolutionaries and to examine their respective organizational capacities up to the fall of the old regime and during the immediate aftermath.

From the Countryside to the City: Structure and Methods

Comparative studies have addressed no less than the origins, process, and outcomes of social revolutions. Nicaragua has received substantial attention for over a decade. It is one of the few cases where economic elites have directly financed successful armed revolt. A widely accepted explanation for broad revolutionary alliances in the developing world is that economic and social modernization without concomitant institutionalization breeds the conditions for collective action. The participation of sectors of the business community in revolution has been linked to the behavior of a corrupt and greedy autocrat who eventually renders the institutional structure of his patrimonial fiefdom brittle and unreformable. It is argued that, once these circumstances arise, cooperation between politically marginal elites and a radical movement is forthcoming.[2]

The threat of revolution in other Central American countries preoccupied regional and international observers when Nicaragua "fell" in 1979. El Salvador developed similarly to Nicaragua based on export agriculture after World War II and entered into national crisis about when revolution occurred in Nicaragua. But, there was never an alliance between the Farabundo Martí National Liberation Front (FMLN) and Salvadoran economic elites during the protracted civil war that ended in 1991. As will be discussed in subsequent chapters, the lack of a repugnant dictator with a reputation for personal enrichment in El Salvador, at first glance, seems to account for divergent patterns of political conflict. However, an approach that goes beyond "regime type" and state structures is required to explain why some Nicaraguan capitalists joined forces with the FSLN while the Salvadoran oligarchy remained unified and fiercely opposed the FMLN.

Special attention will be devoted to how differences in upper-class structure and elite relations affected the trajectory of revolutionary situations in Nicaragua and El Salvador. This analytical strategy follows the "Method of Difference" used by Moore (1966) and Skocpol (1979) in their comparative historical studies of political change and revolution in Europe and Asia. At convenient points, this study will "contrast the case in which the phenomenon to be explained and the hypothesized causes are present to other cases in which the phenomenon and the causes are absent, but are otherwise as similar as possible to the positive case" (Skocpol 1979, 36). Equal time will not be devoted to El Salvador. The "negative" case will be invoked to illuminate the structural features of the Nicaraguan upper class and corresponding elite relations that led to cooperation between capitalists and the FSLN, instead of a clash between an intransigent landed class and guerrillas acting on behalf of the peasantry, as in the case of El Salvador.

Much of the analysis of Nicaragua's unique revolutionary experience is drawn from a set of lengthy interviews with elites who held, or continue to hold, positions in governmental, political, economic, and professional organizations. The interview data focus on responses from "marginal" or "peripheral" elites who were subordinate to, and generally supportive of, the Somoza dictatorship until the early 1970s. Most elite respondents backed the centrist reform movement led by Pedro Joaquín Chamorro and several prominent businessmen at that time. They were not necessarily chosen based on their economic orientations in the "oligarchy," "bourgeoisie," or "business class." Care was taken to question a diverse lot of elites who publicly opposed the regime, but maintained varying attitudes about cooperating with the FSLN.

An attempt was made to interview former representatives of agricultural, industrial, commercial, and financial organizations that existed before the revolution, and current officials of business associations that remained intact after 1979. Given the fact that many Nicaraguan businessmen and professionals had, and to some extent still have, interests in several economic sectors, it was difficult to identify clearly defined "capital fragments." Therefore, the respondents did not necessarily represent "segments of the bourgeoisie." The sample concentrates on economic elites who were making political decisions on behalf of private enterprise, though not always with the full endorsement of all businessmen, as the revolutionary situation gained momentum.

Questions were designed to allow the interviewee to give an oral history of his particular role in the opposition to the dictatorship, why the reformist opposition failed to achieve peaceful political change, and whether and how he assisted the FSLN in the late 1970s. Specific questions about family background, property and investments, and opinions about democracy, capitalism, socialism, inequality, and social revolution were posed. Elites' accounts were complemented by the perspectives of Sandinista commanders and militants who recruited elite collaborators. These interviews were devoted mostly to inquiries about why and when elements of the FSLN deemed it necessary to pursue businessmen and professionals. The responses of individuals who served as liaisons between the FSLN and the business community were especially useful.

The respondents did not request anonymity, though a few personal questions were answered only partially or not at all, in some instances. The interviews usually took the form of a recorded conversation guided by a prepared outline on which marginal notes were made. In cases where interviews could not be obtained either with elites or Sandinistas, newspaper and journal articles, public statements, declarations, and autobiographical material published or recorded from the 1960s to the 1990s were substituted.[3]

Chapters 3 and 4 traverse the development of new state structures and elite relations in Nicaragua after 1950. The intertwining of the Somocista bureaucracy and the business community will be discussed in the context of the expansion of export agriculture and the creation of related industrial and commercial enterprises. Business and politics in elite circles were influenced heavily by the flow of abundant official and private foreign capital to the state banking system and the private sector. The potential for elite conflict increased as peripheral elite groups assumed new economic roles and came to depend more on Somoza-controlled institutions after 1950. Yet, mobilization of business interests against the dynasty did not occur until the 1970s. Sources for both chapters are: studies of Nicaragua's political and economic history conducted primarily by Nicaraguan and North American scholars; interviews with elite political and economic actors involved in modernizing the state financial system and creating independent enterprises and business organizations in the 1950s and 1960s; statistical abstracts compiled by international development banks and the Central Bank of Nicaragua; and primary documentation of political events in the 1950s and 1960s.

Chapter 5 details demographic and social trends in the countryside and the rise of urban middle sectors in the 1950s and 1960s. The overriding theme is how rapid economic and social change occurred without political development. The disruption of rural communities and migration to urban centers were permanent conditions by the early 1960s. The FSLN recruited peasants and rural labor but was unable to establish an effective peasant-intellectual alliance reminiscent of the Russian, Chinese, or Mexican experiences. In El Salvador, the guerrilla movement relied on rural support to expand its armies and sustain its survival. The available data on land distribution over time and the literature on "what makes peasants rebel" will be evaluated in light of Nicaragua's departure from previous patterns of rural conflict.

In Nicaragua, dislocation in the countryside, combined with a high urban growth rate, created intense social pressures after 1960. Urbanization generated greater demands on the Somoza regime for housing, health, and education and created larger domestic consumer markets. Data from international development banks and Nicaraguan research institutions will provide a clear picture of how the expansion of export agriculture and industrialization offered few sources of employment while labor achieved little political organization due to state repression. In the late 1960s and early 1970s, mainstream political parties withered as Anastasio Somoza Debayle coopted his traditional opponents. The conditions for revolution matured as middle and lower classes suffered adverse economic and social effects during agro-export growth under the control of the Somoza family. Although still an immature movement, the Sandinistas began to establish a network of barrio dwellers, university students, and urban workers. At the same time, capitalists not directly linked to the Somoza clique consolidated their control over many industrial, commercial, and financial enterprises.

A similar process of urbanization and industrialization occurred in El Salvador, but under different political circumstances. Guerrilla organizations had not formed by the late 1960s and early 1970s. Centrist and rightist parties were expanding their following among the middle classes. Meanwhile, the Salvadoran oligarchy absorbed new industrial and commercial opportunities, negating the rise of independent capitalist groups. The formation of a center-left urban-based alliance against the regime of General Carlos Humberto Romero in the late 1970s, and the subsequent military coup in 1979, profoundly affected the trajectory of political conflict and the potential for revolution in El Salvador in the 1980s.

Chapter 6 will shift the focus from economic and social change to specific political antecedents that made a revolutionary alliance possible in Nicaragua. The time frame encompasses the earthquake of 1972 to the beginning of the revolutionary situation at the end of 1977. During this period, opposition to the dictatorship was concentrated in a predominantly urban, middle-class movement. The FSLN, elite political parties, and some businessmen competed for the loyalty of mobilized workers, students, professionals, and small merchants. This led to a confrontation between the Sandinistas and elites, who had withdrawn their support for the dictatorship and were advocating Western liberal reform. The guerrilla movement would eclipse the reformist one, leading to cross-class cooperation later in the decade. It was not the existence of dictatorship per se, but rather the ineffective political responses of mobilized elite groups to the Somoza clique's behavior from the early 1970s that allowed the Sandinistas time to forge ties with wealthy dissidents. This chapter relies on interviews with businessmen, professionals, and political leaders who organized the civilian opposition, and interviews with Sandinistas who recruited wealthy supporters. Also, a content analysis of the newspaper *La Prensa* and the "political diary" of Pedro Joaquín Chamorro clarify the effectiveness of the mainstream opposition movement in the mid-1970s. Data from the Central Bank and private-sector organizations, interviews with businessmen, and studies by Nicaraguan academics offer a gauge on business confidence as the national crisis worsened and illuminate whether economic concerns drove businessmen to the violent option.

Chapter 7 is devoted entirely to the specific events and circumstances that culminated in coordinated action between economic elites and the FSLN during the "final offensive" from May to July 1979. A clear understanding of this phenomenon requires an analysis of the political incapacity of organized elites to reform or remove the dictatorship during 1978 and early 1979. The reflections of key figures from the moderate opposition explain when and why elite groups perceived a need for complete political change in order to gain greater control over policy making. Extensive oral history reconstructs the strategies and process by which some businessmen and elite party leaders attempted to increase their political legitimacy within middle and lower sectors. The interviews reveal a general desire for more democratic electoral procedures, respect for individual liberties, and allowing the economy to respond to free-market forces instead of directives from the state. Primary material from business associations and background from *La Prensa* further account for elite political behavior as the Sandinista insurrection became imminent.

Interviews and documents on the Sandinista perspective complete the picture of the nature of political relationships between the Tercerista guerrilla faction and its elite sympathizers in 1978 and 1979. The Terceristas' shrewd tactics and capacity to rally support for armed attacks established tremendous momentum behind the revolution while peaceful efforts toward political change foundered. The Terceristas carefully identified some wealthy individuals they considered favorably disposed to revolution rather than distinct capital fragments eager to rid themselves of contradictions with Somoza. Other elites participated in the revolutionary process because they could not galvanize middle- and lower-class support for a liberal socioeconomic agenda and forge unity within their own organizations around a coherent strategy of political action.

Once the Somoza government was removed, many elite political and economic groups balked at genuine social revolution. Disagreements over the structure of government and the purpose of economic activity led to a rupture of the revolutionary junta within a year. The immediate postinsurrectionary period is characterized by a disparity of goals among components of any broad-based coalition that has just toppled the old regime. The Sandinistas dominated postinsurrectionary politics on behalf of the poor and unrepresented, despite objections from the business community. Elites who remained in the country and attempted to influence the reconstruction of the state were unprepared to defend their interests against the FSLN. Though the initial revolutionary government envisioned an active role for the private sector in rebuilding the economy, business leaders in the Council of State lacked reliable constituencies, particularly in the labor force, that eluded them during unprecedented mass mobilization in the 1970s.

Understanding the politics of the Nicaraguan revolution is the main objective of this study. Theoretical analyses of modernization, the peasant condition, inter- and intraclass conflict, and state structures do not offer enough toward this end. An examination of the elite power structure in Nicaragua after 1950 will shed light on the causes of elite conflict and the effectiveness of elite political strategies for change. Elites do not cooperate with revolutionaries because they perceive a common enemy. Cross-class revolutionary alliances are inspired by the politics of mass mobilization, the organization of civilian opposition, and the onset of civil war.

2

Theories of Revolution and Revolutionary Coalitions

[The] historical roots of a given phenomenon reach very far back into the past. That, of course, is true as a general proposition and is the basic justification of all historical work. Yet, it says little about the actual course of historical processes, in particular whether such a course is revolutionary or evolutionary.
—*Alexander Gerschenkron*

One could argue that the Latin American revolution began when Hernando Cortés landed in the Americas.
—*Richard Millett*

This chapter will place the pattern of the Nicaraguan revolution in theoretical and comparative perspective. The main objectives are to evaluate several theoretical approaches to the study of development and identify variables that best explain the advent of the broad-based coalition of incompatible partners that toppled the Somoza dictatorship in 1979. The general effects of structural economic and social change, regime type, class relations, and elite conflict on the trajectory of revolutionary situations will be considered. Those cases that culminate in cooperation between elite groups and a guerrilla vanguard are rare and deserve special attention. Recent episodes of "successful" revolution in the Third World have featured cross-class action against the prevailing order (Goldstone et al. 1991). This pattern contrasts sharply with other "failures," such as El Salvador, where a class war over the struggle for land engulfed the country during the 1980s. The theoretical focus is fixed primarily on the political behavior of economic elites during the national crisis and the onset of armed insurrection. But, the scope of the analysis will encompass a broad range of conditions that generate political mobilization against despotic rule at nearly every social level.

A vast amount of comparative research has concentrated on political relationships between mobilized social groups and authoritarian regimes, class conflict, state crisis, and elite alienation in the process and outcome of revolutions. Though all of these variables are important, they have not been utilized adequately to explain how and why landowners, businessmen, and professionals would become partners with a revolutionary vanguard to overthrow a regime from which they have benefited.

Modernization, Mobilization, and the Political System

Modernization theory emerged in the 1950s and 1960s as a response to questions concerned with capitalist economies at various stages of industrialization. A central assumption is that economic development follows a linear path from backwardness to modernity (Rostow 1960). Based essentially on the British and North American experiences, modernizationists indicated a positive correlation between increasing industrial vitality and pluralist, competitive political systems. That is, the consolidation of democracy is facilitated by implementing more complex forms of production and by achieving higher rates of economic growth.

Long after winning independence from colonial rule in the nineteenth and twentieth centuries, many countries in Latin America, Asia, and Africa lacked a sophisticated set of institutions capable of reconciling economic growth and greater social complexity. The gap between political modernity and traditional forms of authoritarian rule preoccupied social scientists who examined developing areas from the modernizationist viewpoint (Almond and Coleman 1960). The term "civic" was coined to define democratic forms of political institutions and political culture characteristic of Anglo-Saxon political systems. These served as models for less advanced societies aspiring to the modern world (Almond and Verba 1963).

In his study of elites in Latin America, Lipset (1967) emphasized the key role of values to sustain modernization. He argued that, through exposure to Western liberal education, businessmen could develop strong entrepreneurial habits and generate greater prosperity and social equality. Old attitudes about business relationships and antiquated economic institutions were stifling the capitalist impulse and democracy in Latin America. Johnson (1958), however, placed the burden of modernity on the shoulders of the "middle sectors." He asserted that the proliferation of urban labor and professional groups in South America in the first half of the twentieth century reflected progress toward democratic society. The increasing availability of public education and channels of political articulation for the middle class made it "an aggressive political force." Yet, linkages between political parties and labor unions of the center-left and government took on a populist nature. State intervention in politics and the economy militated against laissez-faire doctrine.

Hopes for democratic consolidation and further industrial growth ran high in Latin America at the beginning of the 1960s. Modernization theory was the intellectual inspiration behind the Kennedy administration's policies toward the region. Prominent Latin Americanists at the time insisted that the massive financial and technical assistance program would "tip domestic political scales in favor of modernizing groups" and strengthen democratic institutions (Valenzuela and Valenzuela 1978, 542). The Alliance for Progress generated unprecedented rates of economic growth and urbanization and more social mobility. Yet, between 1964 and the mid-1970s, several South American countries experienced military coups d'état. In most cases, oligarchies, the church, and the armed forces acted to protect traditional power structures and contain mass political mobilization encouraged by popularly elected civilian governments (see Remmer 1989, chap. 1).

In this same period, industrialization and social mobilization in Central America proceeded under control of established authoritarian regimes, except in Costa Rica. Generally, the five republics achieved less economic and social diversity than most South American countries in the first half of the twentieth century, and populations remained predominantly rural until the 1950s. Dictatorships presided over the fusion of greater agro-export production and new import-substitution industries in the haven of the Central American Common Market for the next two decades (Bulmer-Thomas 1987). The quest for higher production, greater international trade, and access to modern technology launched rapid and comprehensive demographic shifts and modifications in class relationships. These trends led to an intense clash between dictatorial rule and new social imperatives.

Interpretations of political underdevelopment in Latin America have focused on the incompatibility of the corporatist values imbedded in Latin American society with Western ideas and procedures. Wiarda (1982) asserts that the Iberian heritage bound Latin America to a "distinct tradition" from northern European and North American development. Other scholars concluded that the goals of the Alliance for Progress were simply unrealistic: "In developing countries . . . the increasingly ineffective and unpopular traditional authorities cannot be replaced by the institutions of eighteenth and nineteenth century liberalism and laissez-faire" (Deutsch 1971, 391). The incongruence between rapid modernization and exclusionary rule in Central America contributed mightily to protracted political violence in the region through the 1980s. Remmer, in her study of military rule in Latin America, focuses on the relationship between socioeconomic change and "forms of political domination" as a key to explaining political outcomes:

> Composed primarily of countries dependent on export-oriented agriculture with high levels of social inequality, limited industrial development, and literacy and urbanization levels that do not begin to approach those [in South America], Central America has been enmeshed in a cycle of reformist pressure and repressive response that has discredited moderates, radicalized popular-sector forces, and created a political dynamic highly unfavorable to inclusionary rule. (1989, 17)

Though Remmer is referring specifically to the influence of the military in El Salvador and Guatemala in the 1980s, this scenario applies to dictatorship in Nicaragua in the 1960s and 1970s.

Huntington (1968) asserted that economic modernization and social mobilization could lead to political instability. Increasing demands for political participation without sufficiently adaptable, complex, autonomous, and coherent institutions was a recipe for revolution.

> Like other forms of violence and instability, revolution is most likely to occur in societies which have experienced some social and economic mod-

ernization and political development, and where the processes of political modernization and political development have lagged behind the process of social and economic change. (Huntington 1968, 265)

Huntington indicated three regime types particularly vulnerable to revolutionary pressure: traditional monarchies (France, Russia, and China); narrowly based military dictatorships (Mexico, Bolivia, and Cuba);[1] and colonial states (Vietnam, Algeria). Revolution occurred in these cases because "the political system demonstrated little capacity to provide channels of participation of new groups into politics" (1968, 275). The basic principles of functionalist and systems theory are clearly at work here. The inability of the regime to perform the functions of political aggregation, integration, and articulation signifies the absence of an adequate institutional structure (Powell 1982). If the structures do not exist, then the system cannot process demands (inputs) and generate policies (outputs) efficiently to legitimize itself with the citizenry (Easton 1965).

Given this situation, Huntington envisioned the formation of alliances between social groups for the purpose of fundamental change. But, he explains group behavior strictly in terms of the degree to which the regime loses its capacity to maintain the support of the population. "Revolution involves the alienation of many groups from the existing order. It is the product of 'multiple dysfunction' in society" (Huntington 1968, 277). Thus, the collapse of the old regime is a prerequisite for mass mobilization and revolutionary coalitions.

The modernization-breeds-revolution approach associates the wellspring of revolution too closely with the internal workings of institutions (Davidheiser 1992, 472). It neglects how human actions influence various kinds of political change. Olson attributes collective action and revolution to individual perceptions of a changing economic and social environment. Violence is not a product of an inefficient political system, but of intolerable levels of stress due to social dislocation. "It is not those who are accustomed to poverty, but those whose place in the social order is changing, who resort to revolution" (Olson 1963, 531–32).

Olson infers a process of modernization by asserting that individuals are often "left in places in the economic order that are incompatible with their positions in the old order and political hierarchy" (1963, 533). This no-

THEORIES OF REVOLUTION AND REVOLUTIONARY COALITIONS

tion coincides with Gurr's (1970) analysis of how changing conditions can give rise to a disparity between "value expectations" and "value capabilities." The perception that one is receiving fewer resources than he or she deserves fosters a sense of "relative deprivation." Both Gurr and Olson conclude that the impetus for collective action lies in the unreasoned decisions of individuals whose lives have been altered. "Unless there is coercion or some other special device to make individuals act in their common interest, rational, self-interested individuals will not act to achieve their common or group interest" (Olson 1965, 2).

Therefore, irrationality leads human beings to act on behalf of others. Only extraordinary psychological pressures would draw individuals into a broad alliance, seeking collective goals and not just immediate personal gain. Olson and Gurr discount the possibility collective action can emerge from the sober and deliberate efforts of social groups in the pursuit of clearly defined interests. Political contention cannot be reduced to emotional reaction to misery or disequilibrium; it is part of the interaction of group interests engaged in the political process. Revolutionary coalitions are not merely a convergence of disparate manifestations of irrational human behavior (Tilly and Tilly 1981).

> Rational choice theory cannot account for ways group solidarities, moral commitment to the collectivity, and other nonrational values may mobilize people to act independently of individual self-interest. What is rational for the individual is not always consistent with the politically or culturally inspired choices of groups. (Eckstein 1989, 4)

The question remains as to how broad revolutionary coalitions take shape and expand through cooperation between social groups. Like Huntington, Tilly (1973) discussed modernization in terms of state capacity to manage changing social conditions and rising political demands. But, he steers away from viewing revolution as a phenomenon that occurs simply because the regime reaches its limits of control and legitimacy. He stops short of predicting revolution based on the failings of the political system: "To the extent that one judges [institutional] adaptability, complexity, autonomy, and coherence on the basis of the absence or containment of domestic violence and instability, the circle of truth by definition will close"

(1973, 431). Structural changes like population growth, industrialization, and urbanization can influence "agents," i.e., individuals and groups, to act collectively and frame their political choices (Berejikian 1992). But, the pressures of "modernization" on the state and society do not determine how and when revolution will be "successful." As Tilly insists, the formation of a genuine revolutionary coalition depends more on how social groups mobilize and organize resources against the prevailing order (1973, 447).

Tilly introduced the concept of "multiple sovereignty" as the main feature of a revolutionary situation. Multiple sovereignty occurs when "contenders" for power appear advancing exclusive political and economic claims against the government; when a significant number of people commit to those claims; and when the regime is incapable or unwilling to address or suppress claims being made against it (1978, 200). The contenders may be "polity members," including elites who intend to assume power without destroying basic economic and social institutions, and "challengers," who desire a complete break with old structures. Most importantly, Tilly located the origin of revolutionary alliances in the deliberate actions of social groups that consciously challenge the sovereignty of government.

> In a great many situations a single contender does not have enough resources to influence government by itself. A coalition with another contender which has overlapping and complementary designs on the government will then increase the joint power of the contenders to accomplish these designs. (Tilly 1978, 126)

A coalition is the result of negotiations and exchanges between mobilized groups that find it impossible to eliminate the regime without explicit cooperation. The relative organizational strength and capacity for leadership among challengers and polity members determine which interests dominate the coalition and shape the path of change. Class dynamics are inherent in Tilly's (1978) theoretical references to "designs" and interests. Elsewhere, he has analyzed collective action in terms of "people who occupy similar positions with respect to the means of production [pitted] against others who occupy different positions" (Tilly and Tilly 1981, 17). Severe class conflict may militate against the convergence of diverse interests in a revolutionary coalition. Cooperation between the rich and the poor in the developing world may be deterred by interclass grievances especially over the ownership and use of land.

Beyond Class Conflict: Peasants and Guerrillas

Latin American revolutionaries have tried invariably to cultivate seeds of discontent among small farmers and field workers. Yet, recent revolutionary coalitions in developing countries have extended beyond the classic peasant-intellectual combination. The condition of the peasantry has occupied center stage in the theoretical literature on the causes of political violence and revolution. Whether one is interested in the transition from feudalism to capitalism in large European and Asian societies, or the effects of global economic trends on small emerging states in the twentieth century, the role of peasants has been crucial in the process of political change. Social upheaval in Central America in the 1970s and 1980s has been firmly tied to how the spread of export agriculture restricted access to land for food production (Brockett 1990; Williams 1986). Therefore, this section will examine if and how the rural class relationships influence patterns of revolution.

Several scholars have argued that certain kinds of rural inhabitants are the arbiters of revolution. Scott (1976, 1977) offered insight into how small farmers producing for subsistence experience insecurity in the transition to a market economy. According to Scott, the spread of the capitalist mode of production endangers traditional peasant culture, i.e., property rights, religion, and family.

> The social values of the peasantry [that] are precapitalist may give its rebelliousness a quality of tenacity and moral cohesion in the sense that the struggle to restore or defend customary rights [to resources] may evoke a more passionate commitment [to rebellion]. (Scott 1977, 271)

On the other hand, peasants who abandon the village and migrate to urban areas have few opportunities for solidarity as they confront unemployment and resort to informal economic activity.

When peasants move to the city they are demobilized as they lose much of the traditional structure of action. . . . [Migrant workers and day laborers are] less culturally cohesive and hence less resistant to hegemony [imposed by the dominant class]. (Ibid., 289)

Wolf (1969) evaluated the "tactical mobility" of the peasantry based on relationships with landlords and the degree to which the state exercises control in rural areas. "The decisive factor in making peasant rebellion possible lies in the relation of the peasantry to the field of power which surrounds it" (1969, 290). He placed more emphasis on social-structural features of class relations and rural communities than on peasants' desire to protect their culture in explaining revolution. Yet, like Scott, he argued that landless laborers are unlikely leaders of rural opposition and precapitalist small farmers hold the key to revolt. Both saw the causes of rural tension in the process of capitalist expansion that threatens the stability of the "moral economy."

Popkin (1979) challenged the notion that peasants will respond violently to the penetration of capitalism. The conversion of land to commercial purposes was not, by definition, the catalyst of revolution.

Commercialization of agriculture and the development of strong central authorities are not wholly deleterious to peasants, although they may dramatically alter peasant society. This is not because capitalism [is] more benevolent than moral economists assume, but because traditional institutions are harsher and work less well than they believe. (1979, 79)

In other words, the rise of the capitalist institutions in the countryside may benefit peasants who have been exploited by landlords in the feudal order. Capitalism may offer small producers the opportunity to develop independent means of survival depending on their access to credit, primary materials, and markets.

It is difficult to identify the precise historical juncture at which a traditional society begins to develop capitalist habits. The expansion of coffee production for export in the second half of the nineteenth century is generally considered a clear break from a semifeudal economy in Central America (Woodward 1985). Coffee, cotton, sugar, banana, and beef exports integrated the Central American states fully into international markets in the twentieth century. Paige (1975) focused specifically on small agro-export economies consisting of large plantation owners relying on landless wage laborers. He found this class relationship politically unstable. Cultivation for export tends to depress wages and require capital-intensive technology to compete on a global level.

> A typical form of social movement in systems dependent on landed property and wage labor is revolutionary. Such movements involve . . . violent conflict over landed property and direct attack on the rural stratification system. . . . long guerrilla wars are the likely result. (Paige 1975, 58)

As is shown in chapter 5, the expansion of export agriculture in Central America between 1950 and 1970 accelerated the dislocation of the peasantry and urban migration, and created an artificial scarcity of land for food production. Conflict over rights to land intensified in this period. In Nicaragua and El Salvador, we can confirm the existence of severe threats to peasants' entire mode of life, the deterioration of subsistence production under the impact of commercial agriculture, and the formation of a large landless labor force. Despite eventual success in rallying rural support for the revolution, the Sandinistas were not swept into power by widespread uprisings by peasants or rural labor; they sought urban elite and middle-class partners. In El Salvador, the guerrillas established military strongholds in the countryside and refused to court elites. But, they were not able to overthrow the alliance of the oligarchy and the military.

Midlarsky and Roberts (1985) and Midlarsky (1988) have attempted to establish a theoretical link between the availability and use of land and patterns of revolutionary conflict in El Salvador and Nicaragua. They assert that relatively more severe scarcity and unequal distribution of land in El Salvador encouraged a class-oriented war. At the same time, they suggest that less urgent agrarian conditions in Nicaragua allowed for broader social cooperation. Nevertheless, rural class tension ran high in both cases due to the effects of export agriculture on the poor rural population after 1950, as we shall see in chapter 5.

Here, we turn to deliberate efforts by revolutionary movements to penetrate rural communities and mobilize popular support for insurrection. Recent studies on Latin America have focused on the political context in which guerrillas have launched attacks on the state. Wickham-Crowley (1989b) compares the strategies of "winners" and "losers." He claims that revolutionary organizations that forged linkages between the city and the countryside were able to coordinate rural warfare and urban insurrection on the road to victory. In Cuba and Nicaragua, according to Wickham-Crowley, the dictatorship failed to commit sufficient resources to defeating guerrillas, thus allowing them time and space to delegitimize the prevailing political order in rural and urban areas. Therefore, the participation of landed and capitalist groups in the Cuban and Nicaraguan revolutions was the result of the old regimes' inadequate response to the guerrilla movement.

McClintock (1984, 1989) has argued that revolutionaries can emerge from within rural communities and develop strategies to politicize issues of distribution. The ineffective policies of the state to alleviate abject poverty in the countryside tend to encourage and sustain strong ties between peasants and revolutionaries. Sendero Luminoso has targeted urban areas, but has never attempted to recruit wealthy sectors. Clearly, Peru's potential revolutionary situation precludes cooperation between landed elites and the Senderistas. The revolutionary fervor of peasants in Peru is propelled by Maoist influences similar to those found by Migdal (1974) in his study of Southeast Asia. Migdal concluded that armed radicals entered villages from urban areas in Vietnam. The intellectual disposition and ideological conviction of the guerrilla leadership are critical factors in the trajectory of revolution.

The convergence of poor peasants and guerrilla movements is not always immediately forthcoming when agrarian conditions deteriorate. This certainly holds true for Nicaragua and El Salvador. Brockett's studies of Central America (1989, 1990, 1992) emphasize the "temporal dimension" to account for the patterns of political violence. He astutely shows that rural inequality has not always meant that peasants have been prepared to rebel. He asks: "Do changes in the level of rural discontent resulting from growing inequality promptly cause corresponding changes in the level of mobilization and/or violence?" (1992, 173). Timing is crucial for guerrilla movements that covet the dispossessed and disenfranchised in the countryside.

The struggle over land has played an important role in protracted political conflict in Central America. Large landowners and other capitalist interests perpetuated the commitment of the best land to export agriculture while national crises festered in the region. Constant state repression certainly represented export producers' fears of land invasions (Williams 1986). As Moore states, "One cannot understand [peasant revolt] without reference to the actions of the upper classes that in large measure provoked it" (1966, 457). But, the grievances of peasants and guerrillas' ability to forge vast political and military networks offer limited value for understanding the behavior of economic elites during a revolutionary situation.

Reverting to the State: Regime Type and Coalitions

Research in comparative politics has brought back the concept of state autonomy in the spirit of Weber's (1964) theory that bureaucratic functions are performed independently of parochial interests. The state is defined not as an arena only for the interaction of class interests, but rather a set of institutions, separate from societal forces, governed by bureaucrats with "modern loyalty . . . to a superior authority" (1964, 197). Recent theoretical studies have emphasized the state's role in setting priorities for the use of resources. "Autonomous state activity . . . can never really be 'disinterested' in any meaningful sense. . . . Autonomous state actions will regularly take forms that attempt to reinforce the authority, political longevity, and social control of the state organizations" (Evans et al. 1985, 15). Thus, the nature and actions of the state are considered to be the independent variables that account for politics and political change.

This conception of the state has affected the theoretical literature on revolution. Skocpol's (1979) study of France, Russia, and China elevated the variables of state strength and autonomy to prominence. She argues that revolution was possible in these cases because the old regime lost the capacity to manage external military and economic pressures. Greater exposure to international exigencies led to political and fiscal crises for traditional monarchies which facilitated the rise of a revolutionary situation. The imperatives of confronting economic competition and waging war forced the state to extract more resources from dominant and subordinate classes to maintain fiscal equilibrium and political stability. The state's pursuit of autonomous interests led to contradictions with elites. Moreover, changes in the methods of control employed by the central authority alienated large sectors of the population, including peasants, urban workers, and professionals. As the crisis of the state deepened, some bureaucrats, linked to the old regime through patronage, deserted and pressed for political change.

Once the state began to disintegrate, the opportunity arose for mobilized groups to form revolutionary alliances. In France, for example, Skocpol indicates that commercial and industrial leaders encouraged popular opposition to hasten the collapse of the war-weary and financially strapped monarchy (1979, 66–67). She rejects the idea that revolutionary situations are caused by purposeful actions of social "forces" that form an alliance to "deliberately challenge the sovereignty of the existing government" (1979, 298 n. 44). She also discounts the Marxist notion of a class acting "for itself" in the process of revolution (ibid., 17). According to Skocpol, revolutions are not made; they come after "a conjuncture of separately determined processes and group efforts" (ibid., 298 n. 44). Such a conjuncture is brought on by fissures in the state edifice. This view is reflected in Skocpol's description of how pivotal peasant revolts were possible in France, Russia, and China: "It was the breakdown of the concerted repressive capacity of a previously unified and centralized state that finally created conditions . . . for widespread and irreversible peasant revolt against landlords" (ibid., 117). Once uprisings engulfed the countryside, urban elite and working-class groups in the case of France, and communist cadres in Russia and China, seized the moment to eliminate the mortally wounded regime.[2]

State autonomy from society and state capacity to maintain political stability have been used to explain patterns of recent revolutionary episodes in the developing world. Goodwin and Skocpol (1989) pay special attention to the structural features of "neo-patrimonial dictatorship" that characterized many Latin American, Asian, and African countries in the twentieth century. They state that, "Many authoritarian regimes do not bother to mobilize social groups into politics. . . . They leave the prerogatives of the state and the benefits of politics entirely in the hands of rulers and narrow cliques" (1989, 496). This extreme form of autonomous exclusionary rule is deemed inherently incompetent and vulnerable to collapse. Clearly, autocratic regimes are likely to lose political legitimacy when levels of corruption, greed, and repression consistently increase. Thus, Goodwin and Skocpol measure the susceptibility of dictatorship to broad social alliances and revolution in terms of degrees of exclusion and abuse.

> Revolutionary coalitions have formed and expanded in countries in which one finds not only poverty . . . professional revolutionaries, and peasants of a certain sort, but also political exclusion, and severe and indiscriminate repression. Revolutionary movements have actually succeeded in overthrowing those regimes that have been rendered brittle and unreformable by the structural features and strategies of rule characteristic of . . . neopatrimonial dictatorship. (1989, 505)

Goodwin and Skocpol present a model (ibid., 504) similar to Huntington's diagram depicting praetorian political conditions (1968, 79) that suggests that revolution is imminent when political participation is practically nonexistent, and bureaucratic flexibility and control are low.

In the same fashion, Dix (1983) analyzes the Nicaraguan and Cuban cases to demonstrate when urban elite and middle-class groups will participate in revolutionary activity. The nature of the Somoza and Batista regimes enabled radical intellectuals to enlist the support of urban workers, professionals, and businessmen. The "semi-modern" regime controlled economic growth and monopolized new opportunities which alienated a wide range of groups in the "semi-modern" society. Dix's theoretical perspective closely resembles the *modernizationist* argument that revolution is possible when political development lags behind political mobilization that comes with economic and social change.

Dix (1984) also proposes that the "success" and "failure" of revolutionary movements is related to regime type. He explains the divergent paths of revolution in Nicaragua and El Salvador by examining differences in the structure of dictatorship in each country. "The most plausible explanation" for the emergence of a broad social alliance capable of insurrection is "where sufficient regime narrowing takes place to push otherwise nonradical elements of society into a loose negative coalition with a core of revolutionary militants" (1984, 443). The Nicaraguan case is presumed to fit this scenario. But, the way in which Dix uses the term "negative coalition" distorts the interests of mobilized groups that commit their resources to realize potential benefits of genuine change. He states: "The impetus for such a coalition is not a positive goal like social justice or even the affirmation of national identity or independence, but rather ridding of the country of an isolated, corrupt, and repressive clique of rulers" (ibid., 444). Of course, Dix argues that the absence of a coalition between wealthy sectors and guerrillas in El Salvador was because the dictatorship did not become an "increasingly narrow paternalistic clique against which virtually all in the nation could rally" (ibid., 442).

Other scholars have readily incorporated the variable of regime type into explanations for elite behavior during revolutionary situations.

> The instrumentalist state . . . is essentially an instrument of class domination. The state rules in the interests, and often through the persons, of the dominant class. It acts to maintain the conditions necessary for capital accumulation . . . and the suppression of any lower class threats to the system of class hierarchy. . . . This type of state is perhaps best exemplified by the military [regime] in El Salvador. [Another] type of state [is] the autonomous personalist state. The "lider maximo" generally rules in conjunction with the military establishment . . . and the complicity of the dominant class. If the personalist clique of collaborators come to monopolize economic activity, they may well constrain the opportunities for capital accumulation available to other sectors of the class and thus jeopardize their support. (Midlarsky and Roberts 1985, 182–83)

Similarly,

> In the 1970s the upper class would turn decisively against the Somoza regime, from the left [espousing more democratic institutions] and not from the right [obstructing democracy, as in El Salvador]. (Wickham-Crowley 1989b, 515)

> [Business organizations in El Salvador] have moved to the right of the regime. . . . Politically they are leagues away from the revolutionaries, whereas in Nicaragua they eventually moved into a uneasy alliance of convenience with the Sandinistas. . . . Only such patrimonial regimes [like Somoza's] tend to elicit cross-class populist uprisings. (ibid., 518)

All the aforementioned scholars more clearly define how "praetorian" a society has to be before a revolutionary situation develops. The general proposition is that the scurrilous manipulation of power by a despot weakens state capacity to control society and causes resentment among elites. Once this occurs, "a clear correlation emerges [between] patrimonial praetorian regimes . . . [and] cross-class opposition to the patrimonial ruler. . . . [The] emphasis on the vulnerabilities of [patrimonial regimes] to revolution is meant to echo and build on . . . Skocpol's analyses of revolutions in France, Russia, China, and Iran" (Wickham-Crowley 1992, 299–300). Hence, the principal variable that shapes and unites the political opposition is presumed to be the behavior of the dictator which weakens its own political structures and facilitates revolutionary situations.

The hypothesis that vices and ineptitude of certain kinds of dictatorship elicit revolutionary cooperation among diverse social sectors cannot necessarily be nullified. In Nicaragua, Cuba, Mexico, and Iran, repugnant leaders alienated most sectors of the population, including erstwhile elite collaborators who eventually advocated violent means of political change. Of course, Goodwin and Skocpol (1989, 499–500) and Wickham-Crowley (1992, 299–300) explicitly recognize that not all patrimonial regimes have been extinguished by multiclass revolutionary alliances. These scholars and Snyder (1992) elaborate on how autocrats around the world have succumbed to civil-military coalitions with anything but revolutionary intentions.

Obviously, Trujillo in the Dominican Republic and the Duvaliers in Haiti did not suffer the same fate as their Caribbean counterparts, Somoza and Batista. One could assume from this logic that Trujillo and the Duvaliers abstained from some of the more egregious acts committed by the latter dictators, thus not debilitating the state so severely and alienating most social groups. Nascent guerrilla organizations and some elites did call for various degrees of political change in the Dominican Republic and Haiti, yet they never converged to form genuine cross-class revolutionary alliances. Diederich's studies of Duvalier and Trujillo (1969 and 1978, respectively) indicate many of the same features that characterized the Somoza and Batista dictatorships, including high levels of business-related corruption and repression of moderate and radical opposition groups. "Baby Doc" Duvalier eventually attacked old privileged elites in the political and economic sphere (Latin American Bureau 1985, 31–42).

Too much attention has been focused on the nature of the state to explain how and why revolutionary and/or reformist challengers might cooperate to topple the existing order. The literature discussed in this section has not expunged the inherent tautological tendency of Huntington's explanation for the causes of political instability and revolution. Consider this statement: "The probability of revolution . . . depends upon . . . the extent to which intellectuals, professionals, and [the] bourgeoisie are alienated from the existing order . . . the extent to which the peasantry is alienated from the existing order . . . and the extent to which [these groups] join together in fighting against 'the same enemy'" (Huntington 1968, 277).

A main theoretical assertion of this study is that large landowners, businessmen, and professionals do not necessarily encourage revolutionaries even when a dictator and his clique go beyond arbitrary boundaries of "acceptable" greed, corruption, and repression. Arguing that a narrowly based dictatorship is the principal catalyst for a broad revolutionary coalition fails to distinguish elite political and economic interests from those of other components of the opposition. The formation of a revolutionary coalition is not the manifestation of all social groups mobilizing for the same reason. Perhaps, the existence of "umbrella" organizations prior to the fall of dictatorships in the developing world accounts for the proclivity in the theoretical literature to assume that only one political goal is being articulated by all groups opposing the old order (see, for example, Goldstone et al. 1991, chap. 14).

Furthermore, scholars have argued that autocratic features can contribute to the political flexibility and longevity of authoritarian regimes. Strong personal leadership and "one-man rule" have been identified as principal factors in the long-term maintenance of the tenures of Pinochet in Chile (Remmer 1989; Valenzuela 1989; Valenzuela and Valenzuela 1986), Stroessner in Paraguay (Lewis 1980; Miranda 1990), Noriega in Panama (Ropp 1992), and the Duvaliers in Haiti (Diederich 1969; Latin American Bureau 1985, 25). In fact, Remmer groups the Somoza dynasty with Pinochet and Stroessner to demonstrate how "sultanistic" dictatorship in Latin America has been a durable form of exclusionary rule (1989, 37–38).

> Contrary to the views of . . . Huntington [and the scholars mentioned earlier in this section] who [regard] personal rulership as inherently precari-

ous, stable and personalistic forms of authority do not represent opposite ends of a single continuum. . . . The Chilean case emphasizes that in confronting the dilemmas and contradictions of military rule, sultanistic regimes enjoy some distinct advantage over more impersonal bureaucratic ones. Weathering . . . fundamental political realignments [against dictatorship] requires a flexibility uncharacteristic of [highly developed] bureaucracies as well as a capacity to obviate, surmount, or at least mitigate key sources of tension. (Remmer 1989, 143–44)

"Bureaucratic authoritarianism" in Latin America has been equated with the modernization of institutions that constitute a more sophisticated state apparatus than in countries dominated by "traditional" or "oligarchic" regimes.[3] However, the assumption that there is a strict dichotomy between "strong" state structures of bureaucratic authoritarianism and "weak" state structures of personalism obscures the specific political and institutional circumstances that allow despots to endure. Relatively more complex authoritarian regimes do not always ensure political stability by definition.

Davidheiser echoes Tilly (1973) in recognizing the circularity of the reasoning that "if revolution has broken through old structures, the state must have been weak" (1992, 463). A corollary is, then, that neopatrimonial dictatorships are not always more likely to alienate elites, and thus become susceptible to disintegration, than more impersonal bureaucratic forms of exclusionary domination. The Pinochet regime, for example, implemented neoliberal programs favoring trade liberalization and monetary discipline to overturn the protectionist posture and social welfare policies of Salvador Allende's socialist government. "Although many Chilean businessmen went bankrupt because of [emphasis on exports and low tariff barriers], the bulk of the business community remained a strong pillar of the Chilean government [after 1973]" (Valenzuela 1989, 194). Pinochet assembled a group of "neutral" technocrats, known as the "Chicago Boys," through which he personally controlled the economy and isolated the military and rightist political supporters from decision-making processes. This situation translated into a high level of state autonomy.

However, the dictatorship tailored economic policies to favor capitalists in the most dynamic export sectors. Consequently, the state's interests coincided with important fractions of the capitalist class which resulted in a high degree of legitimacy for Pinochet in the business community. Opposition to the regime was asserted from within a broad spectrum of long-established democratic political parties, not from business interests. Pinochet himself provided the mechanism by which power would be transferred to civilian government when a plebiscite law was included in the 1980 constitution. Pinochet used the plebiscite to reinforce his reign. However, elite politicians from the right, center, and left, despite severe divisions that contributed to the overthrow of Allende in 1973, waged a successful campaign for a "NO" vote in 1989. This result forced the dictator to allow a presidential election that brought Patricio Aylwin to power in 1990. Social opposition was inspired primarily by effective party mobilization.

Stroessner coopted Paraguayan businessmen by granting the Federation of Production, Industry, and Commerce (FEPRINCO) representation on policy boards governing foreign trade, utilities, and taxation (Lewis 1980, 155–56). The business community reaped the benefits of authoritarian capitalism which, among other things, held labor unions under state control and actively encouraged joint ventures between foreign capital and Paraguayan investors. "The Stroessner regime mixed appropriate levels of control with sustainable levels of cooptation in order to maintain its hegemony [which] made possible [its] unprecedented longevity" (Miranda 1990, 3, 76). FEPRINCO criticized the dictatorship only after Paraguay entered severe economic depression in the wake of the poor performance of two hydroelectric projects, a global energy crisis, and a dramatic drop in agricultural export prices in the late 1970s (ibid., 135–36). The contraction of previously high growth rates, rising unemployment, and increasing human rights violations mobilized labor, peasant, and church organizations. As the political environment became progressively charged in the 1980s, a faction of Stroessner's ruling Colorado party precipitated an elite split by arguing for democratic reforms (ibid., 130–31). General Andres Rodríquez, Stroessner's closest military advisor, responded to intraparty conflict and mass mobilization by removing the regime through a coup d'état in February 1989.

In Panama, businessmen enjoyed the benefits of "preferential" access to external financing from private banks and official lending institutions established under the regime of General Omar Torrijos in the 1970s. Panama's role as a commercial clearinghouse and financial haven enabled Torrijos to construct an autonomous bureaucratic apparatus and "an aura of national legitimacy" among elites and middle classes (Ropp 1992, 218–21). When Manuel Noriega came to power surreptitiously in 1983, he expanded the control of the Panamanian Defense Forces over economic activity. Noriega made many enemies in the business community as he tightened his grip on commerce in the Colon Free Zone. "The officer corps was beginning to challenge the commercial elite for social status. . . . Given the growing tensions between the regime and urban commercial and industrial elite, it comes as no surprise that some members of that elite spearheaded the movement to get rid of Noriega" (Ropp 1992, 229). After Noriega nullified the electoral victory of Guillermo Endara, who was backed by a large portion of the business community, elites grappled for a peaceful solution until the United States invaded Panama in December 1989. The Bush administration's action preempted what promised to be a lengthy process of Noriega's further consolidation of his personal rule and the consistent rise of broad social discontent.

The regimes discussed above forged distinct relationships with elites engaged in private enterprise. Capitalists generally prospered by supporting dictatorship. Furthermore, in the case of Mexico, the government of Porfirio Díaz "was intimately intertwined with private enterprise," both seeking political tranquility and economic prosperity in the late nineteenth century (Saragoza 1988, 51–52). As Saragoza demonstrates, even though political power was concentrated in Mexico City, Díaz's personal rule did not restrict the Monterrey elite from dominating important regional markets and culling favorable tax and investment incentives provided by the regime. Political opposition by capitalist interests is not necessarily a direct function of a sultanistic dictator's penchant for corruption and tendency to control economic policy making. Like their Chilean and Paraguayan counterparts, businessmen in Monterrey and Chihuahua, for example, were extremely cautious about advocating violent change despite their recognition that the Porfiriato was obsolete (Saragoza 1988, 97; Wasserman 1984).

Several Latin American dictators have shown remarkable resilience to social pressures and keen capacity to quell civilian opposition for long periods of time. Autocrats are vulnerable to collapse when corruption, cooptation, and coercion become liabilities rather than sources of legitimacy in elite circles and popular sectors. Yet, the circumstances under which the regime's base of support erodes and social movements emerge vary widely. Illegitimacy is not necessarily a sufficient condition for the breakdown of authoritarian rule. "What matters for the stability of any regime is not the legitimacy of this particular system of domination but the presence or absence of . . . alternatives" (Przeworski 1986, 51–52). Stable dictatorship rests partially on the maintenance of a power bloc between political, economic, and military elites. If conflicts develop in the power bloc and some elements withdraw their support, the crucial question is what political options are available to leaders of elite opposition. The concentration of research on the effects of neopatrimonialism should be enhanced by an analysis of "how modes of economic organization, and associated class and political relations, shape [potential] revolutionary [alliances and immediate] outcomes" (Eckstein 1989, 48). Paying particular attention to the role of businessmen in political change, this study warrants a theoretical discussion of the development of elite relations within the structure of the upper class, and the conditions under which disgruntled elites pursue a strategy of constructing a viable alternative which includes alliances with other social groups.

Elite Relations and the Organization of the Upper Class

This section will veer away from the nature of the state to explain the outcome of elite conflict and the formation of cross-class coalitions. Our focus will shift to an evaluation of how the structure of the upper class affects patterns of revolution and the possibility of elite support for revolutionary movements. A basic assumption here is that capitalist class interests permeate the state in small economies oriented toward export markets. Then, it is instructive to consider how international economic trends mold the upper class and initiate new elite relations in countries like Nicaragua. The creation of new institutions to facilitate economic growth often signifies a political coincidence between government and private enterprise. Thus, a convergence of landed and capitalist interests around new economic opportunities perpetuates dictatorship. This phenomenon occurred in Nicaragua with the expansion of export agriculture and related industrial and commercial activity after 1950. Under these conditions, a rupture in the prevailing form of political domination depends on relationships between elites who control the state and other elite groups outside central power which depend on the dominant elites' policies.

The dependency school focused on the influence of global capitalism to explain patterns of economic development in Latin America. Lenin's concept of imperialism pervaded the original work of scholars who attempted to demonstrate that capitalism caused underdevelopment in the Third World, not values and institutions bound by tradition (Frank 1967). Santos (1970) detailed the structure of dependent relationships based on international trade. He summarized the dependent condition in terms of how one country's development is determined by trade with and transfers of technology and raw materials from another country. Wallerstein (1982) stretched the meaning of dependency to characterize the international economy. He saw the flow of investment capital from the industrial center to peripheral economies as the driving force behind dependent relationships. Production in the periphery was inevitably oriented toward the export of surplus value to the center. Capitalist interests in developing areas interlocked with those in the industrial center. Thus, elite behavior in the periphery was shaped by the "world capitalist system," not by domestic forces.

Disciples of the dependency school readily adopted Marxist social determinism into their view of Latin American development. Chapters 3 and 4 will address how and why Nicaragua's agro-export economy became indelibly linked to flows of foreign capital and was influenced by fluctuations in international markets. The dependency interpretation will be evaluated in the context of how elite politics changed as more production was devoted to export. However, "we need not necessarily accept arguments that national economic developments are actually determined by the . . . market dynamics of the 'world capitalist system.' We can certainly note that historically developing transnational economic relations have always strongly influenced national economic developments" (Skocpol 1979, 20).

Cardoso and Faletto (1979) refocused the frame of inquiry toward Latin America on how class alliances were formed and political decisions taken in a given historical context. This approach has proven useful in case studies of the effects of export-led economic growth on upper-class structures and elite politics. Evans's (1979) analysis of the relationships between multinational corporations, local industrial capitalists, and the state enhanced our understanding of the political consequences of dependent development in Brazil. Furthermore, Maxfield (1992) contends that much can be drawn from historians and political economists who have studied the impact of international economic conditions on domestic politics in Europe and North America.

Gerschenkron (1962) emphasized how international economic competition during the time at which a country enters a period of industrial modernization influenced regime type in nineteenth- and twentieth-century Europe. Late industrializers required interventionist states and, in some cases, authoritarian rule to develop competitive economies. Other scholars have linked the formation of domestic political coalitions and subsequent economic policy making to the overall health of the international economy (Gourevitch 1986). Rogowski (1989) analyzes how factor endowments affect political alignments during periods of growth and decline in international trade. He argues that political alliances and policy outcomes depend on the scarcity or abundance of land, capital, and labor. In times of expanding trade, scarce factors need protectionism and abundant factors pursue free markets. The conclusion of World War II ushered in a dramatic increase of international trade and investment driven by North American capital (see Rogowski 1989, chap. 4). In the postwar period, the preeminence of the United States in the global economic order directly influenced patterns of political and economic development in Latin America.

According to Torres-Rivas's works (1981, 1983), the penetration of foreign capital melded the oligarch with the entrepreneur in Central America. Export agriculture was the engine behind commerce and industry especially during the apogee of the Central American Common Market in the 1960s (Zuvekas 1992). Chapters 3, 4, and 5 describe the specific political conditions that led to the convergence of land and finance capital in Nicaragua after 1950. Rival Liberal and Conservative elite factions gravitated to new economic institutions poised to receive infusions of capital from the international financial community based in the United States. Export agriculture and related industrialization from the 1950s through the 1970s enabled the Somoza dynasty to consolidate its power over policy making toward private enterprise. As we shall see, the Somoza dictatorship manipulated foreign capital, technology, and export operations with the complicity of economic elites outside the bureaucratic apparatus. As a result, land became artificially scarce for food production, and labor was repressed and underutilized.

Poulantzas (1974) and Abraham (1981) have shown how dictatorships have served as mechanisms to reconcile diverse capitalist interests. Dictatorship can offer a political solution that facilitates elite accommodation through the promise of political stability and economic prosperity. Stepan (1985) interpreted the emergence of authoritarian regimes in Latin America as evidence of the "classic Bonapartist transaction" where the state rises above dominant class interests. However, the capacity of state rulers in export-oriented market economies to pursue interests markedly different from those of the capitalist class is limited (Lindblom 1977). Paradoxically, the dependence of economic elite groups on dictatorship often increases social polarization over time. Social mobilization against the regime can lead to the dissolution of elite arrangements. Chapters 4 and 5 are partially devoted to a comparison of the political significance of clear divisions within the Nicaraguan upper class backing the Somoza dictatorship with the historical unity and political hegemony of the oligarchy in El Salvador.

How do conflicts develop within the upper social strata and when do some elements of the capitalist class press for political change? Marxist scholars have attributed political change in Europe to clashes within the upper class in the transition from feudalism to capitalism (P. Anderson 1974; Poulantzas 1973). These studies indicated inevitable contradictions between dominant landed interests and emerging industrial, commercial, and financial sectors as capitalism expanded. Political change depended on the capacity of new capitalist fractions to achieve hegemony over the state. This suggests that the state is never completely autonomous, but only relatively autonomous. When a class fraction succeeds in elevating its economic interests to political prominence, it effects an overall reorganization of the social structure (Giddens 1973). The existing regime becomes unstable when the hegemonic fraction's grasp on power is tenuous and threatened by another fraction aiming to capture the state and change the relations of production in its favor. This structuralist theory of conflict in the upper class associates the actions of capital fragments directly with objective class interests.

Cardoso's (1967) study of industrial elites in South America emphasized "competition for the control of the state machinery" among capitalist fractions. In some cases, new entrepreneurs producing for the domestic market joined forces with the masses to bring pressure on the state in opposition to dominant exporting groups. But, Cardoso asks: "What type of political conditions framed the basic choices that these groups adopted with regard to social change, and to what extent did their desire to gain power dispose them to accept popular pressure . . . or to placate the traditional governing classes?" (1967, 104–06). During the import-substitution phase in Argentina and Brazil between the 1930s and the 1960s, industrial and commercial groups, in alliance with popular sectors, broke down the traditional power of landed elites and redirected development toward the internal market. Nationalist-populist regimes were erected to reconcile private capitalist interests and the incorporation of the masses into politics (O'Donnell 1973; Roxborough 1984).

Moore states that the social-structural features of the upper class "have constituted and in some parts of the world still constitute the basic framework and environment of political action" (1966, 423). The rise of capitalist groups separate from the aristocratic order and the old bureaucracy had important implications for political development and outcomes of changing societies in Europe and Asia. Some French aristocrats who assumed strong capitalist habits joined the ranks of an expanding layer of "bourgeois elites" that advocated removing the monarchy and obstacles to trade and production (Doyle 1988, 20–28; Moore 1966, 68). Commercial and industrial leaders ascending in the society tapped the momentum of radical urban and rural opposition when they could not seize power alone and transform relations of production to favor the market. This alliance of convenience disintegrated into violent confrontations over the ownership of property once the old regime fell. But, authoritarian rule was dealt a decisive blow by the revolution. In other cases, the weak impulse of nascent capitalists was an antecedent to an alliance with the aristocracy and the military. German commercial and manufacturing groups coalesced with the Junkers and the military bureaucracy against peasants and workers after the failed "bourgeois" revolution in 1848, thus "exchanging [the] right to rule for the right to make money" (Moore 1966, 437).

Marxist structuralists would argue that the outcome in Germany corroborates their suspicion that capitalists are incapable of executing their own "bourgeois democratic" revolution. They fail due to the "the absence of a political organization capable of producing consistent leadership for the revolutionary process" (Poulantzas 1973, 183). Therefore, capital fragments rarely act decisively for themselves.[4] Recent research on the role of capitalist groups in the Nicaraguan revolution has advanced this interpretation.

> The "class for itself" refers to the formation and development of institutions [political parties, guilds, and business organizations] in order to generate specific influence in the political arena, and to carry out projects that organize and drive the national society through the state. From this perspective, a consolidated bourgeoisie . . . [did not exist] in Nicaragua. (Vilas 1991, 14)

Becker (1983, 1990) insists that Latin American businessmen are not destined to be politically impotent and subservient to traditional sources of power in his studies of Venezuela and Peru. "Every human group acts willfully in pursuit of ends consciously perceived. . . . Class is still the logical unit of analysis for studying power relationships in society. . . . What [should be] discarded is simply structuralism's one-to-one correspondence between objective class interests and subjective class consciousness" (Becker 1990, 117). Thus, Becker argues that business organizations can constitute a social force capable of renovating relations between the state and society. "What matters is whether or not [Latin American capitalists] define and pursue their interests in a way that encompasses a progressive transformation of the nation" (1983, 12). Becker sees a process by which Latin American businessmen have become more skillful and confident in the management of their enterprises. In Venezuela, they have learned the "corporate liberal ideology" through exposure to Western business practices and partnerships with multinational corporations. According to Becker, democratic institutions are indelibly linked to the development of a bourgeois social movement consciously orchestrated by progressive business leaders. This perspective on the role of businessmen in political change shares Lipset's

(1967) emphasis on the importance of elite values in Latin American development.

Chapters 6 and 7 show that some Nicaraguan businessmen opposed the Somoza regime in the 1970s not because they wanted to change relations of production. Rather, they expressed their desire to reform political and economic institutions to conform with Western liberal principles of laissez-faire and constitutionalism while social discontent festered. Leaders of the opposition in the business community organized independent economic institutions and associations in the decades before they were alienated by the dictatorship. They, too, espoused the "corporate-liberal ideology," but their influence was restricted to the economic arena, unlike Venezuelan capitalists. The struggle between the Somocista clique and some businessmen associated with two private banking groups was waged more on political grounds than over pure economic interests. Therefore, the agents of political conflict in Nicaragua's upper social strata are better described as elites than as class fractions.

Mosca (1939) saw the ruling class as a dominant elite that controls state authority. He related political conflict to dominant elites trying to maintain the status quo while new groups threaten to change the power structure. He saw rival elites not as factions of the capitalist class, but rather social groups that emerged from new sources of wealth and knowledge (1939, 57–58). Pareto (1979) classified elites as "ruling" and "nonruling," indicating a plurality of elites at the top of the social order. He asserted that elites ruled by superior quality rather than by class domination. Elite theorists of the late nineteenth and early twentieth century were responding to socialist theory of dialectical materialism and the notion that class conflict was the engine of change (Bottomore 1964). Change did not depend on class consciousness, but rather on dominant elites' capacity to rule. Thus, a loss of power was evidence of a loss of ability.

Lachmann (1989, 1990) takes a different tact in analyzing elite conflict. "Social change is effected by the few elites able to act for themselves [and] disrupt the existing organization of rule by withdrawing their support for the [dominant elite group]" (Lachmann 1990, 401). Marxists claim that multiple elites usually represent class fractions and their interests and political capacities are characterized by their relations to production. However, agro-industrialization in Nicaragua after 1950 did not lead to clashes between groups of "extractors" over transforming the relations of production. As we shall see, there were no inherent contradictions between the plantation and modern enterprise; export agriculture promoted industrial, commercial, and financial sectors. Zeitlin and Ratcliff's work on Chile (1975, 1988) suggests that this phenomenon is not unique to Nicaragua.

Class analysis is sufficient to explain why elites converge around direct control of political institutions and act concertedly to repress the lower classes. Still, the upper class can consist of several elite groups that share the same basic economic interests, but possess unequal levels of political authority over the allocation of resources. Domhoff (1990) emphasizes the importance of analyzing the "elite power structure" to understand a nation's politics. Then, conflict in the upper social strata is often better portrayed in terms of changing elite relations rather than confrontation between class fractions or between the autonomous state bureaucracy and the dominant class (Lachmann 1989, 147–49). It is essential to explore how domestic elite relations affect regime stability (Higley and Burton 1989). The outcome of elite conflict when one group monopolizes the state apparatus hinges on the ability of peripheral elites to break the dominant group's hold on power. A nonruling elite group's capacity to prevail is weakened when it has had no direct control over decision-making institutions up to the point when elite relations rupture and competition begins. This theoretical perspective guides an investigation of why some landed and business groups aligned with the Sandinistas in Nicaragua.

Doyle (1988) and Goldstone (1991) have explored the role of liberal political and economic principles in motivating an array of political and economic elites to rebel in France.

> Elites [may] voice their sense that society has gone astray by offering plans for renewal, and sometimes for transformation, of the Old Regime. . . . Elites [may be] capable of offering diagnoses that the Old Regime is not simply corrupt and in need of rectification; they may proclaim it fatally flawed and in need of replacement by a new order. (Goldstone 1991, 409–10)

"Enlightened" elites intent on changing the political and social order need the support of middle- and lower-class groups to implement a specifically articulated program. "Mass conditions and orientations establish fields of opportunity and constraint to which elites must respond [especially during periods of mass mobilization]" (Higley and Burton 1989, 22). Elite opponents attempting to implement democratic reforms are at a distinct disadvantage when civilian political organizations (parties, unions, associations) have been severely repressed and lack vertical and horizontal linkages. These conditions can contribute to the failure of elites to garner enough resources and popular backing to eliminate the regime on their own terms during a revolutionary situation. Consequently, the impetus for change shifts in favor of an existing guerrilla movement, and an alliance between elites and armed revolutionaries is possible.

Dynamics and Breakdown of Revolutionary Coalitions

This chapter has concentrated on the conditions that raise the possibility that elites will chose the violent option offered by guerrillas. It is equally important to consider why guerrillas are disposed to cooperate with elites. In Nicaragua, the Sandinistas identified clear political divisions in the upper class and between elite groups in the mainstream opposition to the dictatorship. Yet, only some Sandinista leaders were convinced that capitalist interests could be won over to the revolution. The formation of broad coalitions is facilitated when radicals deliberately suppress their ideological convictions in the pursuit of elites. Dix promotes this view in explaining why elites withdrew their support after insurrection in Nicaragua and Cuba:

> The moderates were adjuncts to a radical leadership that continued to hold the key levers of revolutionary control. The moderates joined a revolutionary cause that was in being and that embraced more radical objectives than they subscribed to: ridding the country of a particular dictator. Thus the "struggle" between moderates and radicals was less a contest than a tactic of manipulation used by the always dominant revolutionary leadership. (1983, 285)

However, Dix leaves several practical questions unanswered: Why did radicals dominate the coalition after the fall of the dictatorship? Why did moderates join an alliance in which their interests would be subordinate to those of the radicals? Did the coalition fragment simply because of radical ideas on the postinsurrectionary agenda? We cannot ascertain the fragility of the coalition by insisting that one faction becomes too ambitious and supplants the goal of removing the dictatorship with plans for economic and social transformation. Mobilized social groups ultimately advance diverse class interests in the process of reconstructing the state. Debates over the purpose of economic activity and the type of political institutions which will govern the new society are expressions of class conflict. Tilly accurately describes the precarious nature of alliances of incompatible partners:

> The revolutionary coalition is likely to fragment once the initial seizure of control of the government apparatus occurs [because] it takes a larger mobilized mass to seize power than to maintain it; [because] the inevitable divergence of some major objectives of the contenders within the coalition will come to the fore once the common objective of seizure of power has been accomplished; [because] those contenders which have mobilized rapidly up to a point of the revolution are also likely to demobilize rapidly due to the underdevelopment of their organization for the management of the mobilized resources. (1978, 218)

Disaggregating broad-based coalitions and examining which interests are represented, and by whom, is the key to understanding how elites and revolutionaries sustain or lose their desire to cooperate in effecting sweeping political, economic, and social changes after the overthrow of the dictatorship.

The theoretical discussion in this chapter criticizes and complements comparative research conducted by the "third generation" of scholars of revolution (see Goldstone 1980). Illuminating the influence of regime type, the condition of peasant society, structural changes associated with international economic trends, class relations, and elite conflict on patterns of revolution in the developing world is the task at hand for contemporary analysts. The following chapters will build upon the plethora of studies that address the Nicaraguan case. The principal goal is to offer a more precise comprehension of political turmoil and violent change in an underdeveloped, export-oriented republic dominated by dictatorship.

3

Defining the Dynasty and Changing Elite Relations, 1950–1962

The main objective of this chapter is to provide a historical perspective on changing elite relations after 1950. During the period under consideration, the Somoza dynasty consolidated its control over the state. Despite the death of Anastasio Somoza García in 1956, the family would show political resilience and continue to cultivate the support of other economic elites. The main private banking groups that emerged in the early 1950s reshaped the economic structure of the upper class which began to shift elite politics away from the long-standing Liberal-Conservative feud. In this same period, Christian democratic opposition groups and the Sandinista revolutionary movement were born. The dictatorship assumed the tasks of ensuring steady economic growth based on agro-export production and fending off threats from enemies bent on overthrowing it.

Regime Consolidation and New Elite Structures

The advent of the Somoza dynasty in Nicaragua is rooted in political and military intervention by the United States during the first three decades of the twentieth century. From the end of the Spanish-American War to the end of World War I, American presidents used the Marine Corps and special envoys to mediate political disputes between the National Liberal Party (PLN) and the National Conservative Party (PCN) dating back to the mid-nineteenth century, and to establish hegemony over Nicaragua's natural resources (Millett 1988; Munro 1918, 1964; Woodward 1985, chap. 7). In the

1920s and early 1930s, the United States took responsibility for protecting Conservative and Liberal governments from Augusto César Sandino's "Defending Army of National Sovereignty of Nicaragua," a nationalist, anti-imperialist guerrilla movement (Ramírez 1979; Selser 1979).

With the onset of the Great Depression, the administration of Franklin Roosevelt promulgated the "Good Neighbor Policy" and launched a new approach to hemispheric relations. Roosevelt withdrew the Marine Corps from Nicaragua in 1932, leaving General Anastasio Somoza García in charge of the National Guard. Somoza moved immediately to consolidate his power by first ordering the murder of Sandino in 1934, and then forcibly removing his uncle and fellow Liberal, Juan Batista Sacasa, from the presidency in 1936. Somoza assumed executive office after a fraudulent election in 1937. As a result, the next decade and a half of Nicaraguan politics was characterized by mistrust among elites and political insecurity for the Somoza regime.

Through the 1940s, PCN leaders resented Somoza's relentless efforts to close off their access to high-level decisions. Not only did Somoza isolate the Conservative hierarchy from the central power structure (Woodward 1985, 220–23), but he also attempted to reduce the Conservative oligarchy's influence over its traditional sources of wealth: sugar, coffee, and beef production. He expropriated several coffee plantations and cattle ranches from German fascists who resided in Nicaragua during World War II and acquired two sugar mills that directly competed with the Conservatives' Ingenio San Antonio (ISA) refinery and plantation, established in 1890. The dictator was not immediately concerned with using the state to promote agro-exports in the global marketplace. Most large landholders' export production was based primarily on short-term speculation on coffee, cotton, and sesame prices (IBRD 1953, 295). Also, merchants were alienated by license and tax laws passed by the government to monitor commercial import activities and access to capital markets (Wheelock 1985, 178–79). Somoza manipulated customs services and pricing mechanisms to gain control of the movement of merchandise.

In 1944, several disgruntled members of the National Liberal Party (PLN) formed the Independent Liberal Party (PLI). PLI leaders challenged the regime's malfeasance, unfair price controls, and "the betrayal of Liberal principles and/or the lack of professional opportunities in a backward society" (Gould 1987, 362). When Somoza declared that he would run for office again in 1944, violating the constitution, the PCN and the PLI formed an alliance to defeat him (Leonard 1984, 144). However, campaign support was divided between Independent Liberal Carlos Pasos and Conservative General Emiliano Chamorro. The opposition's failure to reach a compromise handed Somoza an easy victory. Over the next three years, the PLI and the PCN called for tax and banking reforms, the reorganization of the National Guard, and increased foreign investment for industrialization. The alliance was weakened by mutual fear of possible deals with the regime (Leonard 1984, 132–36). Despite being forced by law to step aside in 1947, Somoza continued to intimidate his enemies with the National Guard and held onto executive power through other Liberal leaders up to 1950 (ibid., 144–48). The PLI and the PCN were left groping for political space. Nevertheless, the dictatorship was not able to relieve pressure from elite challengers.

The consolidation of the dictatorship began in earnest in 1950 when the PCN negotiated a truce with the PLN. Emiliano Chamorro and the Conservative establishment sold their deference to Somoza in the "Pact of the Generals" for one-third of the National Assembly and the promise of more commercial liberty for merchants and exporters adversely affected by past state restrictions. The constitution was amended to allow for presidential reelection. Explicit language was inserted about individual freedoms and constitutional government to placate the Independent Liberals (Cole 1967, 125–30). Yet, accommodation with the Conservatives and Independent Liberals was not based on trust and an open exchange of ideas. Conservative elites from Granada considered the agreement a means of regaining much of the political prestige and influence over economic policy making lost to the PLN since the early 1930s. Urban professionals and businessmen were concerned primarily with increasing economic opportunities by eliminating government intervention in their affairs (Gould 1987, 362).

Much of the impetus for political truce among Nicaraguan elites stemmed from the United States' plan to stimulate new trade and investment in Latin America based on development assistance. In 1949, the International Monetary Fund (IMF) advised the Chamber of Commerce of Nicaragua that the economy was suffering unnecessarily from deflation and credit restrictions. The chamber assembled a national group of economists, managers, and agronomists to develop a strategy "for the recuperation of economic vitality" through their "disinterested and patriotic collaboration" (P. Gutiérrez 1978, 82–83). The team consisted of men like Luis Carrión Montoya, who had returned from the United States with a degree in business administration from the University of California, and Eduardo Montealegre Callejas, a former IMF official and Nicaraguan banker.[1] Elites from diverse backgrounds coalesced in the spirit of economic modernization and the creation of an active state. The immediate considerations were mechanizing agriculture and increasing the flow of capital to producers which, of course, favored the agro-export sector.

Shortly after the Somoza-Chamorro deal, the World Bank estimated that less than a quarter of Nicaragua's cultivable land was being used as of 1950 (IBRD 1953, 20). The bank's study in 1951 and 1952 reiterated the need for an adequate credit system to strengthen producers' ability to compete in export markets. This was linked to educating farmers on the value of more scientific methods of cultivation and convincing the government to provide more incentives to borrow. "The [Nicaraguan] government [showed] a clear awareness of the need for [agricultural] improvement and it has demonstrated both the imagination and will to move forward with vigorous action" (ibid., 4–5).

Somoza incorporated the economic strategy of financial experts from the Federal Reserve Board of the United States, the IMF, the World Bank, and the Food and Agriculture Organization into his political platform. He portrayed himself as a champion of the "national well-being" and staked the success of his administration on attracting foreign aid and expanding export agriculture (Martz 1959, 168, 172–73). The sudden international attention whetted the appetites of wealthy exporters and merchants who insisted that the PLN allocate resources fairly so they could compete aggressively in international markets. However, Somoza reacted by invoking "emergency executive powers" granted by the 1950 constitution to control the reorganization of the economy beginning in 1952. At this point, the national agenda turned toward the creation of a modern economic infrastructure.

Analysts have interpreted this shift in Nicaragua's development as an important step toward full integration into the postwar liberal economic order. "[Nicaragua] needed to develop supervised credit institutions that could assure productive use of loans, and new institutions were also needed to regulate the export operations" (McCamant 1968, 213). The World Bank allocated $3 million to increase the Ministry of Agriculture's responsibilities for technical assistance in the field and to set up the Ministries of Economy and Foreign Affairs. The Somoza government discriminated in favor of PLN members and North Americans to fill new bureaucratic positions recommended by the World Bank (IBRD 1953, 86–87).

In 1954, the National Development Institute (INFONAC) was founded ostensibly to supply medium and long-term credit to food as well as cash crop producers (IBRD 1953, 29). INFONAC complemented the Banco Nacional de Nicaragua (BNN) which had been the only national financial institution since 1912. The BNN was founded under United States' law and served North American and European investors and the Nicaraguan oligarchy in the first half of the twentieth century. The bank was not nationalized until 1941 when foreigners diverted their capital to the war effort (BNN 1975, 7). The BNN and INFONAC were groomed to be the principal conduits for international lending to agro-export sectors. The dependency school would identify this situation as a stage in the process of the industrialized center drawing the underdeveloped periphery into a dependent relationship. Clearly, this proposition is valid. But, the domestic political effects of prevailing international conditions are of greatest relevance here. The scramble to modernize the state banking system placed Nicaragua's economic future in the hands of tyranny. The dictatorship now held the tools to mollify most elite political opposition with the promise of an economic boom. The expanded capacities of the state would enable the Somoza regime to control credit to the private sector and gain leverage against capitalists eager to increase their fortunes.

Economic elites outside the tight political circle of the Somocista clique did not remain idle in the face of impending economic change. They seized the opportunity to establish independent private banks for the first time in Nicaragua's history. Conservative families from Granada, who represented the lineages of the oligarchy, founded the Banco de América (BANAMER) in 1952. Their immediate goal was to concentrate resources for expanding traditional agricultural and commercial operations. BANAMER's original stockholders were ISA owners Alfredo Pellas Chamorro and Adolfo Benard, who had just completed construction of the largest sugar mill in Central America in 1949 (Gould 1990, 63, 149); Enrique Dreyfus was involved in manufacturing, imports, coffee, and cattle; Felipe Mántica operated in consumer imports, real estate, cattle, and cotton; Ernesto Fernandez Holmann and Carlos Holmann were real estate tycoons and cattle ranchers; and the Baltodano, Cuadra, Chamorro, and Benard families constituted the Nicaraguan coffee oligarchy. By the early 1950s, the coffee elite had been rendered politically impotent by the inability to produce as efficiently as its Central American counterparts (Paige 1987) and factional strife within the Conservative Party stemming from electoral defeats over the past twenty years (Dodd 1992; Leonard 1984). Another pillar of the BANAMER group was the SOVIPE construction and land development company, organized by Alfredo Solórzano, Julio Villa, and Enrique Pereira shortly after the bank opened. The family based consortium was initially intended to balance these interests against the economic strength of the Somoza family in the 1950s (Joaquín Cuadra Chamorro, interview by author, 28 July 1991).[2]

The Banco Nicaragüense (BANIC) was established in 1953 by Liberal factions from the rich Pacific plain around León and Chinandega and the capital of Managua. Families of cotton growers, such as Montealegre, Callejas, Deshon, Gurdián, and Alvarado, converged with the industrial interests of the Guerreros, the Reyes, and the Langs in anticipation of new requirements for technical assistance, machinery, pesticides, and export services. As Gould indicates, the BANIC group was split between a traditional landed class and an emerging industrial bourgeoisie which produced elite conflict within the Liberal establishment (1990, chap. 5). However, as will be demonstrated, the development of agro-export-based industry fostered by the Somoza dictatorship would ultimately blur the distinction between "modern" and "traditional" capitalists.

In the mid-1950s, Eduardo Montealegre Callejas spearheaded the creation of Nicaragua's first home finance corporation, Financiera de Vivienda, as a subsidiary of BANIC. Luis Carrión Montoya moved from successive positions in BNN and INFONAC to become manager of the financiera. BANAMER's SOVIPE and the financiera initiated the construction of several middle-class and wealthy neighborhoods in and around Managua and would continue to expand their operations when the urban population grew at unprecedented rates in the 1960s (Wilkie and Perkal

1984, 88). A past interview with Montealegre Callejas expresses the general outlook of BANIC in this crucial period of economic modernization:

> My initial concern was to find supporters with capital, business connections, governmental influence, and sufficient position in the community to create the goodwill and confidence necessary to ensure the bank's success. A major hurdle was getting government permission to open a bank, a project accomplished by convincing General Somoza [García] that the time had come for this sort of institution in Nicaragua's development. (Quoted in Strachan 1976, 128–29)

At the outset, the founders of both banks were identified with one side of the protracted Liberal-Conservative feud or the other. But, they did not actively represent old partisan interests, per se. BANAMER and BANIC members did not aspire to political office. Rather, they were preparing themselves to exploit economic opportunities anticipated on the heels of the "Pact" and the World Bank's sudden generosity. The basic difference between the two groups was that BANIC assembled Liberal elites around the untapped potential of the cotton industry and welcomed close cooperation with state financial institutions, whereas BANAMER recast the structure of the Granada oligarchy into a formal capitalist organization that guarded its financial autonomy in sugar, cattle, and coffee (Jarquín 1977, 13). Most importantly, BANAMER and BANIC were the bases for distinct elite groups which would develop complex economic relationships with the Somoza dictatorship over the next two decades.

Like the Monterrey elite and the Porfiriato in late-nineteenth-century Mexico, the Somoza government and Nicaraguan capitalists sought an alliance between the state and private enterprise to encourage order and prosperity and espoused "the rhetoric of economic liberalism" (Saragoza 1988, 52). The changing roles of elite groups did not indicate a change in social background, but rather a change in "the character and operation of the [economic and political] system" (Smith 1979, 10; also see Stone 1990, chaps. 1 and 2). The remainder of this chapter will analyze how rapid economic expansion under dictatorial rule affected elite politics up to the early 1960s. The power struggle between Liberals and Conservatives would partially give way to new elite interests configured around export agriculture and the state. Also, the origins of moderate middle-class opposition and the Sandinista revolutionary movement, that emerged to challenge the Somozas while elite conflict waxed and waned, will be introduced.

Export Growth and Political Challenge

The World Bank's study in the early 1950s recommended that loans for cash crops be made on a medium- and long-term basis to encourage growers to build up working capital and reinvest in land improvements. The goals were to establish more consistent production cycles and to sharpen Nicaragua's international competitiveness in all existing export sectors. However, the Somoza government focused particularly on cotton and initiated a rapid credit increase in 1953. The BNN and the Ministry of Agriculture negotiated a $5.3 million loan from the World Bank and the new Ministries of the Economy and Foreign Affairs arranged cotton sales on futures markets in New York. This was extremely beneficial to BANIC members who had just opened a cotton brokerage firm to handle more export volume. BANIC also consulted the Ministry of Agriculture about importing tractors, harvesters, pesticides, and high-quality seed from the United States. Cotton was grown in previous decades, but the state had never directly promoted investment and export.

In 1953, 45 percent of all credit for major crops was allocated to cotton growers compared to 32 percent for coffee and 5 percent for sugar. In that year, one hundred thousand acres of cotton were planted. In 1954, 68 percent of all credit was devoted to cotton, and acreage doubled with the infusion of a $7.5 million loan from the World Bank. By 1955, cotton overtook coffee as the top export crop. This is not to suggest that coffee and sugar lost their traditional economic importance. Coffee exports increased in the first half of the 1950s, and sugar production for export rebounded in this period from a poor performance in the 1940s (Wheeelock 1985, 234). Cotton, coffee, and sugar were responsible for an agro-export growth rate of 12.3 percent between 1952 and 1955; private investment increased 16.3 percent in the same period as growers intensified operation (Jarquín 1978, 2). But, cotton assumed the leading role of the government's vigorous pursuit of economic prosperity (see table 1).

TABLE 1

Bank Credit for Major Export Crops, 1953–1960

	Cotton		Coffee		Sugar	
	$ Millions	% of Total	$ Millions	% of Total	$ Millions	% of Total
1953	42.1	45	30.7	32	5.1	5
1954	94.8	68	31.7	22	3.1	2
1955	103.2	58	50.1	28	3.6	2
1956	134.1	68	42.4	22	3.4	2
1957	88.1	57	47.3	31	4.5	2
1958	84.3	60	42.7	30	4.7	3
1959	52.2	53	29.7	30	2.9	3
1960	63.7	60	27.4	26	3.1	3

Source: Biderman (1982, 185); dollar amounts are current value.

Unlike producers of coffee and sugar in BANAMER, cotton growers in BANIC obtained the majority of their capital from the state. By 1956, government financing covered between 70 and 80 percent of the total cost per acre (Biderman 1982, 87). The BNN's policies generated so much enthusiasm for cotton exports that landowners began renting fields to doctors, lawyers, merchants, and other well-to-do urbanites from Managua and the Occident who took advantage of high prices in the first half of the 1950s. Together they "constituted the first real entrepreneurial class with explicit links to the state" (Jarquín 1977, 12). Under such conditions, a pattern of short-term price speculation and reluctance to invest personal funds pervaded the cotton sector, whereas coffee and sugar producers financed most of their input costs. Experienced cotton growers and newcomers to the scene showed little caution even though the crop was vulnerable to bad weather, insects, and fluctuating prices.

While Somoza nurtured the economy and courted elites, criticism of the regime began to mount from moderate and radical movements among Nicaragua's growing urban professional and student population. Pedro Joaquín Chamorro, a young university-educated Conservative dissident, took control of his family's newspaper La Prensa in 1952 and began publicizing collusion between the PLN and older Conservatives almost daily. As a law student at the National Autonomous University of Mexico (UNAM) in 1948, Chamorro formed the National Union of Popular Action (UNAP) with about two dozen other sons of Conservative families, including Arturo Cruz, Reynaldo Antonio Téfel, and Rafael Córdova Rivas. In his thesis "El Derecho del Trabajo" (The Right of Labor), Chamorro positively evaluated the Mexican Revolution's contribution to the plight of the Latin American worker (Chamorro 1948). Consequently, UNAP refused to support the Conservative Party's platform in the late 1940s and pursued an alternative social Christian program that touted ethical public service and representation of workers in democratic institutions (Edmundo Jarquín, interview by author, 7 May 1991). In 1954, Chamorro and UNAP attempted to remove the dictatorship with the help of some high-level military officers with Conservative political loyalties. The National Guard received an anonymous tip and seized an arms cache before the plan could be executed. Chamorro and Cruz, a graduate of the Georgetown School of Foreign Service, were jailed along with conspirators in the army.[3]

At about the same time, Tomás Borge, Carlos Fonseca, and Silvio Mayorga entered law school at the National Autonomous University of Nicaragua (UNAN) where they organized a radical student movement against the regime. The three men held brief membership in the Nicaraguan Socialist Party (PSN), but soon rejected the passive, orthodox Marxist strategy of the Socialists. They agitated for more militant action. Fonseca was especially instrumental in resurrecting the revolutionary thought of Sandino and recasting his nationalist, anti-imperialist philosophy to spur mass political rejection of Somocismo (see Hodges 1986).[4]

In September 1956, Somoza was assassinated by student leader Rigoberto López Pérez. A state of emergency was declared and all civil rights were suspended. The National Guard rounded up and tortured thousands of suspected enemies of the regime, including Pedro Joaquín Chamorro and Tomás Borge. Carlos Tunnerman, a UNAN-educated lawyer, made a futile effort to defend Borge and other students in a mass "trial" orchestrated by the PLN. Luis Somoza Debayle, the eldest son of the dictator, became president in early 1957 after a rigged election and public outcry ensued. As middle-class opposition intensified, UNAP split into the Nicaraguan Social Christian Party (PSCN) and the Christian Democratic Popular Movement (MPDC), which remained tied to the Conservative Party. The PSCN and the MPDC capitalized on resentment toward the Guard's arbitrary detainment of civilians and enlisted the support of many citizens who had never before been politically active. Meanwhile, the compromised wings of the Conservative establishment remained silent.

Later in 1957, Nicaragua entered a deep economic depression due to a precipitous drop in cotton and coffee prices (Jarquín 1978, 2). The illusion of political peace and economic prosperity in elite circles in the first half of the decade was shattered by the end of 1957. Luis's administration reacted by dramatically reducing agricultural credits and implementing more stringent loan eligibility requirements. This situation did not severely affect coffee and sugar barons in BANAMER who did not rely completely on state resources. Nevertheless, Conservative leaders in the National Assembly objected to the president's unchecked power over economic policy and the means of coercion that, ironically, they had approved in the "Pact of the Generals" in 1950. The Conservatives couched their rhetoric in terms of "civic action" and "parliamentary struggle" in an effort to engage the PLN on the old political battlefield.

> With much pain we have to say that the extraordinary powers that the [1950] Constitution grants to the Executive for the maintenance of order were not created prudently.... The Conservative Party expects that Engineer Luis Somoza will rise above such unnecessary measures ... so that together we can start to reconstruct the [failing] economy. (PCN 1958, 109–10)

The government accumulated a $7 million deficit due to lost export earnings (Martz 1959, 207; PCN 1958, 49). More specifically, much of the imbalance was caused by many cotton growers' inability to repay loans taken from the BNN prior to the planting season. The BNN's role as the main source of capital to the cotton sector trapped growers in a dependent relationship with the dictatorship. Therefore, BANIC members did not openly criticize the credit crunch. Most cotton elites were from old Liberal families and supported the government, even though they were not activists for the PLN's political agenda (Luis Carrión Montoya, interview by author, 2 June 1991).

> The dependency of cotton capitalists on the state explains their political domestication to the dictatorship in the 1950s. Therefore, it was impossible to distinguish the public administration from its political clientele in the Liberal establishment.... But development in the 1950s did not affect the basis of the Conservative oligarchy. Its economic autonomy translated into political autonomy from Somoza. Thus, the vitality of the Liberal-Conservative conflict was maintained. (Jarquín 1977, 16)

The death of Somoza García and the adverse effects of fickle export prices created an air of political insecurity in the late 1950s. In 1959, two efforts were made to topple the dictatorship. The first was launched from the villages of Olama and Mellojones by the MPDC, a group of young Conservatives who led the 1954 fiasco. This time Chamorro, Rafael Córdova Rivas, and Reynaldo Antonio Téfel formed the National Opposition Union (UNO) with the nascent PSCN and PLI leader Enrique Lacayo Farfan, who commanded the military phase of the conspiracy. The MPDC recruited disaffected Conservative members of the Chamber of Commerce who met with Lacayo to coordinate work stoppages and an attack on the National Guard in April and May of 1959. The military action suffered logistical problems and workers refused to strike (P. Gutiérrez 1978, 104). Few laborers identified with Conservative politics and most mistrusted the motives of the Chamber of Commerce which opposed Luis Somoza's offer of a social security plan to all private-sector employees in 1958 (ibid., 85). The Guard killed or captured most of the participants.

In July 1959, Carlos Fonseca and his radical following planned an attack from El Chaparral in southern Honduras designed to surprise the Guard which was preoccupied with the previous incident. Fonseca assembled the "Rigoberto López Pérez" column consisting of Nicaraguan students and peasants and Cuban militants provided by Fidel Castro at Fonseca's request. Castro had rejected a plea for assistance from Pedro Joaquín Chamorro a few months earlier (Arturo Cruz, interview by author, 31 October 1991). The Honduran military discovered the plotters' camp before they crossed into Nicaragua and arrested Fonseca. Though both incidents were unqualified failures, Olama/Mellojones and El Chaparral demarcated a social democratic, reformist opposition and a small revolutionary cadre in Nicaragua. "We began a race to throw out the Somozas between moderate forces, on the one hand, and the Sandinistas, on the other hand" (Cruz, interview, 1991). Chapters 4 and 5 examine efforts toward peaceful change by Christian and social democratic forces and the parallel evolution of the Sandinista political-military strategy in the 1960s and 1970s. In the late 1970s, the Sandinistas would forge a revolutionary alliance around their violent option with social democratic elements and some economic elites who became disillusioned with the Somoza dynasty after two decades of deference and cooperation.

The success of the Cuban revolution and the appeal of Fidel Castro among the working class of Latin America mobilized government officials and businessmen in Central America and the United States behind a plan for economic recovery. In mid-1959, "[the Eisenhower administration] expressed its readiness to provide substantial [financial] cooperation if and when the Central American countries established a complete free trade zone" (Castillo 1966, 86). The prospect of increased external financial assistance for generating new regional and international business was received by Central American leaders as a means of averting social upheaval like what had occurred in Cuba. At the beginning of the 1960s, the regime became mired in bitter class struggle in Chinandega. Liberal factions employed extralegal and physical means to oust squatters from prime cotton fields. The National Guard intervened often to quell campesino mobilization and Somocista ministers mediated competing claims to land among their Liberal elite constituents (Gould 1990, 120–23).

Facing this precarious situation, Luis Somoza staked his political survival on improving economic performance. Luis himself participated in intense negotiations with the Agency for International Development and representatives of the other republics that culminated in the General Treaty of Central American Integration signed in Managua in December 1960. Thus, the legal obstacles to a free trade zone and massive international lending in the isthmus were removed. This was a key step toward repairing the economic foundation of elite relations in Nicaragua. Moreover, the grand notion of combining regional integration and foreign capital would help to obscure the need for serious reform of Nicaragua's political institutions in the 1960s.

At the turn of the decade, younger factions of the Conservative Party tried to mount a campaign to regain executive power lost since the 1920s. The MPDC orchestrated the election of Fernando Agüero to the party's presidency in 1960. Agüero pursued a populist strategy of appealing to Christian values and aggregating progressive professional and labor support around democratization and better living standards. The MPDC wrote emotional speeches for Agüero that were intended to rally support for a centrist alternative to dictatorship. This was reminiscent of the movements of José Figueres in Costa Rica and the Democratic Action Party in Venezuela which flourished in the 1950s (Alvarado 1985, 13). Agüero directly confronted the Somozas' authoritarian rule in an effort to redefine the political discourse of the old party rivalry for the upcoming 1962 election.

The PLN had multiple tasks off competing with the new character of the Conservative challenge, making good on its promise of economic liberalization, and stemming support of the Cuban revolution among workers. The Liberal establishment considered the popularity of John Kennedy in the Americas a great boost for its political legitimacy and tried to tap into the enthusiasm of Kennedy's presidential victory (Millett 1977, 224). Thus, Liberal rhetoric became conciliatory in the early 1960s as the national campaign approached: "The victory of liberalism is tied to . . . the struggle against public, political, and economic despotism . . . and tolerance toward those who are not in agreement [with the government]" (Maltes 1960, 53).[5] Liberal party members called for the "modernization of the liberal movement in the Jefferson mode" and referred to decentralized institutions in the United States (ibid., 113–14; Woodward 1984, 296). Luis Somoza reinstated civil rights, including freedom of the press, that had been suspended since his father's death. He also advanced a minimum wage law advocated by the MPDC and the PSCN, though neither organization had formal representation in the National Assembly. Conservative legislators, still holding one-third of the assembly, rejected the proposal as a threat to traditional patronage between employers and employees (Jarquín, interview, 1991).

Between 1960 and 1962, the Somoza regime assumed a somewhat gentler disposition toward labor mobilization in an effort to gain popular leverage against the Conservatives in the electoral season. On two occasions, unprecedented strikes by construction workers in June 1960 and dock workers at the strategic Port of Corinto in February 1962, the government responded positively to demands for higher wages and better working conditions. Official tolerance can be partially explained by the fact that the economic interests of many BANAMER elites involved in the Conservative opposition were affected by the strikes: SOVIPE in construction and the shipping firms of the Vassallis and Palazios at the Port of Corinto (Gould 1990, 184, 194).

In a disingenuous gesture of respect for democratic procedures, the PLN held a convention and put forth René Schick as its candidate. Shortly before the vote in February 1963, the MPDC warned of impending fraud by the PLN and withdrew from the contest, undercutting Agüero's electoral base. Agüero soon drifted back to the old-line Conservative apparatus, and MPDC members joined the PSCN, although without Pedro Joaquín Chamorro. These events amounted to a failure of the Christian democratic movement to build a solid foundation in Conservative politics from which to remove the Somozas from the commanding heights.

Even though a Somoza would no longer be president of the republic in 1963, the family had achieved several important political victories. The dictatorship weathered the economic storm and turned back two armed attempts to overthrow it in the late 1950s. The Somozas retained control of the state banks and the National Guard which were pillars of executive power. Finally, the economic soil was prepared to receive a flood of international financial assistance and cultivate rapid agro-industrial growth that would benefit the Somozas, BANIC, and BANAMER.

4

Business, Politics, and Agro-Industrialization, 1963–1972

This chapter focuses on how BANIC and BANAMER elites created new industrial and commercial enterprises, ventured into new regional and international markets, established stronger links to private foreign capital, and relied more on favorable economic policies of the state. The meteoric rise of Anastasio Somoza Debayle to power in the late 1960s would draw peripheral elites even closer to the dictatorship, but also set the stage for elite conflict in the 1970s. Somoza used his dual role as president and head military officer to enrich himself and his closest associates while brutally repressing manifestations of political discontent. By the early 1970s, elite politics seemed to reach a stable plateau resting on a healthy agro-industrial economy and limited political disturbances from the lower classes. However, the last Somoza's arrogance began to test the patience of many businessmen and professionals who had acquiesced to the dictatorship in the past.

The Alliance for Progress and the Rise of the Last Dictator

In 1963, Liberal president Schick inherited the pressures of economic recovery after nearly a five-year slump in cotton and coffee prices. The PLN hoped that the Alliance for Progress would be the mechanism to activate the Central American Common Market (CACM) and quell rising civilian unrest. The government and BANIC and BANAMER welcomed the "era of foreign assistance" ushered in by the Kennedy leadership. Schick, in a presidential address in August 1963, lauded Kennedy's "intimate knowledge of Latin American problems . . . and his desire to begin revolutionary programs that will transform our old socio-economic structures" (Schick 1963, 8–9). In this context, he sought to shore up relations with capitalists suffering from the recent lean years and tight credit policies. Not long after the speech, the Chamber of Commerce invited Schick to inaugurate a new conference room. The son of the BANAMER cofounder Felipe Mántica, Felipe Mántica Abaunza, BANIC members Eduardo Montealegre and Salvador Guerrero Montalván, and Mauricio Robelo of the Industrial Association of Nicaragua received a government delegation, consisting of officials from the Central Bank and BNN. This was unprecedented in the history of the chamber, founded in 1928. These men had replaced suspected collaborators in the 1959 Olama and Mellojones plot on the board of directors (P. Gutiérrez 1978, 106, 109–11). The meeting served to relieve tension that accumulated in the tumultuous years of Luis Somoza's rule. The mood was one of mutual anticipation of an avalanche of capital from the international financial community in Washington, D.C.

Up to that point, contact between economic elites and the bureaucracy was limited to credit terms, loan repayment, and customs regulations. Businessmen in BANIC and BANAMER perceived a need to establish more formal channels in order to articulate their interests in private enterprise. Thus, they created the Nicaraguan Institute of Development (INDE) in late 1963. INDE was fashioned as an "apolitical think tank" concerned with economic growth through free enterprise and community development. BANIC members were the first directors and, along with BANAMER leaders, advocated a close relationship with the government and financial institutions (William Baez, interview by author, 31 October 1988). Concurrently, private-sector interests were concentrated in the Superior Council of Private Initiative (COSIP) that included BANIC and BANAMER, established a new Chamber of Industry separate from the Chamber of Commerce, and organized doctors, lawyers, economists, engineers, and architects into professional guilds. The business community quickly forged new institutions to ensure its integration into the design of the Alliance for Progress and Common Market. Business leaders could demonstrate through formal lines of communication that they were "conscious of their responsibility for sustaining economic growth" and worthy of participation in macroeconomic planning (Enrique Dreyfus, interview by author, 30 July 1991).

One of the first projects of INDE and COSIP in 1964 was the construction of the headquarters of the Central American Institute of Business Administration (INCAE) in Managua. Nicaraguan capitalists and professionals, more so than their Central American counterparts, negotiated with the Harvard Business School which sponsored the creation of INCAE. INCAE was specifically designed to train managers, economists, and technicians to fill positions in more complex agricultural, industrial, and commercial operations. INCAE provided private instruction in the principles of liberal capitalism. Essentially, young Nicaraguans from elite families could get a Master of Business Administration in the country while learning the strategies of North American management. INCAE's curriculum was developed by Harvard University and the University of Central America (UCA), founded by the Nicaraguan Jesuit order in 1961. The UCA and INCAE were alternatives to the UNAN whose student body was attracted by Fonseca's Sandinista ideology between 1959 and 1961.[1] Just after the INCAE campus opened, INDE proposed that the government devote a greater percentage of the national budget to university education. Legislation was passed in 1965 that favored UCA and INCAE students over those at UNAN (Baez, interview, 31 October 1988).

Many of INCAE's advocates were products of business, economics, and science programs in North America and supporters of the Alliance for Progress. Eduardo Montealegre attended the Harvard Business School and maintained strong ties with the faculty and administration as well as officials at the IMF for which he worked in the 1940s. William Baez Sacasa graduated from Holy Cross University in sociology and economics. Baez participated in the formation of the Pan-American Development Fund (PADF), an agency of the Organization of American States devoted to financing microenterprise in Latin America. Jaime Bengochea organized the Association of Nicaraguan Industry shortly after he received a chemical engineering degree from the University of Michigan in the late 1950s. The Association was the precursor to the Chamber of Industry. Bengochea inherited his father's pharmaceutical company which was a pillar of the chamber. Enrique Dreyfus was a business student at McCall University in Toronto and became a consultant for a financial services corporation in New York. Dreyfus was also involved in the PADF from its inception. Alfonso Robelo is an engineer from Rensselaer Polytechnic Institute in New York. He would serve as rector of the UCA from 1970 to 1972, and as president of the Chamber of Commerce from 1970 to 1975. Felipe Mántica Abaunza graduated from the Georgetown University business school and cooperated with Dreyfus and Baez in INDE and the PADF. He sat on the UCA board of trustees and was active in affiliated church organizations. Ernesto Cruz, brother of Arturo, was trained in law and economics at Georgetown University and was a principal researcher for INCAE through the 1980s.[2]

During the first two years in office, Schick tried to assume an independent posture vis-à-vis the Somoza family. He reduced the budget of the National Guard and spoke frankly about the need to eliminate official corruption (Booth 1985, 91). This proved politically fatal. In 1966, the Somozas ordered Schick replaced by Vice-President Lorenzo Guerrero and the PLN announced that Luis Somoza would run in the 1967 election. This action reinvigorated the National Opposition Union (UNO), consisting of PCN elements under Fernando Agüero, the Nicaraguan Conservative Youth organization, the PLI, and the PSCN (Vargas 1990, 63–64). Pedro Joaquín Chamorro did not formally rejoin the UNO campaign, but publicly advocated Agüero's candidacy in a "symbolic act of solidarity" against the Somozas (Jarquín, interview, 1991; Institute for the Comparative Study of Political Systems 1967, 23). Luis won the election but died of a heart attack before taking office. National Guard chief Anastasio Somoza Debayle immediately appointed himself president for "security reasons." Chamorro mobilized fifty thousand people in Managua to protest Somoza's arrogance in assuming executive powers while retaining control of the Guard. Soldiers fired on the crowds, killing three hundred, and Chamorro was jailed. Upon his release in 1968, Chamorro sharply criticized Agüero and his closest advisors in La Prensa for bowing to Somoza's intimidation which got him expelled from the Conservative Party. As mentioned earlier, he never considered himself a traditional Conservative activist ever since the party's compromise in the "Pact of the Generals" in 1950. This bitter divorce would lead Chamorro down a new political road marked by public scrutiny and personal frustration; it would end with his death in 1978.

With his father and brother out of the picture, Somoza proceeded to gather up the political treasure of the dynasty. He accentuated his personal power in the bureaucracy by filling key policy-making offices with close friends and relatives. Retired National Guard General Alejandro Montiel Argüello became minister of finance and Noel Pallais Debayle, a cousin, took over INFONAC. Both Montiel and Pallais were partners with Somoza in the Savings and Loan Corporation (CAPSA) that received funds from the central banking system (Departamento de Ciencias Sociales 1982, 244). Guillermo Sevilla Sacasa, Somoza's brother-in-law and descendant of Liberal president Juan Batista Sacasa, who was ousted by Somoza García in 1936, was appointed ambassador to the United States. Somoza also inherited complete control of the Joint Planning Mission of the Secretariat of Central American Economic Integration (SIECA) located within the offices of the president in each Central American country.

This was the basis for assembling a bureaucratic network known as the "minifaldas" (miniskirts). The minifaldas were usually supporters of the Liberal Party, if not members, and graduates of the INCAE or foreign business and technical schools. The president of the Central Bank of Nicaragua, Francisco Lainéz, an INCAE professor, headed a team of economists and technicians responsible for implementing long-term development plans based on theoretical models of competitive markets used in INCAE seminars. "About 100 people . . . designed a liberal economic program on paper," but they never consulted directly with INDE and COSIP as recommended by the Agency for International Development (AID) and SIECA (Baez, interview, 31 October 1988). Several technocrats were trained in the planning program of the United Nation's Economic Commission on Latin America (ECLA) that advocated state intervention in the economy (Wynia 1972, 66). "Lofty sounding social programs, ostensibly concerned with public health, agrarian reform, low-income housing, education, and social security, served mainly as devices to legitimize the system, attract foreign aid, and employ the politically faithful" (T. Walker 1986, 103).

Somoza's direct supervision of the minifaldas enabled him to fend off "[any] serious threat [posed by international planning agencies] to personalistic control" (Wynia 1972, 49). Initially, the facade of a "neutral technocracy" insulated Somoza from international and domestic sources of pressure for socioeconomic reform. The minifaldas played a role similar to that of the "Chicago Boys" in Chile and the "Científicos" in Mexico. They enhanced the personal influence of Pinochet and Díaz over their respective economies while contributing to the durability of the regimes (Maxfield 1990, 39; Saragoza 1988, 52–55; Valenzuela 1989; Valenzuela and Valenzuela 1986). The advent of new institutions to facilitate economic integration in Central America "brought new visibility and dignity to national leaders who perceived themselves as pathfinding diplomats" (Wynia 1972, 49). Of course, Somoza used this situation to avoid relinquishing real decision-making power to international advisers or to private business interests.

Initially, Somoza enjoyed complete legitimacy with the BANIC and BANAMER groups. Peripheral economic elites were benefiting from new lending from the international financial community (see table 2); there was no immediate reason to expect that a formal change in political leadership would affect their interests. Particularly significant was that relations between the regime and BANAMER improved in the first half of the decade. The historic meeting with Schick in 1963 was an important factor. In addition, Somoza as the National Guard chief dispatched soldiers to quash a canecutters' strike after the ISA requested government assistance in 1963 (Gould 1990, 246–50). Nicaragua began receiving a large portion of the United States' sugar quota after the Cuban revolution, and the ISA was a primary benefactor. By 1967, BANAMER members no longer considered

TABLE 2

Loans from Development Institutions, 1961–1970

IBD	$77.4 million
IBRD	$29.7
AID	$69.9
EXIMBANK (US)	$13.1
CABEI[a]	$55.0

Source: SIECA 1973, 23.

a. The Central American Bank for Economic Integration (CABEI) received capital from the IDB, AID, EXIMBANK, Japan, Holland, and Germany in the amount of $222.5 million between 1961 and 1970. CABEI allocated approximately one-quarter of its loans to Nicaragua in the 1960s (Schmitter 1972, 32).

the Liberal Party a threat like they did in the 1950s (Felipe Mántica Abaunza, interview by author, 19 February 1991).

The BANAMER group and BANIC cotton capitalists dependent on the BNN sought continued favorable treatment in the allocation of financial resources and access to local, regional, and international markets that were part of the economic feast laid on the table by the Alliance for Progress. Because the United States government was the largest contributor to the International Bank of Reconstruction and Development (IBRD), commonly known as the World Bank, and the Inter-American Development Bank (IDB), it exercised substantial influence over capital transfers. AID monitored the operations of the Central American Bank of Economic Integration (CABEI) and the SIECA and reserved the right to approve all loan disbursements through the CABEI (Jonas 1974, 43–45).

International development experts in Nicaragua were committed to expanding agricultural production and improving transportation facilities that enabled producers to move harvests to urban centers for processing and to ports for passage abroad (SIECA 1973a, 39). Funds from the World Bank, the IDB, and CABEI went to road construction from the north-central regions and León and Chinandega to the Pacific coast and Managua. AID and the Export-Import Bank of the United States focused on expanding acreage and yields for major cash crops. Legally, the United States agency or development bank in Washington, D.C., could make loans only to the Nicaraguan government which would be responsible for administering funds. Capital had to be deposited in either BNN or INFONAC accounts controlled by Somoza (OEA 1976, various pages). Thus, the Somoza machine was the lifeline to official development assistance. Ambassador Sevilla Sacasa continually shuttled between the United States and Somoza's offices arranging new loans (Washington Post, 19 August 1975, 23). The loans were usually released in the form of credit to renew agricultural cycles.

However, the bureaucracy began transferring foreign aid directly to BANIC or BANAMER which then lent to members who were venturing beyond cash crop cultivation into new enterprises related to export agriculture. Cotton, coffee, beef, and sugar production were the engines of industrial and commercial activity in the 1960s. Many landowners became capitalists who produced manufacture and consumer goods for export and domestic consumption. Therefore, it is not surprising that economic elites

TABLE 3

Share of Export Crop of Total Exports, 1960–1979 (Nicaragua) (in percent)

	1960–1964	1965–1969	1970–1974	1975–1979
Cotton	33	38	25	24
Coffee	24	15	15	25
Beef	6	9	14	10
Sugar	5	5	6	6

Source: SIECA 1981b.

considered the flow of capital from official lenders through state banks to export agriculture a barometer for the entire economy. "When there was a new loan granted for the coming year, capitalists thought times were good; when a new loan was not forthcoming, they were negative" (Cruz, interview, 1991). Table 3 is the basis for examining how BANIC and BANAMER members and Somocistas assumed the role of both oligarch and entrepreneur, especially in the cotton, beef, and sugar sectors.

Agro-Industry and Elite Convergence

The following analysis of the main export sectors reveals much about the relationship among agriculture, industry, and commerce in Nicaragua. Likewise, the structure of ownership of land and capital will be illuminated.

Cotton

Credit and production rebounded from the lean years at the end of the 1950s and the beginning of the 1960s. The National Cotton Commission of Nicaragua (CONAL) was created under the auspices of the Ministry of Agriculture in order to provide technical assistance for increasing yields and information on export prices. Professionals and merchants resumed renting land from absentee owners who preferred to deal with a few tenants growing cotton than with many small food producers. The BNN implemented stricter loan qualification procedures and higher yield requirements which favored wealthy urbanites and the largest landowners (Biderman 1982, 90). Per usual, they borrowed heavily from the state and deposited their profits in separate bank accounts often located abroad (Carrión Montoya, interview, 1991; Biderman 1982, 98). By the end of the decade "some 2,600 Nicaraguans produced cotton. . . . Half the planted area was controlled by approximately 250 family groups who could have formed the nucleus of . . . a modernizing entrepreneurial class" (Paige 1985, 103–04).

However, the social diversity of cotton growers did not translate into a large group of capitalists with direct control over the entire industry. Only a small nucleus of BANIC elites, Somoza, and a few multinational corporations were involved in the industrial and commercial stages outside of planting and harvesting (CIERA 1989, 29).

Five Nicaraguan companies, owned by BANIC and BANAMER, and the John Deere and Caterpillar corporations imported tractors and harvesters. INFONAC and BANIC set up several joint ventures with North

TABLE 4

Cotton Export Production, 1962–1970

	Bank Credit ($ millions)	Cost Covered (%)	Value ($ millions)
1962	82.3	66	32
1963	108.0	68	40
1964	136.9	74	46
1965	220.4	89	71
1966	209.8	75	58
1967	237.1	78	57
1968	243.2	85	60
1969	188.4	83	46
1970	167.8	82	37

Sources: For credit, Biderman (1982, 185–86); value of exports, Williams (1986, 198) and Stevenson (1964, 44, 46, 48, 50, 52); figures are current dollars.

American and European chemical manufacturers to monopolize the sale of pesticides (Baumeister and Neira 1983, 48; Cámara de Comercio 1991, 20; Williams 1986, 201). BANIC members owned the two largest ginning plants, "La Virgen" and DEPSA, and managed the export houses EXPASA and Servicio Agrícola Gurdián. They served North American garment manufacturers and gradually acquired Western European, Chinese, and Taiwanese business (BCN 1970, 32; CIERA 1989, 29). Textiles for local and regional markets were manufactured primarily by FABRITEX of which BANIC and Somoza were majority investors with North American partners. Cooking oil was manufactured from cotton seed for the first time in the 1960s. The Acietera Corona, a majority-owned subsidiary of United Brands, captured most of the North American market. But, the GRACSA and AGROSA plants, owned by the Montealegre, Callejas, and Robelo families of BANIC, and E. Chamorro Industries, a BANAMER enterprise run by Alberto Chamorro,[3] exported to Great Britain, Venezuela, and Central American neighbors and supplied Nicaraguan housewives (BCN 1970, 32; CONAL 1973, 5). These same businesses produced mustard, mayonnaise, and oils for making soap, ice cream, cheese, and reconcentrated milk that were sold in modern supermarkets.

Beef

The dictatorship was well-positioned to dominate meat exports that increased rapidly in the 1960s. Cattle had been raised on ranches isolated from urban centers and port facilities and Nicaragua exported almost no beef in the 1950s (IBRD 1953, 295; Wheelock 1985, 234). In 1957, the Somoza family and most of the largest ranchers initiated the modernization of the beef industry. Through funds obtained from INFONAC and the Association of Nicaraguan Cattle Ranchers (ASGANIC), construction began on the "Matadero Modelo," the first high-capacity slaughterhouse in Managua. Luis Somoza was the president of ASGANIC and co-owner of over fifty cattle ranches, with his brother Anastasio, which they inherited from their father. In 1958, ASGANIC and Somocista officials of INFONAC converged to form the Institute of Cattle Development (IFAGAN) with a nucleus of about eighty ranchers of Conservative and Liberal origins. This gave the Somozas control over the only ranchers' association and its principal source of credit and technical assistance. Ranchers envisioned the development of a modern infrastructure to increase the herd and develop industrial and commercial opportunities.

In 1963, the IDB began a coordinated effort with INFONAC to create more slaughter capacity as quickly as possible. In that year, the Somozas and IFAGAN associates were the primary beneficiaries. Somocistas Pablo Valle, Abner Ríos, Adán Smith, General Arnoldo García, and William Montiel established the second modern slaughterhouse, EMPANICSA, in Condega in the northern department of Madríz. They combined eight of the largest ranches with the complex to corner the meat processing market in the entire area. Anastasio Somoza Debayle opened the CARNIC ranch and slaughter complex just outside of Managua in 1964 with land inherited from his father (Grijalva 1991, document 2).[4] INFONAC began dispensing funds received from the IDB directly to IFAGAN, CARNIC, and EMPANICSA to expand herds and pastures and promote sophisticated breeding techniques in order to meet the quality requirements of the United States Department of Agriculture (Gastón Ramírez, interview by author, 22 July 1991; IDB 1969, 77). Demand for beef in North America increased dramatically in the 1960s as fast food restaurants came in vogue (Williams 1986, chaps. 4 and 5).

Cheap Nicaraguan beef attracted the attention of businessmen in the United States, and the Department of Agriculture began inspecting slaughterhouses nearly every six months. They wanted meat to be processed in the most modern and reliable facilities which, of course, were the property of Somoza or ranchers with links to the Somoza regime through IFAGAN. The Somoza family and the members of IFAGAN dominated the agricultural, industrial, and commercial stages of production up to the 1970s. They bred and fattened their own cattle and transported them to their "Mataderos de Exportación" by vehicle, thus bypassing the traditional role of collectors who used to bring the herd to slaughter on horseback. By 1971, 2 percent of all ranchers owned 960,000 manzanas (1 manzana = 1.7 acres) of pastureland and grazed 2,074,596 head of cattle, more than 80 percent of the herd (LATINOCONSULT 1975, 5–4).

Wealthy ranchers also controlled municipal auctions where cattle were sold for domestic demand. The vast majority of small- and medium-sized ranchers relied on local markets and were paid low prices for their cattle by the owners of the main slaughter operations (G. Ramírez, interview, 1991). The meat was sold to restaurants and vendors at inflated prices or processed into salami and hot dogs. Excess fat and tissues were used to manufacture soap, candles, and animal feed. Hides were either exported to

TABLE 5

The Beef Export Sector, 1950–1970

Value ($ millions)		Head (thous.)		Pasture (manz.)	
1950	0.29	1950	900	1960	2.7 mil.
1963	8.4	1965	1,670	1970	4.0 mil.
1966	10.2	1970	2,500		
1967	12.5				
1968	15.9				
1969	21.0				
1970	26.9				

Sources: For value of exports, see Williams (1986, 206) and IRBD (1953, 294–95; for population, see Wilkie and Perkal (1984, 322); for pastureland, see Biderman (1982, 114) and Warnken (1974, 216); figures are current dollars.

the United States, Germany, or other Central American countries, or cured into leather for making shoes, saddles, and clothing that reached local, regional, and international markets (BCN 1970, 33). Another slaughterhouse, IGOSA, was opened in Rivas in 1971 by independent ranchers. IGOSA provided some diversity and competition in local markets. But, CARNIC, IFAGAN, and EMPANICSA yielded no export business and accounted for 86 percent of total production through 1975 (LATINOCONSULT 1975, 5–4).

Sugar

Production for export and domestic markets was the domain of the Pellas-Chamorro-owned ISA complex of plantations and refinery and Anastasio Somoza Debayle. When the United States suspended trade with Cuba after Fidel Castro came to power in 1959, Nicaragua obtained a large portion of the North American sugar quota. The value of exports rose from a paltry $0.5 million in 1956 to $6.0 million in 1963, and reached $15.2 million by 1972 (Biderman 1982, 120–21; Wheelock 1985, 234). During the same period, Nicaraguans began to consume more sugar in various forms, for example, soda pop, liquors, candy, and bakery goods, that presented a whole range of new investment opportunities for the ISA and Somoza. The Pellas family, with other BANAMER members and foreign investors, established the "San Antonio" Sweets Factory and the National Liquor Company. Furthermore, BANAMER owned the "Milca" soda pop plant that purchased its sugar from the ISA. Sugar accounted for 20.7 percent of the primary materials used in the manufacturing sector by the mid-1970s (see CIERA 1989, 90, 151). The ISA eventually controlled 50 percent of local and international business while Somoza garnered 30 percent through the state sugar company, CANSA (Biderman 1982, 121). Few capitalists penetrated the sugar sector either in cultivation or industrial enterprise. The elite structure remained essentially the same as it was in the 1940s.

Coffee

Coffee remained an important export crop thorough the 1960s. Export earnings consistently increased from $17.5 million in 1963, to $26.3 million in 1965, to $32 million in 1970. Coffee presented few risks to growers in terms of sensitivity to pests, weather, and price volatility. But, coffee did not provide the multitude of industrial and commercial spinoffs like cotton, beef, and sugar. The operation of coffee plantations did not change from traditional practices of planting and picking by hand. There was little room for the application of technology. Milling beans into grain or instant forms was the only industrial derivative. The largest mill, Molinos de Nicaragua, was owned by the Baltodano family of BANAMER, and Emilio Baltodano managed the Café Soluble "Presto" plant that produced instant coffee for local consumption and export after 1965. The Bank of Caley-Dagnall, established by English coffee barons in Matagalpa and Juigalpa in the 1880s, was a limited independent source of capital for growers in the northern region.

Still, BANAMER came to control the two main coffee export houses, Casa Palazio and Comercial Internacional Agrícola, for the largest producers in the country. Granada-based coffee growers were an active economic force as part of the BANAMER group and maintained financial autonomy from the state through the 1960s. However, the political influence of the coffee oligarchy that emerged within the Conservative Party in the late nineteenth and early twentieth centuries was successfully isolated from central power by the Somoza dynasty (Paige 1985, 95; Wheelock 1985,

165–67, 189). Growers were not efficient entrepreneurs like their Salvadoran counterparts who attained political unity in the 1930s. Rather, the Nicaraguan coffee elite was primarily a contingent of rich farmers whose wealth depended on stable prices and relatively inelastic international and local demand, not processing and export (Paige 1987, 179).

Class and Elite Dynamics: A Comparative Perspective

From the early 1950s to the early 1970s, the economic interests of elite factions expanded and overlapped in agricultural, industrial, and commercial sectors. BANIC and BANAMER members, and Somoza himself, were oligarchs, industrialists, and exporters, thus leading to a "coincidence of interests between the national bourgeoisie and the oligarchy" (Torres-Rivas 1981, 245–46). No immediate contradictions between land and capital emerged during the expansion of capitalism in Nicaragua after World War II. The cotton fields, sugar plantations, and cattle ranches were the lifeblood of most industrial and commercial activity (see figure 1). The "landed class" did not necessarily exist separately from the "modern entrepreneurial class," a condition not unique to Nicaragua as shown by scholars of other Latin American countries (Roxborough 1984; Zeitlin and Ratcliff 1975). Figure 1 also demonstrates that there was not a strict dichotomy between capitalists producing for export and those producing domestic consumption (CIERA 1989, 88; Ortega 1990, 12). Industrialization, spurred by the Alliance for Progress and the Central American Common Market, left the agrarian economic structure intact and allowed for some import substitution.[5]

In sum, agro-export-led development in Nicaragua did not create sources of conflict within the capitalist class based on relations of production and competing economic interests. There was little chance for a "bourgeois revolution" emerging from clashes between capital fragments like those discussed by Moore (1966), Poulantzas (1973), and P. Anderson (1974) in Europe and Asia, and by Cardoso and Faletto (1979) and O'Donnell (1973) in South America. Nicaragua's version of a "marriage of iron and rye" developed naturally from the phenomenon of capitalists in export agriculture readily venturing into related industrial and commercial enter-

BUSINESS, POLITICS, AND AGRO-INDUSTRIALIZATION

FIGURE 1

Nicaraguan Agricultural Exports and Related Industry (through 1978)

		Exported to[a]
Cotton	Processed fiber ("white gold")	US, EC, As
	Textiles	CA, US
	Lint (bedding, pillows)	US, EC
	Seed — Cooking oil	
	Seed — Margarine	US, GB, Ve, CA
	Seed — Oil for pasteurization of cheese, milk, cream; mustard, mayonnaise	
Beef cattle	Slaughtered meat	US
	Hides	US, GE, CA
	Leather for clothing, saddlery	US, CA
	Animal feed, soap, candles	Domestic consumption
Sugarcane	Refined sugar	US
	Liquors	US, EC
	Soft drinks, baked goods, candy	Domestic consumption
Coffee	Harvested beans	EC, US
	Instant powder	EC, US

Source: Author.

Note: Most products listed were also produced for local markets, depending on international prices and demand.

Key: As = Asia; CA = Central American Common Market; EC = European Community; GB = Great Britain; Ge = Germany; US = United States; Ve = Venezuela.

a. Countries are listed in order of quantity of exports.

prises. Of course, the "marriage" was encouraged and arranged politically by Nicaraguan elites. The political consequences of this situation for workers and peasants will be considered in chapter 5.

In the case of El Salvador, new industrial and commercial opportunities in the 1960s were absorbed by old landed families who dominated export agriculture, too. Yet, the process of industrialization was not accompanied by changes in elite relations and the emergence of new business organizations. The reasons for this are grounded in the political ascendance of the Salvadoran coffee elite from the late nineteenth century (T. Anderson 1971, chap. 1; Paige 1985, 94–99; Woodward 1985, chaps. 6–8). In the 1920s and 1930s, the wealthiest coffee growing families consolidated their power over the state and took the form of a cohesive oligarchy (T. Anderson 1971, 8–10). The descendants of the coffee elite preserved their political unity and economic dominance during postwar economic expansion. Certainly, the number of actors in export agriculture was more than the notorious "fourteen families" by the 1960s. However,

> twenty-three of the twenty-six family groups producing ten thousand quintals [of coffee] or more were also engaged in [new] processing opportunities. In addition, these twenty-six included twelve of the fourteen largest producers of cotton. . . . [Therefore] one gets a fairly precise idea not only of the extent of the concentration but also of the overlap in ownership in different aspects of the exploitation of coffee and of the main agricultural exports. (Baloyra 1982, 25–27)

Table 6 demonstrates the primacy of coffee in the Salvadoran economy between 1960 and 1979. Though cotton and, to some degree, sugar diversified export production during this period, the overwhelming importance of coffee perpetuated the historical dominance of a core of elite families. Thus, the industrial and commercial potential evinced by export crops was destined to fall into the hands of the oligarchy.

Most traditional landowners added to their portfolios by simply increasing production and investment. So, names synonymous with the coffee oligarchy, like Regalado, Dueñas, Alvarez, Alfaro, Guirola, and García-Prieto, were commonly found in the industrial and banking sectors (Colindres 1976). Like in Nicaragua, industry was spurred by increasing consumer demand and expanding trade within the CACM. Food and beverages, textiles, clothing, oils, and leather were some of the extensions of coffee, cotton, beef, and sugar production. Some medium-sized local capitalists emerged in urban markets, but large private enterprise clearly favored the families

TABLE 6

Share of Export Crop of Total Exports, 1960–1979
(El Salvador) (in percent)

	1960-1964	1965-1969	1970-1974	1975-1979
Coffee	57	47	43	47
Cotton	29	12	11	10
Sugar	2	3	6	6
Beef	—	—	1	1

Source: SIECA 1981b.

who controlled the use of land and the flow of capital since the turn of the century.

The largest private banks founded by the coffee elite before and after World War II—the Banco Salvadoreño (Guirola), the Banco de Comercio (Dueñas, Regalado, Alvarez), the Banco Agrícola Comercial (Escalante-Arce, Sol), and the Banco Capitalizador (Alvarez, Alfaro)—dominated all lending to agriculture, industry, and commerce (SIECA 1973a, 252–53). Moreover, the Central Reserve Bank and the National Mortgage Bank were managed by bureaucrats from these same families. "In 1971 the country's thirty-six largest landlords controlled 66 percent of the capital of the 1,429 largest firms" (Dunkerley 1988, 344). The only business organization that included industrialists, the National Association of Private Enterprise (ANEP), was headed by coffee growers (Williams 1986, 47). Consequently, industry and manufacturing became concentrated in fewer and larger firms in the sectors mentioned above. Food and beverage processing, and textile, shoe, and pesticide manufacturing together constituted about 77 percent of the industrial value added between 1969 and 1978 (Bulmer-Thomas 1987, 209–11). The oligarchy as a cohesive whole maintained control over the economy through civilian political and ministerial offices and the military (Dunkerley 1988; Montgomery 1982; Webre 1979). Elite disputes over access to resources and decision making were highly improbable under these conditions. Dictatorship in El Salvador took the form of the bureaucracy acting on behalf of a unified landed class that had completely penetrated the state apparatus.

> Economics has been reflected in politics through the saga of ruling classes. ... Conditions under which production has been organized have forged different class values [in Central America], and those values have made members of ruling classes in some countries more aware of their position than their counterparts in others. Class consciousness makes for greater cohesion and explains much about past and present attitudes of their members. ... [In El Salvador ruling groups], when threatened, are prone to close ranks and fight for what have traditionally been their prerogatives. [Elites in Nicaragua were] less cohesive and more vulnerable to [internal conflict and] social groups from other categories. (Stone 1990, 4, 9; see also Wickham-Crowley 1992, chaps. 11–12)

By the 1960s, the Nicaraguan upper-class was best characterized in terms of distinct elite groups organized around private enterprise, with Somoza presiding over the state, rather than a unified capitalist class. The business community was derived from several generations of the Liberal and Conservative families who represented the vestiges of the oligarchical structure. As in El Salvador, wealth was concentrated in the hands of capitalists with backward and forward linkages in the agro-export economy. But, policy decisions were not made directly by an entrenched oligarchy with a long history of political hegemony. As explained earlier, the minifaldas managed the economy by Somoza's directives. BANIC and BANAMER members viewed cooperation with Somoza's technocrats, with whom they often shared similar family backgrounds, as good business strategy (Carrión Montoya, interview, 1991). Dictatorship in Nicaragua reconciled elites from rival political origins who converged around the same basic economic interests.

Cardoso and Faletto (1979) argue that alliances between businessmen, the state, and transnational capital have been responsible for "dependent development" in Latin America. The Brazilian experience in the 1960s and 1970s is a commonly used example. Evans (1979) demonstrates how Brazilian capitalists relied on political links between the "technobureaucrats" and foreign investors for their economic opportunities. The local economic elite pushed for industrialization after World War II. After the military coup of 1964, the state opened the doors to direct foreign investment (DFI) by the United States in manufacturing which reached $2 billion in 1973; this amount was nearly 25 percent of the United States' DFI in Latin America (Evans 1979, 25, 167–68). Local businessmen deferred to the state's promotion of foreign majority participation in the economy while they invested in minority shares of new enterprises. More than half of the two hundred manufacturing subsidiaries operating in Brazil by 1967 were owned entirely by foreigners. In the 1970s, there was a "tendency for [existing] joint ventures to degenerate into wholly-owned subsidiaries" (Evans 1979, 204–05). Therefore, the alliance of the bureaucratic apparatus with foreign and national capital constituted the structural basis for dependent development in Brazil.

Did this same situation occur in Nicaragua? Though the Brazilian economy is much larger and more complex, a general comparison is instructive. Studies have shown that foreign capital invaded Central America in the postwar period, indicating a scarcity of domestic capital (see Rogowski 1989). DFI steadily increased in all republics especially after 1960 (Torres-Rivas 1983, 184). But, in Nicaragua, direct participation of multinational corporations (MNC) reached only $76.3 million by 1969, a mere 10 percent of the total DFI in the region (SIECA 1973a, 100). As the Central American Common Market blossomed in the late 1960s, foreign investors penetrated some manufacturing and export sectors which posed unwelcome competition. But, BANAMER and BANIC members secured high tariff barriers and export licenses from the Somoza government to defend treasured local and regional markets (Strachan 1976, 125). By the mid-1970s, DFI represented only 4.3 percent of the gross domestic product (GDP), the lowest in Central America (CIERA 1989, 36).

Thus, the entire economy was not the reserved enclave of outside interests, and there were few wholly owned subsidiaries in Nicaragua. Somoza and other economic elites entered into several joint ventures with MNCs, but rarely did foreign ownership of stock exceed 50 percent (CIERA 1989, 154–55). Nicaragua's "situation of dependence" was not like that of Brazil's. BANIC and BANAMER capitalists borrowed from the BNN and INFONAC, international development institutions, and private banks in the United States to finance their own industrial and commercial operations (BCN 1979, 28). They usually relied on MNCs to provide primary materials, machinery, pesticides, technical assistance, and export services. The Latin American Agribusiness Development Corporation (LAAD), a consortium of companies including John Deere, Caterpillar, Dow Chemical, Ralston Purina, Monsanto, United Fruit, the Luxembourg-based ADELA Chemical, Chevron, and Texaco (Goff 1970), did business with Somoza and other economic elites at numerous stages of production through the state-run Nicaraguan Investment Corporation. This evidence qualifies the notion that Nicaraguan agro-industry was a "happy hunting ground" for DFI (Schmitter 1972, 44).

The political consequence of state protection from foreign competitors was that peripheral economic elites owed allegiance to the Somocista bureaucracy.

> From the point of view of the dictatorship, the state was the means by which to sweep capitalists into a process of political domestication.... The nature of industrialization generated by the Central American Common Market helps to explain the political weakness of the ... private sector vis-à-vis the Somoza regime. (Jarquín 1977, 19)

Nevertheless, Somoza's legal umbrella allowed businessmen to carve out important niches in the economy. By 1970, most investment in industry and commerce came from BANIC and BANAMER (SIECA 1973a, table 46). Food and beverage production accounted for nearly 40 percent of the manufacturing output in Nicaragua. The liquor, cooking oil, milling, refinery, bottling, and milk companies of BANIC and BANAMER constituted the majority of the "Fortune 30" that supplied domestic and regional demand. Only the Somozas' slaughterhouses, CARNIC and IFAGAN, and Nabisco and United Brands were on the list (CIERA 1989, 155). These businesses were among the 6 percent of the industrial enterprises that accounted for 90 percent of the value added by 1972 (ibid., 34).

BANIC and BANAMER eventually accounted for 35 percent of the total national assets and 32 percent of loans and investments. Most short-term (six to eighteen months) and medium-term (eighteen months to five years) loans originated in private North American banks that helped finance many BANIC and BANAMER companies (SIECA 1973a, tables 46 and 51; Strachan 1976, 50). They prospered in the haven of the Central American Common Market as intraregional trade grew 15 percent per year between 1963 and 1968 (Wionczek 1972, 408). In the same period, gross domestic product increased at an average annual rate of 5 percent and the manufacturing sector grew at more than 10 percent (IDB 1969, 2, 12).

Furthermore, the modern industrial, commercial, and financial framework resting on the agro-export foundation generated wealth for industrial and chemical engineers, architects, agronomists, corporate lawyers, managers, and economists. By the 1970s, the professional guilds of COSIP were filled with the sons of old elite families who studied at the UCA and INCAE and obtained graduate degrees abroad. They occupied vital positions and held stock in the most profitable companies owned by BANIC and BANAMER. As one Nicaraguan businessman put it, they were the "yuppies" of the society and made up the first full generation with higher education and modern urban lifestyles (Jaime Bengochea, interview by author, 22 April 1991).

Many were involved in community projects and educational foundations. Under the auspices of AID, INDE set up a college scholarship fund known as EDUCREDITO (Educational Credit System). Men like Alfonso Robelo, Felipe Mántica, Enrique Dreyfus, and William Baez sat on an advisory council that chose the recipients who attended the UCA, INCAE, or foreign universities (Mántica Abaunza, interview, 1991). In July 1969, the business community participated in the creation of the Nicaraguan Development Foundation (FUNDE) with grants from AID, the IDB, and the Pan-American Development Fund. Younger members of COSIP touted FUNDE as "a bloodless revolution" that established an independent source of credit for rural workers and subsistence farmers (Baez 1970, 47). A few hundred people were organized into "model" cooperatives for food production and microenterprise. FUNDE was a diplomatic recognition by some peripheral elites and AID that the state banking system completely ignored the needs of rural inhabitants. But, in no sense did this amount to a concerted movement in the private sector to confront Somoza and force fundamental political and economic change.

Up to the early 1970s, the business community saw no reason to question the legitimacy of the Somoza regime. But, after Somoza Debayle came to power, some businessmen expressed resentment about the dominance of the minifaldas over economic policy making. Strong complaints were registered even by elites inside Somoza's Liberal machine. In late 1969, Alfredo and Ramiro Sacasa Guerrero of BANIC, Pedro Quintanilla, ex-minister of education, and Luis Carrión Montoya formed the Liberal Constitutionalist Movement (MLC) in protest of Somoza's blatant nepotism and cronyism in the administration. They were especially incensed about Noel Pallais's jealous management of INFONAC (Carrión Montoya, interview, 1991). The Sacasas and Carrión were high officials in the state banking system during its formative years. Alfredo Sacasa was the president of INFONAC from 1954 to 1964, and Carrión Montoya was INFONAC's business manager under Somoza García's regime in the 1950s (El Semanario 1 (31): 9; U.S. Dept. of State 1988, 43). Ramiro Sacasa ran Somoza's presidential campaign as chairman of the PLN in 1966 and 1967 (Institute for the Comparative Study of Political Systems 1967, 24).

The MLC emphasized classical liberal ideals of private initiative and free competition and raised anew the issue of the constitutionality of Somoza Debayle's presidency. Though the MLC's hue resonated well with INDE officials, exporters, industrialists, and bankers were quite content to allow the state to renew agricultural cycles while they continued to invest in a multitude of agro-industrial and commercial ventures. They were profiting from the increasing purchasing power of the middle sectors and selling at high prices to a limited market (Baloyra 1983, 313). Peripheral economic elites left the political stage to the dictatorship and concurred with its desire to limit popular organization (see chap. 5). Figures 2, 3, and 4 indicate how the most important economic sectors were divided between Somoza and members of the private banking groups, most of whom remained aloof from day-to-day politics (Strachan 1976, 79).[6] The willingness and ability of some elites to contest the dictatorship in the political arena when Somoza's greed exceeded their levels of tolerance after 1972 will be considered in chapters 6 and 7.

This chapter has traced the maturation of economic elite relations in the 1960s. The BANIC and BANAMER groups built diverse industrial and commercial portfolios from their bases in export agriculture. The expansion of the economy, combined with the concentration of political power in the hands of Anastasio Somoza Debayle, led to a convergence of elite interests around private enterprise and the state. However, unlike in El Salvador,

FIGURE 2

"Somoza Incorporated" (circa 1970)

| National Development Institute (INFONAC) + National Bank of Nicaragua (BNN) | Nicaraguan Investment Corporation (CNI)[a] | Wells Fargo + Bank of America |

Agro-Industrial Enterprises

IFAGAN, CARNIC (cattle slaughter)

FABRITEX w/ BANIC, United Brands (textiles, cooking oil)

National Sugar Company (CANSA)

Hercules Powder Company, ADELA (Lux.), Pennsalt[b]

Commercial Enterprises	*Industrial Enterprises*	*CAPSA (Savings and Loan Corp.)*
LANICA (airline)	METASA (sheet metal)	Home construction, appliances, home loans
Mercedes Benz dealership	PROLACSA (Nestlé)[c]	Customs services, warehouses
Novedades (newspaper)	National Cement Company	Architecture, engineering projects
International Hotel, Mercedes Hotel Montelimar and Xiloa resorts	Cigars (INFONAC)	Partnership with Montiel Argüello, Pallais Debayle, Lacayo, Terán, and Blandón[d]

Source: Author.

a. CNI was founded in 1964 with the assistance of the Agency for International Development (AID) to promote joint ventures in Nicaragua, especially with LAAD chemical, machinery, feed, and commercial export companies. Bank of America and Wells Fargo invested in several ventures established through LAAD and CNI.

b. Joint ventures in pesticides and chemicals through INFONAC.

c. Joint venture.

d. Somoza's PLN clique.

FIGURE 3

Financial Portfolio of Banco de América (BANAMER)

National Bank of
Nicaragua (BNN)

+

National Development
Institute (INFONAC)

Wells Fargo + Bank of America + First National Bank of Boston

Agro-Industrial Financial Corporation (FIA)

Nicaraguan Investment
Corporation (CNI)

+

Latin American Agri-
business Corp. (LAAD)

Commercial Enterprises	Investors
Ingenio San Antonio, Nicaraguan Sugar Estates, Licorera Nacional (rum), Ingenio Amalia, Compañía Azucarera	Pellas-Chamorro, Bernard
E. Chamorro Industries (oil, soap)	Chamorros of Granada
AGROTEX (textiles)	Multiple investors[a]
Molinos de Nicaragua, Café Soluble "Presto" (coffee processing)	Baltodano
M. I. Lacayo Rolter (shoes)	M. I. Lacayo
Embotelladora "Milca" (Coca-Cola)	Multiple investors[a]
SOVIPE (construction)	Solórzano, Villa, Pereira
Cerámica Industrial	Dreyfus, multiple investors from BANAMER and BANIC in joint venture with American Standard[a]
Cerámica Chiltepe	Dreyfus

FIGURE 3

(continued)

Commercial Enterprises	**Investors**
CASA Pellas (Toyota dealership, spare parts, refrigeration, air conditioning)	
Santa Monica (real estate and commercial investments)	
• "Plaza España" (supermarkets, office space)	Felipe Mantica
• CASA Dreyfus (retail imports, hardware)	Enrique Dreyfus
• Central Comercial Camino Oriente (office and recreational complex)[a]	Multiple investors
Julio Martínez (automobiles, hardware, supermarkets, retail imports)	Martín Benard (machinery imports)
J. Vasalli (machinery and chemical imports, customs services)	
Almacenadora de Pacífico, Carlos Holmann and Co. Ltd. (customs services)	
Nicaragua Machinery Company	Pellas, Mántica
SOVIPE Commercial (home appliances, Villa architecture)	
Comercial Internacional Agrícola (coffee exports, chemical and machinery imports)	Baltodano
BIRSA (real estate development)	Fernández Holmann

Diverse Investments Corporation (CID)
- Time deposits abroad
- Insurance, credit cards, and savings and loans guaranteed by Bank of America, Wells Fargo, and First National of Boston

Source: Author.

a. Company stock was sold to *accionistas* who held their assets in the bank (interview with Arturo Cruz, 31 October 1988).

FIGURE 4

Financial Portfolio of Banco Nicaragüense (BANIC)

```
                    Chase Manhattan + Morgan Guaranty + Multibank
National Bank of                          │
Nicaragua (BNN)                           │
    +                                     │
National Development    ─────────────▶    │
Institute (INFONAC)                       │
                                          ▼
                  Nicaraguan Development Investments (INDESA)
                                          │
                                          │       Nicaraguan Investment
                                          │           Corporation (CNI)
                                ◀─────────┤                +
                                          │       Latin American Agri-
                                          │       business Corp. (LAAD)
                                          ▼
```

Commercial Enterprises	Investors
GRACSA, AGROSA (cooking oil), GEMINA (flour, meal)	Montealegre, Callejas, Robelo[a]
FABRITEX	Robelo, Montealegre, Callejas w/Somoza, United Brands
Compañía Cevecera Nicaragüense (beer)	Sacasa Guerrero, Montalván
Desmotadora "La Virgen," DEPSA (cotton ginning)	Gurdián, Montealegre
Embotelladora Nacional (Pepsi-Cola)	Sacasa Guerrero, Montlaván
Compañía Lactea "La Completa" (milk processing)[b]	
Cerámica Industrial	w/ BANAMER and American Standard[b]
EXPASA, EXPASA Quimica (cotton exports and technical services)	Blandón, Gurdián

FIGURE 4
(continued)

Commercial Enterprises

INQUISA (chemical imports)

ALMACENTRO (customs services)

MAISA (machinery imports for cotton processing)

Investors

Somoza, Hercules Powder Company, Pennsalt (joint venture)[b]

Lang

Reyes

Financiera de Vivienda

CONTECSA (commercial/industrial parks, housing tracts)[b]

La Protectora

- Time deposits abroad
- Insurance, and savings and loans guaranteed by Chase Manhattan, Morgan Guaranty, and Multibank

Source: Author.

a. Sales to General Mills and United Fruit.

b. Company stock was sold to *accionistas* who held their assets in the bank (interview with Luis Carión Montoya, 2 June 1991).

---

most economic elites were isolated from bureaucratic circles which controlled policy making. Neither BANIC nor BANAMER was part of a unified oligarchy with a long history of political and economic dominance. The development of the Somocista state and the emergence of distinct capitalist interests outside the dictatorship gave rise to potential for competition within the Nicaraguan upper class. On the one hand, the continuous reign of the oligarchy in El Salvador maintained homogeneity in the wealthy strata after 1950. On the other hand, though Somoza and the business community had not clashed over access to resources and policy making by the early 1970s, the structural conditions for elite conflict were present.

5

Class Structure and Political Organization: Land, Labor, and Opposition

This chapter will focus on dramatic changes in the social configuration of middle and lower classes in Nicaragua during agro-industrialization from the 1950s to the early 1970s. Rural dislocation, urbanization, and the nature of popular resistance to the Somoza dictatorship will be considered in the context of existing political institutions, i.e., the state, political parties, and labor unions. The main emphasis will be on the degree to which middle and lower classes had access to, and were organized in, the overall political system. A brief analysis of these political circumstances in El Salvador is made for approximately the same period. The aim is to establish a comparative perspective on different patterns of coalition-building against authoritarian rule in each country in the late 1970s.

Rural Class Conflict and Peasant Revolution

Agrarian transformation that dislocates peasant communities is a central feature of the theoretical literature on revolution. Several studies have suggested that revolution results from autonomous peasant violence that surges out of conscious class struggle in the countryside. The debate centers around which kinds of peasants really account for revolutionary "success." Wolf (1969), Scott (1976), and Popkin (1979) analyze the conditions under which small subsistence producers experience economic insecurity in the transition to commercial agriculture. In contrast, Paige (1975) focuses on rural class relationships in small capitalist economies that depend heavily on export crops. He argues, among other things, that an agro-export economy that consists of wealthy landowners who employ landless, often temporary, laborers who earn only wages may be inherently politically unstable.

> The homogeneous poorly paid, concentrated mass of workers that Marx saw as the vanguard of the revolution are found not in industrial societies, but in commercial export-agriculture in the underdeveloped world. It is such societies that the greatest incentives for class based organization and class conflict exist. (Paige 1975, 34)

Rural conditions in El Salvador and Nicaragua somewhat approximated this description at about the end of the 1960s or the beginning of the 1970s (Brockett 1990; Dunkerley 1988; Williams 1986). Obviously, rural rebellion did not occur in either case at that time. Skocpol states that, "[Peasant vanguard] parties . . . have been created and led by urban-educated middle-class people. In no sense have they been the autonomous organizational creations of agrarian lower classes" (1982, 358). This raises the task of explaining the structural conditions that facilitate cooperation between peasants and a guerrilla movement against the dominant landed class.

The classic peasant-intellectual combination has been considered the axis for overthrowing the existing order (Huntington 1968, chap. 5). Several scholars have emphasized the deliberate efforts of guerrillas to penetrate rural communities and politicize misery (Migdal 1974; Wickham-Crowley 1989b). On the other hand, McClintock (1984, 1989) has focused on how the deterioration of rural living standards can encourage radical elements from within peasant villages. A common feature of this literature is that the regime's unwillingness or failure to address severe inequality and deprivation in the countryside exacerbates class divisions and perpetuates attacks on landed interests. Of course, this precludes any kind of political cooperation between the rich and the poor during a national crisis. It is relevant here to ask whether relative agrarian conditions explain the emergence of a revolutionary alliance that included elite economic groups in Nicaragua and not in El Salvador.

Social upheaval in El Salvador was defined along class lines, pitting the oligarchy and the military against the peasantry and the guerrilla army of the Farabundo Martí National Liberation Front (FMLN) in the 1980s. In Nicaragua, the Sandinista National Liberation Front (FSLN) failed to mobilize a coordinated rural uprising and pursued an urban-based insurrection with assistance from some landowners and businessmen in the late 1970s. Midlarsky and Roberts (1985) and Midlarsky (1988) have attempted to establish a theoretical link between the severity of rural inequality and divergent revolutionary paths in El Salvador and Nicaragua. They make inferences about qualitative differences by analyzing land tenure and availability.

> Rural class-based revolutions are more likely where the land is scarce [like in El Salvador]. . . . Where the land is less scarce [like in Nicaragua] . . . other types of revolutionary behavior can arise and broad-based coalitions are more likely. (Midlarsky 1988, 493–94; see also Midlarsky and Roberts 1985, 166–67)

The impulse of the Alliance for Progress expanded cotton, coffee, beef, and sugar production and energized the Central American Common Market. This produced spurts of high agricultural growth rates in El Salvador and Nicaragua. Land became scarce for food production as plantation owners acquired more land and committed more hectares to export operations.[1]

Although land tenure statistics show that Salvadoran peasants faced a more serious problem of access to land, conditions in Nicaragua were hardly desirable (Wilkie and Perkal 1984, 92, 96). The agro-export boom led to evictions of poor farmers and fundamentally changed the traditional interdependent relationship between landowner and peasant/laborers in both countries. This is reflected in the reduction of the economically active population in agriculture from 62 percent in 1960 to 45 percent by the early 1970s in both cases (Taylor and Jodice 1983, 209). A greater number of people were affected by changes in agrarian production relationships in El Salvador than in Nicaragua. El Salvador's population was always about twice that of Nicaragua's during this period. But, the data on agrarian conditions militate against the notion that there was markedly less potential for rural class conflict in Nicaragua than in El Salvador (Gould 1990, 122, 178).

TABLE 7

Rural Economic Change, 1960–1979
(in percent)

	El Salvador	Nicaragua
Annual Agricultural Growth		
1960–1965	3.8	11.0
1966–1970	3.8	0.6
1971–1975	4.5	5.7
1976–1979	1.9	3.5
Growth of Agro-Exports		
1960–1965	12.5	14.7
1966–1970	−0.4	2.4
1971–1975	8.6	7.6
1976–1979	2.7	2.3

Sources: SIECA 1973a, 1973b, 1971a.

TABLE 8

Land-Use Area, 1970
(in percent)

	El Salvador	Nicaragua
Food	16.3	10.1
Export	62.0	59.6[a]
Idle	19.6	29.6

Source: SIECA 1972.

a. Includes grazing.

What was happening to the Nicaraguan peasantry during the expansion of export agriculture in the 1950s and 1960s? In the 1950s, cotton became particularly threatening to small farmers. The agricultural priorities of the state began to reshape the agrarian class structure as cotton spread quickly along the rich Pacific plain. Food producers, particularly those growing corn and beans, found themselves in direct competition with cotton capitalists for the first time. Peasant families that depended on small plots for survival came up against government officials and growers who manipulated credit and title policies. Evictions were not new phenomena. In the early twentieth century, Conservative governments sold "ejidal" (common) lands in Granada and Carazo, traditionally rented to peasants by townships or municipalities, to foreigners for coffee exports (Brockett 1990, 26). But, the arrival of cotton to Chinandega, León, Posoltega, and El Viejo forced poor farmers to move eastward to mountainous regions in Nueva Segovia, Madríz, and Matagalpa where land was scarce (Biderman 1982, chap. 7). Cotton quickly dismantled the vestiges of the old ejidal system in the Occident where coffee had not reached overwhelming proportions. In the late 1950s and early 1960s, organized peasant groups regained some fields but were violently removed by the National Guard (Gould 1990, esp. part 2; Williams 1986, 56–57).

The plight of peasants in the Occident became even more urgent when private landholders increasingly rented land to urban professionals after cotton prices rebounded in the early 1960s. These part-time cotton capitalists had better access to bank credit than food producers. The concentration of land in the cotton sector was threatening to replace subsistence farmers all together. By the mid-1960s, 72 percent of the legal titles granted by the government in León and Chinandega were for cotton cultivation (Williams 1986, 57). The percentage of arable land occupied by cotton farms in the country rose from 16 percent in 1960 to 25 percent in 1967 (Warnken 1974, 14). But, the number of cotton farms actually fell from 3,676 in 1963 to 2,888 in 1971, with those of over 500 manzanas (1 manzana = 1.7 acres) constituting 48 percent of the planted area (CONAL 1979; Warnken 1974, 14, 43). Elite growers and the Somozas considered the deposits of "white gold" their private reserves. They prevented displaced food producers from entering the prized vaults. Instead of providing food producers an opportunity to convert land and secure an alternative source of income, "cotton became another word for eviction" (Williams 1986, 55).

Many corn and bean farmers who lost their land in the 1960s joined the ranks of cotton labor. The number of temporary cotton workers rose from about 44,000 in 1960 to somewhere between 150,000 and 200,000 in the 1970s, depending on the success of the harvest for a particular year (Biderman 1982, 94). Imported machinery restricted manual job opportunities only to the harvest period. Although thirty man days per acre per year were needed to pick cotton (Williams 1986, 118), tractors and disc-plows did the work of ten men in tasks like field preparation and weeding. The number of machines rose from 500 in 1950 to 2500 in 1967 (Biderman 1982, 93), all of them purchased from companies owned by LAAD and the BANIC group. Consequently, a large portion of the peasantry was transformed into a seasonal, salaried, nomadic labor force with no formal political or social organization. An interview with a manager of a cotton farm in the early 1970s is revealing:

> The labor force of the cotton farm was 400 people.... They were not organized in any syndicate because the majority stayed on the premises for only three to six months.... 60 percent of the laborers would come and go year after year which did not permit them any type of organization. (Quoted in Ogliastri 1986, 8)

Sugar production in the Occident augmented the onslaught of cotton on food producers in the 1960s. As mentioned earlier, the Ingenio San Antonio and the Somoza-controlled National Sugar Company benefited from the reallocation of the United States' import quota after the Cuban revolution. Plantations doubled in size from 23,000 manzanas in 1960 to 58,000 manzanas by the early 1970s, and 85 percent of sugar was grown around León and Chinandega (Biderman 1982, 120). Some cotton fields were converted to sugar when cotton prices fell temporarily in the late 1960s.

After the violent incidents in the Occident in the late 1950s, Pedro Joaquín Chamorro sympathized with the popular struggles in *La Prensa* (Gould 1990, 97). The MPDC expressed serious concerns about deteriorating rural living standards due to export expansion. In response to a labor protest on May Day 1961, Luis Somoza promised campesino leaders to initiate an agrarian reform program and minimum wage legislation (ibid., 127). President Somoza was caught between the rising tide of popular mobilization and intraelite conflict over political stability and the profitability of cotton production.

> The lack of a clear governmental policy on the agrarian question arose out of the disunity of the Chinandega elite. The split between the Reyes and Campuzano-Deshon factions, exacerbated by campesino agitation, produced tensions throughout the Somocista power structure. . . . The two factions openly struggled to define regime policy toward the campesino movement. (Gould 1990, 131)

The agrarian reform law of April 1963 was the last major action of Luis Somoza's administration before René Schick took office in May. Somocistas reasoned that the new law would "create more property owners and fewer communists."[2] In 1964, AID helped the Schick government establish the Nicaraguan Agricultural Institute (IAN) which oversaw a project designed to stabilize and pacify the rural population. However, the legitimacy of the policy was immediately called into question by campesinos when Schick appointed Tomás Montealegre as minister of agriculture, Horacio Montealegre as IAN executive secretary, and Alfonso Callejas Deshon as minister of development. The Montealegre, Callejas, and Deshon families and other elite landowners manipulated the regime to secure their dubious claims to contested land in the cotton belt (Gould 1990, 254–58).

The IAN reverted to settling rural class conflict by forcing dispossessed peasants to migrate to settlements in remote areas and giving them titles to idle land. Between 1964 and 1973, 63 colonies with a total of 2,600 families covering 41,000 manzanas were organized in Nueva Segovia, Jinotega, Matagalpa, Chontales, Río San Juan, and Zelaya, far away from the fertile Pacific plain where cotton, sugar, and coffee were grown (Camacho and Menjivar 1985, 416). On the agricultural frontier, 16,500 titles for land were distributed to individual farmers. The IAN amounted to a disingenuous effort to address the profound contradiction between export and food production. The National Guard patrolled the settlements daily to ensure that peasants did not cultivate outside designated areas.

Mass colonization was certainly the manifestation of upper-class fears that the radical ideology of the Cuban revolution would penetrate the countryside and lead to mass revolts. The impact of the program was limited at best. Over the next decade, discontent festered as a result of the marginalization of the rural population. Between 1964 and 1973, 240 land invasions were reported in the departments of León and Chinandega in the heart of the cotton belt (Biderman 1982, 140). Many peasants "escaped" from the colonies and returned to the fertile Pacific coast in search of land, but encountered only brutality. The National Guard was ordered to crush any attempts at "squatting" in order to protect "property rights" (Paige 1985, 107–08). This situation could be considered evidence of potentially explosive class polarization.

Cattle grazing presented another barrier to peasants' access to land even as they began to migrate to the northern mountains. Reacting to increased export demand, ranchers began stringing miles of barbed wire around previously unoccupied lands in Matagalpa, Madríz, and Estelí. Before the cattle boom, most of the herd was located in flat, open areas in Chontales and Boaco, south of the mountains, and tended by Nicaraguan "cowboys." The average ranch size was only 25 manzanas in 1963 (Warnken 1974, 43). By the end of the decade, ranches of less than 500 manzanas accounted for only 11 percent of pastureland (ibid., 1974, 216). As the dense forest of Matagalpa was cleared to make room for new herds, ranchers and the Somoza regime collided with the Sandinistas.

Carlos Fonseca, Tomás Borge, and Silvio Mayorga operated the FSLN out of northern Nicaragua and southern Honduras in the early 1960s. They were from middle-class families in the city of Matagalpa and had little experience with peasant communities in the remote surrounding areas. Fonseca's father was the administrator of Anastasio Somoza García's rural properties in Matagalpa that included cattle ranches. Borge was the son of a drugstore owner in Matagalpa and participated in Liberal politics in León in the 1940s and early 1950s (U.S. Dept. of State 1988, 13, 15). All three leaders emerged out of the radical student movement started by Fonseca at the UNAN in the mid-1950s. But, the initial activities of the FSLN were devoted to establishing guerrilla cadres in the mountains around Matagalpa and attracting the support of rural labor and peasants (Booth 1985, 138–41). The strategy of relying on occasional forays in small towns proved completely unsuccessful for the guerrillas. An attack at Bocay on the Río Coco in 1963 was easily thwarted by the National Guard. The operation suffered from the lack of strong ties with villages that could provide refuge, poor lines of communication, and limited knowledge of the dense forest of the northern regions.

The Sandinistas did not strike again until 1967 at Pancasan on the eastern edge of the department of Matagalpa. The National Guard mobilized four hundred troops and several U.S.-made airplanes to repel the guerrillas. Mayorga was killed in the fighting which dealt a severe blow to military leadership in the field (FER 1975, 12). Ranchers expressed concern about the security of their ranches and herds after the incident. The Guard obliged them by declaring Matagalpa a counterinsurgency zone and rounding up hundreds of peasants suspected of being "communist sympathizers." The repressive presence of the Guard was welcomed by members of IFAGAN and the Somocista partners of EMPANICSA who slaughtered cattle from the Matagalpa region.

The physical and strategic immaturity of the FSLN precluded a "peasant revolution" reminiscent of the Russian or Chinese experience and the influence of radical ideology in the countryside (see McClintock 1984; Skocpol 1979, 1982). Moreover, the dispersion of the rural population due to constant migration of dispossessed farmers and seasonal labor hampered the development of grassroots organizations that could defend their interests. In 1970, there were only twenty-two agricultural unions with a total membership of 1,158 out of an economically active population in agriculture of 240,000 (Paige 1985, 106). After the disaster at Pancasán, the Sandinistas retreated into self-evaluation in San José, Costa Rica. "The majority maintained that it was necessary to return to the city and from there [begin to build] a popular army out of a strong student and urban-based resistance" (FER 1975, 12). This is not to suggest that the FSLN abandoned the peasantry. According to Sandinista commander Henry Ruíz, the problem was not that rural inhabitants were useless to the revolution, but rather that the FSLN had yet to discover how to mobilize them: "In the wake of Pancasán the idea of . . . [prolonged popular war utilized by Mao and Giap in Asia] . . . was adopted borrowing from the Chinese and Vietnamese experiences. . . . But there remained several concepts that were obscure to us in theory . . . for example, how to plant the seed of political consciousness in the peasantry" (Ruíz 1980, 13).

Over the next two years, the FSLN developed a concrete revolutionary agenda. In 1969, the "Programa Sandinista" called students, workers, and peasants to arms, and advocated the nationalization of wealth "usurped" by Somoza and North Americans, agrarian reform, an independent foreign policy, and socialized health, housing, and education.[3] While the guerrilla leadership as a whole remained convinced that a peasant war was attainable, Fonseca drifted toward the idea of broad popular insurrection (Invernizzi et al. 1986, 54). He wrote that, "We are disposed to march together with Nicaraguans of diverse backgrounds who are interested in the overthrow of the dictatorship" (quoted in Tirado et al. 1982, 29). Rural existence revolved around temporary harvest work for six months at most and simple survival for the rest of the year (CIERA 1989, 136). As life became more and more unbearable, many people migrated to urban areas, usually to Managua, León, Masaya, and Estelí, and entered the so-called "informal sector" (Gibson 1987, 22). The cotton boom, the encroachment of cattle grazing, and the expansion of sugar plantations unraveled the social fabric of peasant communities. Though most Sandinistas did not recognize it at the time, the opportunity for peasant revolution was lost.[4]

A similar phenomenon of dislocation took place in El Salvador after World War II. Conflict over land pervaded Salvadoran politics decades before the agro-export boom in Central America. Ejidal rights had been severely restricted in the late nineteenth century when the wealthiest Salvadoran families began expanding coffee production to take advantage of high prices and technological improvements. These conditions facilitated the oligarchy's solidarity through the first decades of the twentieth century (Paige 1987). There were no unresolved political disputes, like those between the Liberals and Conservatives in Nicaragua, to destabilize the workings of government and invite North American intervention (Paige 1985, 94–99; Woodward 1985, chaps. 6, 8). After a brief dip in prices during World War I, the value of coffee exports rose from $7.3 million in 1915 to $22.7 million in 1928 (T. Anderson 1971, 8). When prices fell again between 1929 and 1931 with the onset of global depression, the coffee elite exploited hard times to further consolidate their economic power. Many small and medium producers defaulted on debts owed to the Central Reserve Bank. Their lands were confiscated by the state and distributed to the members of the Coffee Growers Association, an exclusive organization of the largest producers. Also, the oligarchy used its dominance over the coffee monoculture to acquire municipal lands through courts that favored private property (ibid., 9–10).

In this atmosphere, Agustín Farabundo Martí constructed a communist movement among peasants and workers. As a university student in El Salvador, Martí was inspired by the Mexican and Russian revolutions in the early part of the century. He joined the army of Augusto Sandino in Nicaragua in the late 1920s to fight for self-determination in Central America. Upon returning to El Salvador in 1930, Martí developed a platform around land reform, better wages for rural and urban workers, and the legalization of unions. Between January and March of 1932, Martí led several revolts in Ahuachapan and Sonsonate on the fertile Pacific plain against the unbridled power of the coffee barons. In December 1931, General Maximiliano Hernández Martínez had removed popularly elected President Arturo Araujo in a coup justified by allegations of economic mismanagement. At the behest of the oligarchy, Hernández ordered the massacre of 17,000 peasants who demanded access to plantation lands over the two-month period. Martí was arrested and executed along with two other Communist leaders in March 1932. This violent episode is an antecedent of rural class conflict after 1950.

Coffee remained the dominant export crop through the 1960s. The area under cultivation increased from 96,000 hectares in 1933 to 140,000 in 1966 (1 hectare = 2.43 acres). When cotton production increased in the 1960s, food producers had to compete with the same oligarchy that controlled two major export crops. Cotton never occupied more than 10,000 hectares before 1950. By 1965, 110,000 hectares were planted on the Pacific coast (Durham 1979, 32–33, 36). The combination of massive coffee plantations, new cotton farms, and a population growth rate of 3.5 percent between 1961 and 1971 had a devastating effect on the production and availability of food (ibid., 22). Rural tension in El Salvador has been interpreted as a classic example of Malthusian theory that predicts that consumption will inevitably exceed the capacity of agriculture when the population is growing rapidly (Midlarsky 1988; Midlarsky and Roberts 1985). However, it is more accurate to attribute the inability of food production to keep pace with demand to the expansion of export agriculture.

Between 1961 and 1971, the boom years for cotton, the landless population increased from 75,000 to 138,000; the number of peasants with less than 1 hectare rose from 155,000 to 183,000 in the same period (Durham 1979, 50). El Salvador occupies 21,000 square kilometers whereas Nicaragua occupies 148,000. By 1970, there were 250 people per square kilometer in El Salvador compared to 80 in Nicaragua (Taylor and Jodice 1983, 102). There is no vast agricultural frontier in El Salvador that could have absorbed, at least partially, the exodus of peasants from coastal regions to relieve the scarcity of land for food crops. Instead, many of the landless and land-poor chose to cross the border into Honduras. In 1969, 300,000 poor Salvadoran farmers were cultivating Honduran land. Territorial disputes between the two countries erupted in the "Soccer War" in the same year and the Honduran government expelled 130,000 settlers (Durham 1979, 50). They returned to already overpopulated areas in the isolated eastern regions containing little available land. The province of Chalatenango is a prime example (Pearce 1986). The wave of refugees sparked a series of breaches of large estates. The military responded with the usual blast of force, igniting the countryside once again. The political circumstances and migratory trends discussed above are essential for understanding why conditions ripened for organizing Salvadoran peasants against large landowners in the 1970s.

Large landowners and other capitalist interests associated with export agriculture in El Salvador and Nicaragua certainly wanted to repress challenges to land and wage policies posed by peasants and rural labor. The somewhat more urgent agrarian conditions in El Salvador compared to Nicaragua would have less impact on the character and intensity of rural class violence than the opportunity for peasants to be mobilized into a revolutionary organization. So, to claim that "the relative availability of land may have alleviated [Nicaraguan] upper-class fears of joining a revolutionary coalition [compared to the Salvadoran upper class]" (Midlarsky and Roberts 1985, 189), does not account for different patterns of coalition-building against authoritarian rule and the nature of insurrection in each case.

The next section will analyze the maturation of the Salvadoran guerrilla movement and address the question of why it did not converge with the urban, middle-class opposition to the military dictatorship of General Carlos Romero, or attempt to recruit economic elites in the late 1970s. This will serve as a vehicle to contrast the formation of a cross-class revolutionary alliance in Nicaragua in chapters 6 and 7.

Opposition and Political Outcome: Civil War in El Salvador

The role of centrist and rightist party politics in El Salvador is useful for evaluating patterns of conflict and change that led to the protracted civil war in the 1980s. The birth of the Christian Democratic Party (PDC) in the Alliance-for-Progress era generated legitimate opposition to the historical alliance between the Salvadoran military and the oligarchy. The Christian Democratic platform of economic reform through redistribution, fair elections, and representative democracy galvanized diverse social groups that established patronage with the party during a series of elections in the 1960s. Because the PDC had relative electoral success especially in urban areas, José Napoleon Duarte and other party leaders rejected offers of power-sharing by military governments (see Dunkerley 1988, 360; Montgomery 1982, 75; Webre 1979). They exercised political pressure through popular support at the ballot box until this became hopeless in 1972. The National Conciliation Party (PCN) and the oligarchy committed massive electoral fraud to deny Duarte the presidency in the March vote. Thus, the PDC reverted to more open rebellion against the PCN. Merchants, professionals, teachers, students, urban workers, and some rural laborers rallied around Duarte, who had become somewhat of a living martyr in their eyes. The Union of Catholic Workers (UNOC) operated in urban neighborhoods and rural villages on behalf of the PDC promoting unions, self-help organizations, and peasant leagues.

The PDC was complemented on the left by the National Revolutionary Movement (MNR), born in 1959, and the National Democratic Union (UDN), established in 1967. In the 1960s and early 1970s, these parties attracted various middle-sector groups to calls for reform of the capitalist system and evolutionary socialism. Most labor support for these parties was organized under the United Confederation of Salvadoran Workers (CUTS). Union membership reached 44,000 in 1970 which strengthened the PDC's electoral base when it formed a coalition with the MNR and the UDN in 1972 (Booth 1991, 50). Labor organization increased with an average urban growth rate of 4.2 percent in the 1960s (Wilkie and Perkal 1984, 88). The various unions, guilds, and associations in the CUTS were not disposed to open insurrection and radical revolution; they wanted to agitate within the system for reform (Baloyra 1982, 50–52).

Between 1972 and 1975, opposition parties and unions placed tremendous pressure on PCN president General Arturo Molina. "Progressive" elements of the military pushed Molina to address political and economic demands in order to defuse widespread criticism. A planning ministry was created in 1973 to bolster exports while protecting small and medium-sized domestic enterprises. This was directed at merchants within the PDC's constituency. Public employees in the CUTS organized several strikes to protest wage deterioration due to inflation in 1974 and 1975. Even more urgent was the issue of agrarian reform. In June 1975, Molina promulgated the Salvadoran Institute of Agrarian Transformation (ISTA) to redistribute land in Usulután and San Miguel provinces dominated by coffee. Moderate proposals encouraged the creation of new peasant cooperatives which coalesced in the United Popular Action Front (FAPU).

Immediately, the National Association of Private Enterprise (ANEP) and the Front of Agriculturalists of the Eastern Region (FARO) "accused the PCN regime of circumventing parliamentary procedure, introducing centralized planning, attacking private enterprise, and importing false foreign doctrines that would destroy the fabric of national society" (Dunkerley 1988, 374). Over the next year, ANEP and FARO used their influence in the legislature and the military to purge advocates of redistribution within the officer corps and the private sector. Molina tried to counter in July 1976 with a decree called "The First Project of Agrarian Transformation." Once again, the business community reiterated previous arguments while seizing the moral high ground. Economic elites invoked nationalism and anticommunism in attacking the decree as sacrilege against economic liberty. Support for what Molina's administration euphemistically called "expansionary redistribution" vanished in this propaganda barrage (see ANEP 1976; Webre 1979, 194–96).

Recognizing defeat, Molina endorsed hard-line anticommunist General Carlos Romero as the PCN's candidate for the presidential election in July 1977. Romero was a well-known specialist in counterinsurgency tactics (Webre 1979, 196). Thus, ANEP and FARO appealed directly to the military and Romero to check the activities of all opposition parties, labor unions, and peasant organizations. After the election, the infamous "death squads," the National Democratic Organization (ORDEN) and the Armed Forces of National Liberation for the War of Extermination (FALANGE), were given full license to smash mass demonstrations, strikes, rural protests, and any other manifestation of popular will (Montgomery 1982, 95). The ensuing violence ignited the political atmosphere, and a process of polarization occurred between 1977 and 1979.

The Romero regime became isolated because of its brutal tactics, for example, the assassination of progressive priests and blatant administrative corruption. Romero's behavior prompted some military officers, a few former ANEP members led by Mario Andino, and most political parties representing urban middle sectors to question the legitimacy of his government. In August 1979, the PDC, the UDN, and the MNR joined with the Popular Leagues and ten labor groups, amounting to over seventy thousand employees, to form the Foro Popular (Booth 1991, 50). "The Foro was significant in that it demonstrated the possibility of an alliance between elements of the larger opposition parties and the popular organizations" (Baloyra 1982, 85). Even though it called for substantial changes in the political and economic system, the Foro was not a cross-class revolutionary coalition of economic elites and guerrilla groups. It was a centrist reform movement with roots in the PDC's political following.

On the one hand, guerrilla armies cultivated strong ties with the rural population. The National Resistance (RN) gained the support of cotton, coffee, and sugar laborers organized in the Union of Rural Workers (UTC). The Popular Forces of Liberation (FPL) focused on small farmers in the Christian Federation of Salvadoran Rural Workers (FECCAS) that grew out of popular mobilization by the PDC from the 1960s. The UTC and the FECCAS participated in land invasions orchestrated by the Popular Revolutionary Bloc (BPR) and pressured the regime for better land, credit, and price policies for subsistence farmers. The UTC and the FECCAS moved consistently leftward on the political spectrum. By 1979, revolutionaries saw no need to cooperate with more moderate groups in the cities.

> [The revolutionary cadres and their followers] rejected the view that there existed in El Salvador a national bourgeoisie capable of overthrowing the "feudal" oligarchy and carrying through a national democratic revolution. ... [They] rejected a revolutionary strategy that implied sacrificing the momentum of the mass movement in the interests of a tactical alliance with sectors of the armed forces and the bourgeoisie. (Pearce 1986, 134)

Although concerted military action had not begun at this juncture, the guerrilla leadership had recruited and armed thousands of landless peasants (North 1986, 203). The FMLN was able to sustain military action against the oligarchy and its private armies throughout the 1980s.

The high degree of cohesion of the landed class and its immediate influence over the political process are important variables for explaining class-based social conflict in El Salvador. A unified ruling class that manipulates political institutions, dominates political culture, and mandates economic policies is a clear "target" at which the poor rural masses can direct their anger (Stone 1982, 375–83; 1990, chap. 5). Salvadoran coffee elites consolidated their political control over the economy in the first half of the twentieth century. A "cosmopolitan upper-class" emerged in the 1920s that consisted essentially of descendants of the coffee oligarchy. About two dozen families preserved the structure of the old oligarchy and multiplied their economic interests during the period of agro-industrialization between 1960 and 1980 (see chap. 4). From the 1932 massacre onward, the omnipotence of the Salvadoran oligarchy was embodied in security forces and the judicial system which dealt harshly with the peasantry.

In Nicaragua, the Somoza dictatorship terminated the political life of the Conservative oligarchy and subdued new elite economic groups in the 1950s and 1960s. The state and the National Guard were the Somozas' personal instruments of power to which BANIC and BANAMER deferred up to the early 1970s. It is important to point out that the Somoza regime protected itself, primarily, and elites on the political periphery, secondarily. In El Salvador, repression was the act of a politically unified landed class (Paige 1987, 177–81).

The main business organizations in El Salvador were simple extensions of the oligarchy and were hardly potential partners for social change. The Foro platform included several recommendations that were anathema to Salvadoran economic elites. The Foro demanded the dissolution of the death squad's ORDEN and FALANGE which were serving as the FARO's private army. It wanted to guarantee that peasants had ownership rights to land in areas where export agriculture was dominant. Also, the recognition of the right to strike, wage increases, and price controls on consumer goods were advanced. Surely these provisions did not attract ANEP and FARO (Foro Popular 1979, 843–45). Naturally, the oligarchy redoubled its historical reliance on the military to defend economic privileges.

The coup of October 1979 by a group of junior army officers preempted further political deterioration of Romero's rule. The PDC and most of the Foro members aligned with these officers in hopes of implementing political and economic reforms. But, the civilian junta of Guillermo Ungo, a Social Democrat, Román Mayorga, rector of the University of Central America, and Mario Andino, a former ANEP member, met immediate resistance from Jaime Gutiérrez and José García, the officers who executed the coup. In reaction to the junta's plan for redistributing land in favor of poor farmers, Gutiérrez and García argued that "the ministers [appointed by the junta] were going too far with the proposed reforms" (Montgomery 1982, 21). This contradiction stood squarely in the path toward a peaceful resolution of the class struggle over land and the possibility of genuine civilian democratic government. Consequently, when the three-man junta and its cabinet resigned in January 1980, a five-man junta was created that included two military officers, two Christian Democrats, and an "independent" (ibid., 162). The Basic Agrarian Reform Law promulgated in March 1980 scarcely resembled the more comprehensive proposal made in late 1979. The law "failed to strike at the heart of oligarchic economic power, was easily circumvented by practical or even legal means, and it escalated violence in the countryside" (Dunkerley 1988, 392).

Rural insurrection began in earnest with the convergence of five guerrilla armies in January 1980. They created the FMLN in October 1980 to prepare a general offensive. The radical threat elicited a diplomatic flurry from the United States. In its last year, the Carter administration tried to encourage the moderate elements in the junta by supporting agrarian reform and nationalization of the banks and export marketing (Brockett 1990, 154). The Carter policy resulted in strengthening the oligarchy's resolve against "radical change" through its control of the Ministry of Agriculture, unifying the left against American intervention in domestic politics, and making real political and economic reform elusive (Blachman et al. 1986, chap. 12). Just after the FMLN's "final offensive" in January 1981, the Reagan administration took over the White House. Military aid to El Salvador was greatly increased to achieve the goals of eliminating the guerrilla army and protecting the oligarchy from rural insurrection throughout the 1980s.

It should be noted that the advent of civilian government dominated by Duarte and the PDC, beginning with the constituent elections in March

1982, helped to counter pressures toward more urban support for revolutionary activity. Several legislative and presidential victories for the Christian Democrats in the 1980s provided legitimate political space between the revolutionary left and the oligarchy. The Reagan administration advanced a dual policy of a war of extermination on the FMLN and a Christian Democratic alternative. However, the PDC did not achieve democratic consolidation and could not prevent the Salvadoran oligarchy from sponsoring "death squads" to defend its control of the economy (Dunkerley 1988, 400–13; Montgomery 1982, chap. 6).

Labor, Party Politics, and the Left in Nicaragua

In the 1940s, Anastasio Somoza García courted the incipient socialist labor movement that had slowly emerged under the tutelage of Mexican activists who traveled widely in Central America in the 1920s and 1930s. The Nicaraguan Socialist Party (PSN) formed in 1944 as Somoza advanced a Labor Code granting legal status to workers' unions. Most organizing took place in the capital and culminated in the Federation of Workers of Managua (FTM) that attached itself to the PSN in the same year. Unions of electricians, plumbers, carpenters, garment workers, mechanics, drivers, and customs agents were established under the FTM banner. Somoza encouraged unionism as a means of protecting his tenuous hold on power and fending off political challenges from the Conservatives and Independent Liberals. "The greatest period of union expansion in pre-revolutionary Nicaragua [was] from August 1944 to June 1945" (Gould 1987, 365). While the PCN and the PLI were forming an electoral alliance during this period, Somoza lured labor leaders with the promise of free political association and wage guarantees. At the same time, PLN activists penetrated the ranks of the PSN and built a broad network of patronage between the nascent syndicates and the regime. However, this marriage of convenience lasted only until Somoza secured his claim to the presidency and tamed the Conservative Party in 1950.

In a direct reaction to the "Pact of the Generals," some PSN leaders sought more autonomy from the dictatorship and founded the General Confederation of Workers (CGT). They feared that the PLN's rapprochement with the Conservative Party would stifle labor organization. Nevertheless, workers in the CGT did not openly oppose Somoza in the first half of the 1950s. The PSN rejected the militancy of the UNAN student organizations led by party members Carlos Fonseca, Tomás Borge, and Silvio Mayorga. The contradiction became transparent when the Socialists appealed for calm after Somoza's death in 1956: "We oppose the alteration of the constitutional order by force. . . . we insist on a civic struggle backed by the masses in order to gain the recognition of democratic liberties, better salaries, and just reforms to labor legislation" (quoted in G. Gutiérrez 1988, 101). From this point, Fonseca embarked on a project to adapt Sandino's revolutionary ideology of social Christianity, socialism, and antiimperialism to the contemporary political context (Hodges 1986; Palmer 1988). Fonseca's alienation from the PSN and his bitter experience at El Chapparal in 1959 straddled the Cuban Revolution. Castro's Latin American nationalist posture and Sandino's defiance of North American intervention inspired Fonseca to advance Nicaragua's unique revolution.

> Fonseca came to understand that the making of a successful revolution required more than the standard revolutionary repertoire of Marxist-Leninist theory and strategy. Without native roots and a popular and nationally-based ideology. . . . Marxism-Leninism in Nicaragua was destined to remain the thought of a political sect. (Hodges 1986, 163)

The FSLN was created officially in southern Honduras in July 1961 out of the remnants of the "Rigoberto López Pérez" column. Fonseca, Borge, and Mayorga concentrated on rebuilding reliable student cadres in the UNAN which had been broken by the National Guard in 1959 and 1960 after El Chapparal. Meanwhile, the PSN continued to participate in mainstream politics that ultimately divided the membership. Luis Somoza appealed to workers through a series of decrees on the minimum wage, social security, and vacation with pay in the early 1960s (see chap. 4). PSN leaders close to the regime praised Luis and declared victory for the Nicaraguan people who "spilled a lot of blood in the achievement of an atmosphere of democratic freedoms" even though Liberal and Conservative assemblymen declared the laws unbinding (G. Gutiérrez 1988, 95, 100; Jarquín, interview, 1991).

Populism was perpetuated by Somocista activists only as a tactic to improve the PLN's image during the election season and counter the political assault of Fernando Agüero and the MPDC. CGT ranks tripled between 1960 and 1962 (Gould 1990, 185–86). However, before the election of René Schick in 1963, founders of the CGT, who mistrusted the Somozas since 1950, rebelled against Socialists supporting the PLN. The confederation split into an "official" faction with links to the dictatorship and an "independent" faction (CGTi), attracting the Syndicate of Carpenters, Bricklayers, and Masons (SCAAS) (Gould 1990, 184–86). The CGTi also courted sugar, cotton, and coffee laborers and pressed for negotiations on a new labor code to address working conditions brought on by the introduction of complex machinery in factories and fields. These concerns were ignored by Liberal and Conservative agro-exporters and industrialists (Gould 1990, 190, 255). During the late 1960s, the National Guard consistently used violence to intimidate PSN organizers of new unions in factories and hospitals and on sugar and cotton plantations. In January 1967, the CGTi mobilized rural workers in the mass protests led by Pedro Joaquín Chamorro against Anastasio Somoza Debayle. They were among the three hundred people killed by the National Guard (G. Gutiérrez 1988, 99).

Under these repressive conditions, the number of workers willing and able to join unions remained insignificant. By 1970, there were 26,000 professional and technical workers, 4,700 administrators and managers, 57,000 clerical workers, 55,000 service personnel, and 110,500 industrial workers. Only 30,000 people out of a total economically active population of more than 500,000 were organized in unions; 4,000 were members of the "official" CGT (IDB 1969, 12; Wilkie and Perkal 1984, 262). As discussed in chapter 3, most professional, technical, and managerial positions were occupied by upper-class graduates of the UCA and INCAE who shunned political affiliations.

Furthermore, because manufacturing increasingly depended on imported, capital-intensive technology in the 1960s, most factories required only a few workers with specialized skills. Industrial employment increased only 3 percent during the decade (Wilkie and Perkal 1984, 262), thus limiting the physical and logistical possibilities of union organization (Gaston Castillo Fletes, interview by author, 17 September 1991). In general, formal employment in industrial, commercial, and service sectors was not sufficient to absorb the pressures of urbanization caused by the spread of export agriculture and forced migration from the countryside. Nicaragua's average urban growth rate was 6.7 percent between 1960 and 1970 (Wilkie and Perkal 1984, 88). The outskirts of Managua and other cities became ghettos of the under- and unemployed who relied on informal economic activities for survival.

Many studies have shown that this was a common phenomenon in Latin America particularly during the Alliance for Progress. Despite the accelerated industrial growth after World War II, the relative size of the informal proletariat declined by only 4 percent between 1950 and 1980. In particular, "the proportion of self-employed persons remained static over time, a clear indication that the mass of itinerant workers . . . [were] not being absorbed into formal employment" (Portes 1985, 29).

Export-led development shifted the population from a rural to an urban or semiurban existence. The proliferation of middle sectors and the urban poor translated into more complex social problems associated with housing, health, and education. Advocates of the Alliance for Progress and architects of Central American integration in the 1960s insisted that economic growth would encourage democratic political alliances in the region. It was presumed that, over time, economic success would necessitate political modernization and open a passage to pluralist society.

> Industrial entrepreneurs have not yet differentiated themselves as a group from traditional agricultural exporters. . . . nor have the industrial workers realized how closely associated their interests are with those of agricultural workers and subsistence farmers. . . . To the extent that the workings of the domestic economy grow in importance and its various sectors become increasingly interdependent, conditions will develop for a great coalition of these groups to take its place in the main underpinnings of the political system. (Castillo 1966, 176–77)

This view did not acknowledge that agro-industrialization in Nicaragua was accompanied by the convergence of the Somoza dictatorship with capitalists producing for export and internal consumption against workers and peasants. Economic elites averted agrarian reform, railed against the organization of labor, and avoided direct foreign competition in critical sectors. Consequently, export-led development did not weave together the interests of businessmen and labor as hoped for. The process of urbanization somewhat broadened internal markets and employment. But, demand was restricted by the structure of income. While the manufacturing sector grew at an average rate of 10 percent, wages dropped 8 percent between 1967 and 1970 (CIERA 1989, 32; Wilkie and Perkal 1984, 268).

Moreover, moderate and leftist political parties offered no real political efficacy for the average citizen.[5] The PSN and the PSCN were microparties run by intellectuals with a small following and without the electoral success of the Christian Democrats in El Salvador (T. Walker 1970). The PDC attracted middle- and working-class support and formed a viable coalition with the MNR and the UDN for the 1972 presidential election. Duarte galvanized civilian opposition in the Foro Popular and offered a legitimate reformist alternative to the guerrilla movement which, if anything, helped avert revolution in the 1980s. Christian democratic elements in Nicaragua emerged from within the Conservative Party and never amounted to more than a few dozen people voicing their concerns on the fringes of national politics. The original nucleus of the MPDC failed twice, in 1962 and 1966, to overcome the PLN's machinations and dethrone the Somoza dynasty (Booth 1985, 106–08; T. Walker 1970, 18–56).

The UNO coalition of 1966 did not advance a coherent economic and social reform program like the PDC, the UDN, and the MNR in El Salvador. Conservative and Independent Liberal elites wanted to limit popular mobilization even though they opposed the PLN. The issue of leadership is important here, too. Agüero was "very jealous" of Pedro Joaquín Chamorro and was criticized for "personalist attitudes" by MPDC members in the early 1960s. Agüero eventually alienated many young Conservative activists, like Reynaldo Antonio Téfel, who quit the party and joined the PSCN in 1964 (Institute for the Comparative Study of Political Systems 1967, 20, 23, 25). The Agüero-Chamorro rivalry did not abate until UNO formed late in the 1966 campaign, which diverted energy away from defeating the Somozas (Cruz, interview, 1991). Some observers of Nicaraguan politics have speculated that Chamorro possessed the charisma to lead a centrist coalition to challenge authoritarian rule like Duarte in El Salvador. It took a political and a natural disaster to motivate Chamorro to try to do so.

In 1970, the MLC made a formal challenge to Somoza's presidency based on the constitutional prohibition of a military officer holding executive office. Ramiro Sacasa directed several legal arguments to the Supreme Court, leading many Nicaraguans to believe that he wanted to launch a campaign for the presidency under the Liberal banner (Chamorro 1990, 325 n. 18). Somoza defused the political confrontation by offering to share power with Fernando Agüero and his Conservative faction. Somoza and Agüero met in a now-infamous bar called the "Kupia Kumi" in November to negotiate an agreement in which Agüero, the National Guard General Roberto Martínez Lacayo, and Adolfo Lovo Cordero, a PLN member, would form a "transitional junta" to replace Somoza. At the time, Lovo Cordero had investments in BANIC's holding company INDESA and Somoza's CAPSA savings and loan bank; he was also an original contributor to FUNDE's rural credit fund in 1969 (Baez 1970, 47). The junta dissolved the National Assembly in early 1972 and was supposed to take over legislative functions until the next election could be "legally" held in 1974. Pedro Joaquín Chamorro said that, "we should be content because the farce of Agüero has ended." Chamorro labeled Agüero a traitor of the Nicaraguan people in *La Prensa* (29 November 1970, 1). Of course, Somoza anticipated returning to office in 1974. It was prearranged that Agüero and his close Conservative friends would control 40 percent of the assembly in exchange for the extension of the presidential term through 1981 (*La Prensa*, 27 March 1971, 1).

Clearly, the pervading political conditions could be described as "praetorian"; demands for political participation exceeded the degree of institutionalization (Huntington 1968). But, there was neither a peasant-based insurrection led by intellectuals, nor a mass urban rebellion threatening the regime. The road to collective action began in December 1972. An earthquake demolished downtown Managua, leaving nearly 250,000 people homeless. Approximately 400,000 square meters of commercial buildings and warehouses, 340,000 square meters of office space, four hospitals, and 740 schoolrooms were destroyed (Vilas 1985, 102). No social group was spared from economic hardship and personal loss. The wealthy, the middle class, and the poor required an immediate, comprehensive response to the tragedy from the Somoza regime. They would all be bitterly disappointed.

The class structure of the Nicaraguan society changed dramatically between 1950 and 1970. This chapter has demonstrated the effects of export agriculture on the peasantry and the changes in the configuration of urban middle sectors brought about by agro-industrialization. A peasant revolution in the Chinese or Mexican spirit was not possible in Nicaragua at the end of the 1960s due to the uprooting and dispersion of the rural population. A "proletarian" rebellion was equally remote as most workers were denied political channels of organization and expression by state repression and scarce employment. In addition, Conservative and moderate political parties failed to mobilize support for their strategic electoral coalition in order to defeat the PLN. The earthquake set in motion a complex series of events that would sweep capitalists, elite politicians, professionals, workers, students, and peasants into a revolutionary situation.

6

The Political Roots of Cross-Class Cooperation, 1973–1977

This chapter will analyze how and why the Sandinista and reformist movements against the dictatorship intersected by 1977. The origins of a revolutionary alliance of socially diverse groups can be traced back to efforts to overthrow the Somoza dynasty in the late 1950s. From the death of Anastasio Somoza García in 1956, Sandinista university students and small cells of Christian democrats in the Conservative Party pressed for political change. Neither the military actions masterminded by Pedro Joaquín Chamorro and Carlos Fonseca in the 1950s, nor the Sandinista guerrilla campaign in the 1960s, could crack the foundation of the Somocista edifice. Equally ineffective were the electoral tactics of centrist political parties and the UNO coalition in 1966 and 1967. Perhaps, the failure of opposition to the dynasty, in its various forms, served to link reformers to revolutionaries, and vice versa. The political and economic crisis that followed the earthquake activated a process of mass mobilization unprecedented in Nicaraguan history. But, entering 1973, it was yet to be determined how widespread dissent would be harnessed and utilized against Somocista despotism.

After the earthquake, all state powers were vested in the "Emergency Commission" led by Somoza, military officers, and Liberal bureaucrats. Somoza became the de facto president, reducing the "transitional junta" to a symbolic body. Agüero objected to Somoza's manipulation of the disaster and publicly rebuked him for reneging on their original deal. Conservative politicians compromised with the dictatorship, continued the charade of "legal opposition" in order to maintain their right to "parliamentary action" (Vargas 1990, 62–64). While Agüero threatened to resign from the junta, they moved to protect their claims to legislative seats in the 1974 election. With the blessing of the Granada establishment, Somoza replaced Agüero with Edmundo Paguaga. Paguaga represented the "Zancudo" (mosquito) Conservatives who had been "soaking the national budget" ever since the "Pact of the Generals" in 1950 (Chamorro 1990, 324 n. 9, 325–26 n. 20).[1]

By mid-1973, Conservative politics broke into four pieces: the Zancudos, who continued to cooperate with Somoza, the Conservative Democratic Party, the Authentic Conservative Party, and Chamorro's Conservative National Action Party (ANC), which he founded with his former UNAP colleague Rafael Córdova Rivas. The skeleton-like buildings in what was downtown Managua were a proper metaphor for the condition of the Conservative Party. The business community, political parties, and the few existing labor unions saw the disappearance of the traditional structure of the Liberal-Conservative rivalry as an opportunity to redefine the national agenda in terms of political pluralism and more democratic economic policies. These sectors would coalesce in pursuit of peaceful change. The FSLN, on the other hand, prepared an urban insurrection that would draw upon nearly all social groups.

Political Mobilization and Elite Responses

Somoza's opportunism and corruption during relief efforts and economic recovery during the mid-1970s have been well-documented. He siphoned off funds from AID and other international organizations and pillaged state institutions, like the National Social Security Institute and the National Lottery (*La Prensa*, 1 August 1978, 18; Wheelock 1985, 171–72). Somoza and the CAPSA (see figure 2) group established new enterprises by funneling BNN and INFONAC resources into their newly created Bank of Central America. These included two textile import-export companies, two concrete mix plants, a lumber mill, a food processing factory, several consumer goods import and customs agencies, and three private investment corporations (*Barricada*, 18 September 1991, 8; *La Prensa*, 3 August 1978, 26). The National Guard gained control over land for new housing tracts, import-export licensing, distribution centers for consumer goods, and transportation between hastily constructed camps on the outskirts of Managua and the remaining commercial centers. The dictator's greed far exceeded that of his father and brother who ruled Nicaragua in previous decades (Millett 1977, 237–38). Capitalists in BANIC and BANAMER were able to restore their inventories and equipment quickly through insurance policies held with North American and British companies. General contractors associated with SOVIPE (see figure 3) of BANAMER and CONTECSA (see figure 4) of BANIC were especially anxious to move forward with a multitude of construction projects. Businessmen anticipated rekindling the prosperous economic furnace of the previous decade. However, they now faced an unexpected obstacle: the dictatorship.

In March 1974, Alfonso Robelo, Felipe Mántica, William Baez, and Enrique Dreyfus organized the First Convention of the Private Sector under the auspices of INDE's self-defined role as the voice of private enterprise in the community. This event marked the formation of a "political hierarchy" within the business organizations (Bengochea, interview, 1991). Up to the early 1970s, the private sector was "amorphous" with no deliberate political coordination between the various guilds and associations. Businessmen had been satisfied with the regime and intentionally avoided the political arena.[2] Among the two thousand participants were entrepreneurs, merchants, engineers, and other professionals who purportedly represented a cross-section of the forty thousand members of COSIP and INDE. The immediate objective was to "start to perform the function" of a viable check on the PLN that the debilitated Conservatives could not or would not do (William Baez, interview by author, 7 December 1988). However, many elites expressed reluctance to endorse the gathering as a "political statement" against Somoza (Enrique Bolaños, interview by author, 25 June 1989).

Since the earthquake, INCAE scholars advocated a more limited role for the state in the economy. Their main thesis rested on the devolution of decision making to private interests and the autonomous operation of market forces. Ernesto Cruz, an INCAE founder, wrote a paper for the convention entitled "Development Strategy for the 1970s." He defined the legitimate functions of the state as the maintenance of constitutional order, provision of physical infrastructure and social security, fair allocation of public funds and contracts to private business, and the preservation of macroeconomic equilibrium (Cruz 1974). Specific complaints were leveled against the bureaucracy for fixing prices on consumer goods, imposing new restrictions on import-export activities, and mismanaging public works projects. In sum, the debate focused on securing agreements with the government in which opportunities arising from economic recovery would be given largely to private enterprise. The products of INCAE's researchers in this period clearly expressed the "corporate liberal ideology" discussed by Becker (1990).

Business leaders were also concerned with quelling unrest in the urban labor force. A series of strikes by SCAAS occurred in 1973 and 1974 after Somoza imposed a sixty-hour work week at the behest of many contractors in the Chamber of Construction. SOVIPE executive Enrique Pereira threatened to break the strikes with violence and by hiring "scabs." The Independent General Confederation of Workers (CGTi) signed an agreement on behalf of the SCAAS for a 10 percent raise in exchange for accepting longer hours (Alejandro Solórzano, interview by author, 28 May 1991).[3] It was a pyrrhic victory for construction workers. The increase failed to offset the nearly 20 percent of purchasing power lost by wage earners between 1972 and 1974 (Booth and Walker 1989, table 4). Moreover, 3,000 hospital workers walked off the job in 1973 to protest the slow response of government to repair facilities for treating an overwhelming number of patients.

Other strikes occurred in 1974 in municipal transport and maintenance services, electronic assembly factories, and food processing plants, totaling thirty thousand people. Many employees were fired and forced to enter the informal sector which swelled to 25 percent of the urban economically active population (Gutiérrez 1988, 97–99). Official unemployment rose to 20 percent in urban areas, and 50 percent of the labor force was making less than $225 a year by 1975 (INCAE 1975, 1976; Jarquín 1978, 4). Business leaders made references to improving employer-employee relations in the formal convention program, but no concrete resolutions were put forward (*La Prensa*, 2 March 1974, 6). The problems of rural working conditions and land distribution were completely ignored. Certainly these were critical social issues. By the end of 1974, 32 percent of rural inhabitants lacked land and 22.5 percent had less than 5 manzanas (1 manzena = 1.7 acres), resulting in more people looking for temporary jobs in export agriculture and migrating to the cities (Jarquín 1978, 4).

Somoza briefly attended the March 1974 meeting on the invitation of INDE. He reacted by calling the participants "school children" (*La Prensa*, 11 March 1974, 1). He also alluded that many of his erstwhile elite supporters were making money from artificially low customs appraisals on imports and avoiding state taxes. This was intended to "justify" the selective application of tighter licensing and customs regulations administered by the National Guard (Jarquín 1977, 20). Defiantly, the organizers concluded that there was a "fortified consensus" around rebuilding the economy, resolving labor disputes, and demonstrating "the social sensibility of the exemplary Nicaraguan private sector." Enrique Dreyfus insisted that Somoza's desire "to make himself a billionaire [was] the political spark" that compelled the business community to break its silence. Felipe Mántica expressed a similar sentiment by simply saying that "the private sector was getting tired of Somoza taking control of everything he could get his hands on." Moreover, Jaime Bengochea explained elite reaction as a result of "Somoza's lack of respect for the ethics of the exercise of power" established with the business community over the past two decades.[4]

Somoza's violation of "business protocol" certainly accounts for how some businessmen became dissatisfied. Export-led industrialization under dictatorial rule created wealth for entrepreneurs and professionals who benefited from favorable state policies and clearly demarcated their economic territory in the 1960s. Members of the main business groups who participated in the convention needed to offer logical reasons to stop Somocista capital from garnering more of the economy. Appeals for economic liberalization were made in order to confront the Somoza clique for abusing its monopoly on decision-making power. The rhetoric emanating from INDE, INCAE, and some sectors of COSIP could be construed as evidence that economic elites had transcended "pre-industrial values" (Lipset 1967, 9). Yet, the sudden focus on the importance of fair competition, risk-taking, and long-term investment was somewhat hypocritical and did not make them more likely to embrace fundamental political change. After all, the Nicaraguan business community had been influenced by North American and European financial and educational institutions that espoused laissez-faire capitalism for years. The national crisis would fester for the rest of the decade before most businessmen would call for the overthrow of Somoza.

Between March and September 1974, several dissident political leaders instigated a mass abstention for the upcoming election from which Somoza was sure to emerge victorious. Pedro Joaquín Chamorro and Rafael Córdova Rivas of the ANC, Rodolfo Robelo of BANIC and the PLI, Ramiro Sacasa of BANIC and the MLC, and Uriel Argüello of the PSCN adopted the slogan "No hay por quien votar" (There is no one to vote for). They attracted business, labor, professional, and even Conservative support that resembled the content of the UNO coalition of 1966, except without Agüero and the Zancudos. The "Document of the 27" declared the election illegal. Chamorro was arrested by the National Guard and held incomunicado until after the vote. Although several economic elites endorsed the statement, Alfredo Pellas and Eduardo Montealegre advocated Somoza's candidacy and dismissed the action as a misguided form of protest (Mántica, interview, 1991). Somoza assumed the presidency without incident in November 1974, and the Zancudos prepared to open a new session of the assembly. The opposition's strategy was basically a revival of the old centrist party alliance that had gone stale in the late 1960s. Though most of the same prominent figures lent their names to a list of dissenters, none mounted a campaign to offer a viable alternative to the regime by delineating a specific policy agenda (Córdova Rivas 1983, 27).

At this point, the Sandinistas launched a new campaign in urban areas designed to attract more middle-class sympathizers (Jarquín, interview, 1991). In December 1974, the Sandinistas burst into the public eye with a dramatic raid on a party at the home of Chema Castillo, a wealthy cotton grower and former minister of agriculture. The guest list was a "who's who" of the diplomatic and corporate scene in Nicaragua. Ambassador Guillermo Sacasa, Guillermo Lang, a manager of the BNN, Noel Pallais of INFONAC, Alejandro Montiel Argüello, the foreign minister and CAPSA partner, Filadelfo Chamorro, a BANAMER executive and construction magnate, Danilo Lacayo, manager of the ESSO company in Managua and INCAE director, and Benjamín Gallo, a director of the Chamber of Industry, were taken hostage (Departamento de Ciencias Sociales 1982, 244–45).

Despite recent acrimony between Somoza and some businessmen, the government maintained good relations within important elite circles established over previous decades. These men were central actors in planning and executing the national economic recovery. The FSLN exchanged the hostages for the release of Daniel Ortega from jail, a large ransom, and an airplane to escape to Cuba. The daring act left Managuans buzzing with excitement and speculation about the strength of the Sandinistas. In response, Somoza established the War Council which used martial law to incarcerate hundreds of citizens suspected of being collaborators, suspend all rights of public assembly, and censor all nongovernmental publications (Chamorro 1990, 324 n. 8).

Subsequently, the Authentic and Democratic Conservative factions joined Pedro Joaquín Chamorro and the leaders of the antielection movement to form the Democratic Union of Liberation (UDEL). UDEL's composition was similar to the Foro Popular in El Salvador in that it rallied urban white and blue-collar groups in favor of peaceful evolutionary change. However, the political parties in UDEL could not claim a track record of electoral success or a comprehensive social platform like Duarte and the PDC. UDEL amounted to a few hundred people asking for a "national dialogue" with Somoza and the National Guard (T. Walker 1986, 99–102). Many businessmen perceived Chamorro's willingness to include the PSN and the CGTi as a sign that he was gravitating to the left. At his sixtieth birthday party in March 1975, Alfredo Pellas joked that, "If *La Prensa* would not have been censored, construction workers would have a better chance for more concessions from the contractors." Enrique Pereira of SOVIPE joined in the conversation, warning Chamorro not to encourage more labor unrest. Chamorro retorted: "You have won the battle [so] don't declare war. It is impossible to destroy the SCAAS, and if you try it, you are going to provoke an invincible guerrilla" (Chamorro 1990, 60–64).

At about the same time, other elites approached UDEL as a potential outlet from further conflict. Alfonso Callejas Deshon, a BANIC cotton baron and PLN member who served as Schick's minister of development from 1963 to 1966 and as Somoza's vice-president from 1967 to the deal with Agüero, spoke with Chamorro about his intentions. They agreed that "the country has only one exit . . . the end of the regime" (Chamorro 1990, 38–40). However, neither was sure that it could be done peacefully and quickly. Francisco Lainéz, former president of the Central Bank, established a friendship with Chamorro after he was fired by Somoza in 1971 for opposing the pact with Agüero. Lainéz was generally considered a puppet of the dictatorship while he led the minifaldas, but Chamorro valued his voice in the opposition and trusted his motives: "The Somocistas have never been able to stain the honor of [Lainéz]" (1990, 98). Just after the 1974 convention, Lainéz opined in an editorial about the capacity of the business community to take concerted action: "Each business group has worked independently of the other and has not attempted to join forces and better share the responsibilities that they should assume [in the national economy]" (*La Prensa*, 17 March 1974, 2). Lainéz had direct knowledge of how BANIC and BANAMER associates deferred to the bureaucracy and was not convinced that they were prepared to alter dramatically their relationship with the state (T. Walker 1986, 103).

Nevertheless, Lainéz and Callejas are not examples of what Trimberger (1978) identified as the emergence of "elite revolutionaries from the autonomous bureaucratic apparatus" in Japan, Turkey, Egypt, and Peru. Trimberger delineated two criteria for determining whether bureaucrats can become advocates for revolution: they are not recruited from the dominant landed, commercial, or industrial classes; and, they do not form close personal and economic relationships with these classes (ibid., 4). Lainéz and Callejas are completely disqualified because they maintained links with INCAE and BANIC while they were state officials, and because they never used "their control over state resources . . . to destroy the existing economic and class order" (ibid., 5). The presence of Lainéz and Callejas in the bureaucracy was a product of elite convergence around the state and private enterprise. While in office, they were hardly candidates for a conspiracy to undermine established institutional practices for allocating financial resources; they perpetuated the state's policies. Skocpol found that state organizations "[competed] with the dominant class in appropriating resources from the economy and the society" in France, Russia, and China (1979, 30). But, in Nicaragua, the distinction between the state and the dominant class was blurred by the development of elite relations around export agriculture and related industrialization after 1950.

Elites abandoned the regime due to moral and legal objections to Somoza's unabashed charge to enrich himself politically and economically. Greed, corruption, and cronyism obviously explain Somoza's loss of legitimacy with upper-class groups who had explicitly or implicitly endorsed the dictatorship (Dix 1983, 1984; Goodwin and Skocpol 1989). Businessmen and professionals organized in COSIP, INDE, and the banking groups clashed with governing elites from the same "dominant capitalist class" who were abusing power. Loyalists in the PLN and other collaborators had privileged access to bureaucratic offices, yet they shared many of the same economic interests in agriculture, industry, and commerce with BANIC and BANAMER associates. When the few elites in the bureaucracy, like Lainéz and Callejas, split from the dictatorship, they advocated reforming the state, not eliminating it. Like other mobilized elites who wielded little political influence, they wanted to restrain Somoza but were reluctant to call for the outright destruction of political institutions. They chose to align with UDEL whose components and objectives were not revolutionary.

Under these circumstances, Somoza monitored the activities of his wealthy critics in the private sector. In February 1975, the Chamber of Industry (CADIN) petitioned the government to lift the state of emergency, arguing that the Sandinista threat had passed. Enrique Dreyfus, president of CADIN, complained that the Minister of the Economy, Juan Martínez, was using the emergency as a pretense to scold outspoken industrialists and favor Somocista factories (Dreyfus, interview, 1991). Somoza threatened to dissolve CADIN if its members did not stop "intervening in politics" (Chamorro 1990, 28, 46); Dreyfus withdrew the request immediately. Somoza also punished critical comments from Jaime Morales, manager of BANIC's INDESA corporation, by censoring the "Correo de INDESA," a weekly BANIC newsletter published in *La Prensa* (Chamorro 1990, 26). BANIC and BANAMER often placed announcements and advertisements in the newspaper and members of both groups held *La Prensa* stock. Since the earthquake, elites anonymously expressed their disgust with Somoza in articles written by professional journalists.

Jaime Wheelock describes *La Prensa* as an "ideological investment" of BANIC and BANAMER. But, it is not accurate to include Pedro Joaquín Chamorro in the formal leadership of either financial group (Wheelock 1985, chap. 6). Chamorro was not a large investor in BANIC and BANAMER enterprises, though his brother, Xavier, did own 1 percent of INDESA and briefly managed the corporation with Morales. Chamorro's father was born in Granada and founded the newspaper after World War I. After his father died, Chamorro's mother went to work in a garment factory in New York so he could attend law school at the UNAM in the 1940s. Though his "apellido" (family name) is associated with the Nicaraguan oligarchy, Chamorro held an aversion to the Conservative establishment since 1948, when he formed the dissident Conservative youth group, UNAP. As discussed earlier, many capitalists balked at Chamorro's reputation as an advocate of workers' rights which he acquired during his education in Mexico (Cruz, interview, 1991; Jarquín, interview, 1991).

Chamorro became disgruntled with businessmen who continued their usual economic affairs with the state regardless of increasing corruption. While UDEL was organizing rallies in 1975, members of BANAMER pursued private communication with the dictator. Ernesto Fernández Holmann Enrique Pereira met with Somoza several times to discuss better cooperation between the government and the private sector on reconstruction projects. Fernández Holmann was involved in selling real estate for new commercial and residential developments, and Pereira pursued the lucrative construction contracts (Cuadra Chamorro, interview, 1991). Chamorro talked with Fernández Holmann and Pereira after one meeting and concluded that "they are incapable of issuing complaints on behalf of the country . . . they are only interested in economic questions seen from their own angle" (1990, 30). He did not believe that recent signs of restlessness in the business community would lead to serious open conflict with Somoza (ibid., 64). Arturo Cruz put it well in describing the inherent weakness of UDEL: "The business class [did not] coalesce with the middle class led by Chamorro [in UDEL]" (Cruz, interview, 1991).

Business Confidence and "Unfair Competition"

The conventional interpretation of why some business leaders wanted more direct participation in economic policy making is that Somoza was treading on their traditional economic territory. However, even though the Somoza group became active in a broader range of economic activities, BANIC and BANAMER members retained profits in most agricultural, industrial, and commercial sectors, enjoying a "relative economic bonanza" after 1973 (Reinaldo Hernández, interview by author, 1991). Paige's interviews with coffee and cotton growers reveal a similar attitude toward the business climate in the mid-1970s (1989, 118–20). Lending to the private sector from state and external sources increased in the mid-1970s. Total credit to the private sector went from $607 million in 1974 to $1.01 billion in 1977. In the 1977 fiscal year, BNN accounted for $206 million and INFONAC for $92.8 million, while private foreign banks contributed $271 million in 1977 (BCN 1979, 28).

As usual, the majority of state financing went to export agriculture (BCN 1979, 29). A slump in cotton production in 1973 prompted a study from INCAE that addressed problems of fluctuating international prices for exports and rising costs of primary inputs. It was necessary, the report concluded, "to adopt measures to stabilize the agroindustrial system of cotton and permit [capitalists] . . . to adjust their production decisions better to international conditions" (Cruz and Hoadley 1975, 25). INCAE's research on the cotton sector fit well with the general thrust of the business convention. Because the Central Bank and several foreign companies controlled most cotton sales on futures markets in the United States, INCAE and many growers advocated organizing autonomous export cooperatives. "This [effort] did not reach fruition because of the increase in international prices in the 1975 and 1976 cycles, which alleviated tensions [with the state] and reduced the internal cohesion of the producers" (Baumeister and Neira 1983, 48). Moreover, the BNN reacted to higher prices by expanding credit for input costs from $20 million in 1975 to $30 million in 1977 (BNN 1975, 1977). Better harvests were achieved in 1976 and 1977, and even a few new capitalists entered the market and made quick fortunes (Paige 1989, 113). Yet, growers remained vulnerable to market fluctuations which affected them again in 1978 (see table 9).[5]

Similar phenomena of temporary recession and criticism of state policies occurred in the beef sector. Ranchers in FAGANIC became anxious after a down year in 1974 and pressured the government to address the problem of coordinating production with changing prices to maintain profit margins (see table 9). "During 1975, the beef enterprises of Nicaragua passed a critical period mainly because of low international prices. . . . So the Central Bank and the BNN renewed their contract with the [Argentina-based] Latinoconsult for three more years of technical assistance [to expand the herd and the slaughter to make up for lost profits] (BNN 1975, 30–31). Specialists from Latinoconsult and officials from INFONAC conducted a comprehensive study in which the formal conclusions in-

TABLE 9

Cotton and Beef Exports, 1973–1978

	Cotton		Beef	
	$ Millions	Manzanas	$ Millions	Pounds
1973	65	259,300	44.7	59,557
1974	117	254,369	22.1	32,567
1975	105	204,601	28.0	50,349
1976	121	283,005	40.0	54,399
1977	152	310,846	48.6	56,465
1978	146	248,175	70.1	80,635

Sources: Value of cotton: Williams (1986, 198); manzanas of cotton, BCN (1979, 65); value of beef: Williams (1986, 206); pounds of beef, BCN (1979, 75).

cluded integrating more ranchers into the export sector and creating more slaughter facilities and access roads (LATINOCONSULT 1975, 4–7).

In late 1975, construction began on new slaughterhouses in Nandaime (San Martín) and Juigalpa (Amerrisque). San Martín and Amerrisque represented the potential for more diversity in the beef sector because neither facility was associated with ASGANIC that formed the Somocista slaughter facility IFAGAN with INFONAC in 1958. Amerrisque was owned by José Argüello Cardenal and several minority investors from León who controlled 850 shares valued at $7 million (Grijalva 1991, document 2). Enrique Miranda and Wilfredo Marín were the principal investors in San Martín. Miranda, in a recent interview, emphasized that San Martín "did not have Somocista partners" and kept its distance from the dictatorship (*Barricada*, 30 August 1991, 9). Furthermore, the IGOSA plant, established in 1971 in Rivas, was operated independently by the Barrios family and other local capitalists (*Barricada*, 4 September 1991, 4).[6] Together, San Martín, Amerrisque, and IGOSA produced one-third of the nation's beef (LATINOCONSULT 1975, 1–5). However, their sales were generally restricted to the limited domestic market because CARNIC, IFAGAN, and EMPANICSA retained about 80 percent of export production (G. Ramírez, interview, 1991). Naturally, more state credit was allocated to the large Somocista operations when international prices rose in 1976 and 1977 (BNN 1977).

State capital continued to flow to the sugar and coffee sectors, too. The export value of sugar reached $52.8 million in 1976, three and a half times greater than the value for 1972. In 1976, $23.1 million was granted to the ISA and Somocistas producing for the National Sugar Company (CANSA) (see figure 2, p. 000) (Biderman 1982, 120, 185–86). More emphasis was put on coffee production in the mid-1970s in response to unstable prices and production in the cotton sector. The number of quintals of coffee harvested went from 890,000 in 1974 to 1,251,000 in 1977 (BCN 1979, 67), with credit from the BNN totaling $155 million in 1977 (Biderman 1982, 185). Consequently, coffee overtook cotton as the most valuable export crop by 1978 (SIECA 1981a). As explained in earlier chapters, foreign exchange earned from agro-exports ensured fiscal equilibrium.

Thus, the government took advantage of rising coffee prices in the second half of the decade. Greater emphasis on coffee exports mostly favored Conservative growers who dominated the largest plantations in Granada and Carazo. In mid-1977, export producers in general were sanguine about the future, despite the increasingly chaotic political atmosphere. "[The] Nicaraguan bourgeoisie . . . was thinking of the economy, not politics, and was placing heavy bets on a favorable [harvest season]" (Vilas 1985, 94).

The potential for clashes between Somoza and other elites was most prevalent in the flow of capital to industry and commerce. According to the IDB, private investment expanded 37 percent in 1975 (IDB 1975, 304), and the overall system of credit grew nearly 40 percent in 1976 (IDB 1977, 343). These data are deceptive, at best. It is not clear how much "private" investment was due to Somoza routing BNN and INFONAC funds to his Bank of Central America, and how much investment originated in BANIC and BANAMER. In the mid-1970s, the BNN administered new loans from the IDB, AID, and the World Bank (see table 10), and held $60 million from foreign banks, including the Bank of America, First National of Boston, the Bank of London, and Wells Fargo (BNN 1975, 16; Menjivar 1974, 108). While the BNN mainly served as the conduit for credit to cotton, coffee and sugar production, and cattle grazing, INFONAC devoted resources to physical infrastructure, like highway construction and telecommunications services. The Somocista bureaucracy jealously guarded these

TABLE 10

Official Lending, 1973–1978 (in $U.S. millions)

	IBRD	IDB	AID
1973	11.0	34.7	22.5
1974	8.5	10.5	12.4
1975	—	9.4	40.1
1976	16.2	16.8	16.4
1977	22.0	33.1	20.0
1978	13.6	32.0	15.1

Source: Bendaña (1978, 41).

kinds of projects from other capitalists. For example, the IDB approved a $16 million loan in 1976 to build a highway around Managua that was designed to pass through Somoza's property. Therefore, all the concrete was provided by Somoza's companies, Concretera de Pacífico and Concreto Premezclado (*Washington Post,* 19 February 1976, B20).

Between 1975 and 1977, INFONAC's portfolio reportedly included diverse investments in agricultural processing and industry (BCN 1977). Most investment, according to Central Bank information, was committed to long-term projects (five to ten years) averaging $179 million in industry and $70 million in agro-export operations over the three-year period. Somoza and his associates, like Adonis Porras, Cornelio Hüeck, the National Guard General Humberto Corrales, and Donald Spencer, essentially loaned INFONAC funds to themselves. INFONAC financed the activities of Aislite (a construction materials factory), Textiles de Managua and El Porvenir (fabric import-export houses), CARNIC (see figure 2, p. 000), and the two concrete companies mentioned above (*La Prensa,* 1 and 3 August 1978, 18 and 26, respectively). State banks were powerful economic instruments bolstered by the generosity of the international financial community. Thus, Somoza permitted no one to participate in the feast without his consent. In late 1976, he fired Luis Pallais Debayle as head of INFONAC after Pallais stole cash from the Xiloá resort and created phantom companies without the dictator's knowledge (Chamorro 1990, 218). Pallais was replaced by Donald Spencer, a Nicaraguan whose father was from the United States.

As Somoza built his fortune, he increasingly invited foreign investors to participate in his businesses through a stock market, the Actividades Bursatiles de Fomento, and an international finance corporation, Corporación de Finanzas Transmundial (*La Prensa*, 3 August 1978, 26). This prompted some local capitalists to sound a warning about protecting economic sovereignty. In late 1975, Ernesto Fernández Holmann gave a speech to the American Chamber of Commerce of Nicaragua attended by North American and Nicaraguan businessmen with joint investments: "A policy of unrestricted action by transnational companies can bring [Nicaraguan] business to ruin. . . . Foreign investment must be oriented toward sectors that are not part of the national reserve. . . . Foreigners must never be permitted to involve themselves in decisions of national interest" (Fernández Holmann 1975, 7). This was a clear expression of anxiety over the government's willingness to permit private foreign capital more freedom than in previous years.

Nevertheless, direct foreign investment remained a small fraction of the GDP (CIERA 1989, 36) and Somoza never came to monopolize all viable economic activity or resources. Local entrepreneurs enjoyed an increase of opportunities as the economy grew at an average annual rate of 5.5 percent through 1977; the industrial product alone increased over 10 percent for 1977 (Gibson 1987, 24; Vilas 1985, 92). BANIC and BANAMER continued to make short- and medium-term loans and partake in plentiful external financing from North American private banks (BCN 1979, 29). Therefore, it was nearly impossible to find evidence of an economic crisis consisting of stagnation or decapitalization caused by Somocistas forcing out or scaring off other businessmen in industrial and commercial sectors. In fact, private investment reached 25 percent of fixed gross investment in 1977, its highest level in the decade (Vilas 1985, 93).

Felipe Mántica took several loans from BANAMER and received funds from the IDB earmarked for commercial development to build new offices and supermarkets near upscale neighborhoods where income and consumption were high (Mántica, interview, 1991). Reinaldo Hernández expanded his hardware business in the early 1970s with loans from BANIC. His chain of stores became one of the largest suppliers of tools, paint, and small equipment in Nicaragua by 1975 (Hernández, interview, 1991). The Cerámica Istmica and the Cerámica Chiltepe, owned by Enrique Dreyfus and other BANAMER members, were the principal suppliers of bathroom and kitchen fixtures to SOVIPE which dominated home construction in the mid-1970s (Dreyfus, interview, 1991). The GRACSA plant, owned by Alfonso Robelo and other BANIC investors, was the largest producer of cooking oil in the country. GRACSA generated the fifth highest value added in the food and beverage industry in the 1970s, behind the ISA's Licorera de Nicaragua and Nicaraguan Sugar Estates, BANIC's Cervecera de Nicaragua (beer), and Somoza's CARNIC (CIERA 1989, 155; CONAL 1973, 2). Thus, large capitalists, whether critics of the regime or not, were able to maintain profitable enterprises after 1974.

Building Bridges for the Future: Elites and the Sandinistas

Economic elites usually aired their opinions about the behavior of Somoza as "responsible leaders of the private sector." Initially, they were careful not to portray themselves as aspirants to political power. They confined their comments to questions of "policy," and left "politics" to the UDEL's public forum.[7] A general sense of "civic action" motivated many capitalists who were involved in defining INDE's role as the promoter of "community development" in the early 1960s. Jaime Bengochea explained elite dissent as a reaction to Somoza's "insult to [our] bourgeois sense of fairness and consensus" around the need to restructure the political system so that no one could "mandate economic policies" (Bengochea, Interview, 1991). Reinaldo Hernández added a more personal tone to Bengochea's broad view: "Never in my life had I voted in a truly democratic election [on the national level]. . . . I yearned for a democratic climate. . . . Many young entrepreneurs like me had been exposed to Western political and economic philosophy while studying abroad" (Bengochea, interview, 1991). Hernández received a degree in business administration from the Ibero-American University in Mexico which, like INCAE, emulated business programs in the United States.

Businessmen and professionals got involved in debates over what to do about the dictatorship not because they were losing land or money, but rather because they wanted to seize the economy from complete state control, institute liberal economic reforms, and realize a political process more accessible to a broader range of middle-class interests. In response to questions about business-labor relations in the 1970s, Jaime Bengochea, Reinaldo Hernández, Felipe Mántica, Enrique Dreyfus, and William Baez recognized that workers desperately needed organization and formal channels of communication with employers and the state. However, many COSIP members in the various chambers insisted that if workers were allowed to organize, they must do it in an orderly fashion to avoid confrontation with their employers and "mob politics" (Gilberto Cuadra, interview by author, 9 April 1991).

Tilly's (1978) notion of the capacity of contenders for power to mobilize resources against the prevailing order anchors the analysis from here. Assessing the role of economic elites in the process of political change in Latin America has generated much debate. Some scholars recognize the capacity of the business groups to constitute "a social movement of the bourgeois class that is oriented toward reforming the balance between the state and civil society" (Becker 1990, 115). Others doubt that businessmen can generate "a hegemonic democratic movement which sees civilian society as its source of power, political parties as its instrument, and a democratic regime as its objective" (Cardoso 1986, 150; see also Cardoso 1967). Economic elites looked upon UDEL as a means to mobilize mass support and force change on the dictatorship without bloodshed.[8] The difficulty upper-class leaders would encounter in appealing to working-class concerns was predictable based on severe class antagonisms fueled by land and labor disputes over the last two decades (Gould 1990, 188).

Between 1975 and 1977, the business community did not pound the state with consistent waves of protest; criticism was sporadic. Political campaigning was left to the nucleus of UDEL which toured the country holding rallies and workshops in towns and villages. The leadership was an amalgam of what Goldstone would call "marginal elites" with "upper-class education . . . restricted from active participation in the highest levels of government . . . [and] seeking to implement an alternative social order" (1991, 414). Yet, there was never a consensus about one particular program for the future of Nicaragua. As discussed earlier, Chamorro met resistance from BANAMER and BANIC since UDEL's inception. The energy of the opposition movement was sapped by mistrust among business leaders, Conservative factions, socialist labor activists, and Social Christians, who failed to achieve a large national following.

Emilio Alvarez, Edmundo Chamorro, Luis Pasos, and Nicolas Morales, all products of the Christian democratic tendency in the Conservative Party, worked with Chamorro to try to unify Conservative factions and draw the Zancudos into UDEL officially. The Zancudos were supporting UDEL by 1976, but they did not attend public rallies. Chamorro was pessimistic about the sincerity of all Conservative factions and considered their unification in UDEL "too theoretical" (Chamorro 1990, 146). Conservative representatives remained fixated on strengthening the "Party" first and then showing their solidarity with UDEL. Luis Pasos stated that many Conservatives, especially the Zancudos, "did not like fraternizing with Socialists" (Chamorro 1990, 250). Moreover, labor groups were divided along political and ideological lines. The CGTi and the CTN demonstrated little solidarity on behalf of the working class during UDEL functions. In late April 1976, Chamorro lamented that, "the two federations . . . are going to celebrate the first of May (Labor Day) separately" (ibid., 176). Several dissatisfied members of the CGTi accused the leadership of "allying with the bourgeoisie" in UDEL and forsaking the plight of the Nicaraguan worker (Solórzano, interview, 1991). They broke from UDEL and formed the Frente Obrero which advocated the violent overthrow of the regime instead of fruitless political posturing. In the words of Chamorro, "UDEL está poco penetrada en la gente" (UDEL [was] not embedded in the people) (1990, 320).

While UDEL struggled to muster popular will, the leadership of FSLN entered a crucial period of internal conflict and change. The raid on Chema Castillo's house in December 1974 brought the strategy of recruiting elites and the urban middle-class to the forefront of the guerrilla movement. In the early 1970s, Carlos Fonseca and Humberto Ortega initiated the development of a broader network of clandestine operations that went beyond the northern jungles of Nicaragua. Through the work of Herty Lewites, they established links with Latin American communities in Los Angeles, San Diego, New York, and San Francisco through which they secured reliable sources of money and weapons.[9] Although the Maoist philosophy of prolonged popular war waged from the countryside was still dominant, the military action in 1974 gave birth to a new Sandinista cadre that did not rule out the importance of "bourgeois" elements in the revolution.

In early 1975, Sergio Ramírez, then secretary general of the Council of Central American Universities in Costa Rica, made contact with the Sandinistas. He was impressed by the new urban focus of the FSLN which he considered the "correct revolutionary thesis" (Sergio Ramírez, interview by author, 25 April 1991). Ramírez's recent reflections on his initial meeting with the Ortega brothers are enlightening:

> Daniel and Humberto Ortega introduced to me a renovated [revolutionary] perspective. I was far from the thinking of the Sandinistas before they raided the house of Chema Castillo. The Sandinista Front seemed to exclude my lifestyle [as a university professor], and I felt this way in spite of a broad and profound friendship with Carlos Fonseca. When I met with the Ortegas in Costa Rica [in 1975], they proposed to me [their] new view of the revolution and I joined. (*Ventana*, 15 July 1991, 9)

Ramírez's father was a coffee planter and a member of Somoza's Liberal Party while he was growing up in the 1950s. Ramírez attended law school at UNAN, where he met Carlos Fonseca. While in school, Ramírez was a defender of the dictatorship. But, his position began to change as he pursued a literary career for the journal *Ventana*, which he founded in Costa Rica in 1964. Ramírez joined the Council of Central American Universities after a brief stay at the University of Berlin in the early 1970s. By that time he was an adamant critic of Somoza (S. Ramírez, interview, 1991; U.S. Department of State 1988, 20). The meeting of the minds between the Ortegas and Ramírez would prove to be a critical event in the formation of a broad revolutionary alliance.

Ramírez's first project was to publicize Somoza's corruption and greed in the United States. Carlos Tunnerman, who had just resigned as rector of the UNAN, and Miguel D'Escoto, a Maryknoll priest living in New York, helped Ramírez document Somoza's ill-gotten properties. D'Escoto, who received a degree in journalism from Columbia University and was head of communications for the Maryknoll Order, gave the information to Jack Anderson, a syndicated columnist for the *Washington Post* (Carlos Tunnerman, interview by author, 5 August 1991). Anderson concluded that, "After a thorough study of the available evidence, we nominate Somoza as the most grasping of the world's great grabbers" (*Washington Post*, 18 August 1975, C23). A series of articles by Anderson in 1975 summarized the reports from Ramírez, focusing particularly on the complicity of international financial organizations based in Washington, D.C. Funds from AID and the Overseas Private Investment Corporation, an affiliate of the World Bank, were linked directly to loans made by INFONAC to build the Intercontinental Hotel and the METASA metal factory.

Somoza accused Pedro Joaquín Chamorro of writing the articles and sending them to Anderson. Chamorro wrote a strong letter to Somoza saying that he did not need help from "Yankees" in order to tell the truth about the dictatorship (Chamorro 1990, 100). In spite of the letter, Somoza tightened official oversight of *La Prensa*. Ambassador Sevilla Sacasa also threatened Anderson with a libel suit, but did not proceed after Anderson asserted that he had much more well-documented damaging information on the corruption of the Somoza government (Tunnerman, interview, 1991).

Concurrently, factions of the FSLN engaged in open conflict over which political-military philosophy should guide the revolution. The cautious strategy of prolonged popular war (GPP) was bearing no fruits. Its principal advocates, Tomás Borge and Henry Ruíz, were confronted first by the Proletarios (TP). Jaime Wheelock and Luis Carrión challenged the notion of excessive voluntarism, arguing unsuccessfully for more focus on urban slums. Borge expelled the TP from the organization in October 1975 (Gilbert 1988, 8). Wheelock and Carrión continued to operate in poor barrios without the backing of the FSLN.

In 1976, the Sandinista leadership was dealt a severe blow by the National Guard. In February, Tomás Borge was captured and imprisoned for "illegal political activity." In November, the Guard carried out a massive assault on the Sandinista army in the northern mountains, killing Carlos Fonseca and Eduardo Contreras, the top commanders of the military brain trust. Also, Henry Ruíz was isolated in the mountains after retreating from a battle. As a result, the Ortegas and Sergio Ramírez, known as the Tercerista (third) faction, took control of the guerrilla movement and delineated a plan for strategic alliances and mass insurrection in the "General Political-Military Platform of Struggle of the FSLN." In this new blueprint for the revolution, they avoided leftist rhetoric, encouraged the creation of mass organizations including workers and peasants, acknowledged the utility of courting businessmen, and called for Sandinista unification (Christian 1985, 37). The Terceristas' efforts to present to potential elite collaborators a pragmatic option for eliminating the Somoza dynasty was instrumental in constructing a cross-class coalition. In much the same fashion as Fonseca rejected the PSN in the late 1950s, the Teceristas transcended the strict ideological discipline of the GPP and the TP.[10]

The Terceristas set out to capture the allegiance of several prominent business, professional, and religious figures. Immediately, they found support in the Ingenio San Antonio. Dionisio Marenco and Alfredo César, both middle-level managers in the sugar plantation and refinery complex, helped to instigate a general strike of the ISA's five thousand workers in April 1977. They bargained successfully with Alfredo Pellas and other partners for higher wages and better working conditions (Chamorro 1990, 262, 338 n. 156; Hernández, interview, 1991). This event facilitated the penetration of Sandinista political cadres among cotton, coffee, and sugar laborers and led to the formation of the Association of Rural Workers (ATC). ATC militants, like Carlos Centeno and Edgar García, were at once Christian radicals and Sandinistas who became "revolutionaries in the fields" (Booth 1985, 118; Gould 1990, 273–75).

At about the same time, Ricardo Coronel Kautz, an agronomist and manager of the ISA's cattle ranches in the southern region of Río San Juan, helped the Terceristas expand the pool of elite sympathizers. "Coronel Kautz was one of the most enthusiastic promoters of cattle breeding on the agrarian frontier of southern Nicaragua and of beef exports, sharing with other young conservatives of his class and generation a restless search for new political ideas and intellectual patterns" (Vilas 1992, 327). In May 1977, Humberto Ortega, Sergio Ramírez, Miguel D'Escoto, Herty Lewites, and Ernesto Castillo, a prominent lawyer, arranged a meeting with Coronel Kautz, Felipe Mántica, a close friend of Castillo's through church organizations, Joaquín Cuadra Chamorro, and Emilio Baltodano, owner and manager of Café Presto, to discuss a formal alliance.

The group pooled $30,000 to buy weapons for guerrilla attacks programmed for the coming months and created a "provisional government" that would replace the Somoza regime. Felipe Mántica was designated "president," and Sergio Ramírez was chosen "prime minister" of a "cabinet" made up of the remaining participants (S. Ramírez, interview, 1991). Ortega and Ramírez thought it best to place a respected businessman at the helm of the revolutionary government in order to build the confidence of other elites they intended to approach. Emilio Baltodano expressed the nature of the relationship between the Terceristas and men like himself:

> It horrified me to be a businessman and see what we had done to the people. . . . [but] the Terceristas did not believe all businessmen were enemies of the people. . . . Humberto Ortega warned us to keep the meeting a secret so the other [Sandinista factions] would not accuse [him] of selling out to the bourgeoisie. (*Barricada*, 18 March 1991, 1 and 12B).

The Terceristas intentionally opened the FSLN to businessmen and professionals. Sergio Ramírez, Ernesto Castillo, and Miguel D'Escoto extended invitations to Casmiro Sotelo, an architect, and Carlos Gutiérrez, a Nicaraguan dentist living in Mexico, to follow the example of other members of the "patriotic bourgeoisie." It should be mentioned that, at the time of the meeting in Costa Rica, Joaquín Cuadra Chamorro and Emilio Baltodano had sons in the small Sandinista army in southern Honduras. Joaquín Cuadra Lacayo and Alvaro Baltodano were graduates of private Catholic schools who "left the rich life to be brothers to the poor and oppressed" (Argüello 1979, 91).[11] Both were recruited by the Terceristas after the raid in December 1974 and maintained contact with their fathers as they planned an urban war. On a trip to Honduras before he went to Costa Rica, Cuadra Chamorro had a pivotal conversation with his son: "He explained to me that socialism was not possible immediately in Nicaragua and this sounded very serious to me. . . . The guerrillas wanted to ally with other groups. . . . I saw my role as one of rescuing the youth [in the FSLN] from radicalism" (*La Prensa*, 2 August 1978, 30). Cuadra, Baltodano, Mántica, and Coronel seemed convinced that an alliance with "pragmatic revolutionaries" was the best option for removing Somoza instead of the ideological schemes of the GPP and the TP.

While the foundation of the revolutionary alliance was cast in mid-1977, business confidence that typified the postquake period began to show signs of weakness. Alfredo Pellas and Eduardo Montealegre received threats from Somoza that he was going to "break the spine of capitalists" in their banking groups (Cuadra Chamorro, interview, 1991). Somoza was particularly perturbed about bad publicity being disseminated in the United States regarding human rights abuses and malfeasance. In April,

Dionisio Marenco and Fernando Guzmán, also an industrial manager and Sandinista sympathizer, presented documentation of National Guard violence to the United States Congress. Moreover, Fernando Cardenal, Pedro Joaquín Chamorro's cousin, submitted several accounts of misuse of international loans to the General Accounting Office. Somoza attributed this activity to his new enemies in the BANIC and BANAMER groups associated with UDEL leaders. Consequently, Pellas and Montealegre began preparing contingency plans to protect the banks' assets from state seizure. Cuadra Chamorro, Pellas's long-time legal advisor, began setting up a trust fund outside of Nicaragua in which BANAMER capital could be deposited in case of emergency. The BANIC group resolved to transfer money to North American banks with which it had business.[12]

An encounter between Pedro Joaquín Chamorro, Alfredo Pellas, and Enrique Pereira confirms the worries of large capitalists in this period. Pellas was preoccupied about possible reductions in North American assistance that might result from the testimony given by Marenco, Guzmán, and Cardenal. Congressmen in the United States recommended to official and private financial institutions to take special precautionary measures in awarding new loans to Nicaragua. Although international aid flowed unabated through 1978 (see table 10), Pellas and Pereira asserted that UDEL was influenced too much by leftist politics. They suggested that Chamorro could have reunified the Conservative Party and become president of the republic had he not been identified so closely with socialists, communists, and social democrats in UDEL. In addition, Pereira insisted that the private sector's initiative against the regime was futile and that the Conservative Party held the only prospect for ousting Somoza peacefully (Chamorro 1990, 258–62).

The Revolutionary Situation Begins

A series of meetings in Cuernavaca, Mexico, at the house of Carlos Gutiérrez in August and September 1977, advanced the coordination of Sandinista military strikes planned for October. They intended to attack seven National Guard posts and bring all-out war to urban areas. According to Sergio Ramírez, the Sandinistas received about $100,000 in contributions from their wealthy associates and support groups in major cities in the United States (S. Ramírez, interview, 1991). During this time, Felipe Mántica established links with Carlos Andrés Pérez, then-president of Venezuela, and arranged a $100,000 monthly stipend for arms and supplies for the guerrillas (Mántica, interview, 1991).

The group also sent Miguel D'Escoto and Ricardo Coronel to Washington to recruit Arturo Cruz who was working for the IDB. Cruz initially became involved in international banking after he graduated from Georgetown University in the late 1940s. His first job was as a clerk for the IMF. He worked with Enrique Dreyfus in his commercial business in the 1950s and assisted in the establishment of the Aceitera Corona, a cooking oil manufacturing plant owned by United Brands and several minority investors in Nicaragua. Cruz briefly managed the concern which became the second largest producer of cooking oil behind GRACSA in the early 1970s (CONAL 1973). Nevertheless, Cruz shuns the label of entrepreneur: "Something that makes me mad is when someone says that I am a businessman.... My profession is development banking.... I met with Ricardo Coronel right here in my office [at the IDB] and his words had a great effect on me" (Cruz, interview, 1991). It should be mentioned that Cruz was offered only the stewardship of the Central Bank in the new government and not formal membership in the group. However, "Cruz insisted that he be a full member of the group or nothing at all" (S. Ramírez, interview, 1991). When his request was granted, Cruz returned to Mexico with Coronel and D'Escoto and secretly joined the revolution.

Between 14 and 17 October, Sandinista teams blasted and machine-gunned their way into National Guard compounds in San Carlos, Masaya, and Ocotal. As news of the fighting reached Managua, banks, schools, and government agencies closed down in anticipation of battles in the capital. They never came. The National Guard managed to kill or capture about one hundred guerrillas, some of high-school age. The mass uprising foreseen by the Terceristas did not materialize. Immediately after the attacks, Ortega and Ramírez gave their elite collaborators the option of ending their association with the FSLN; none exercised it (Cuadra Chamorro, interview, 1991). Instead, they issued a firm statement of support for revolution from Costa Rica:

> We do not vacillate in making a call to all conscientious Nicaraguans to find a national solution to the crisis ... a solution which cannot ignore the participation of the FSLN if we desire the guarantee of a permanent and effective peace. (Quoted in Carmona 1983, 188–89)

The proclamation was signed by Felipe Mántica, Joaquín Cuadra Chamorro, Ricardo Coronel, Arturo Cruz, Emilio Baltodano, Casmiro Sotelo, Miguel D'Escoto, Ernesto Castillo, Carlos Gutiérrez, Carlos Tunnerman, Sergio Ramírez, and Fernando Cardenal, who became known as "Los Doce" (the Twelve). Los Doce did not profess any particular elite economic interests despite the preponderance of businessmen and professionals. "The group was a phenomenon of friendship, not of special interests" (S. Ramírez, interview, 1991). Conversations with former Los Doce members for this study indicated a common effort to downplay financial motivation or even personal political aspiration. They insist that the group represented the basis for a cross-class alliance not inspired by immediate economic considerations emphasized by Moore (1966) in his analysis of the French case. Solidarity between the Terceristas and elites, and their commitment to non–Marxist-Leninist political change, was reflected in the "provisional government" that, in 1977, they hoped would serve as an alternative to the dictatorship.

When Los Doce's statement was published in *La Prensa* on 18 October, sixty businessmen sent a communique to the newspaper showing solidarity with their colleagues in the group (Arias 1980, 148). The communique included many of the participants in the 1974 convention, but none asked to join Los Doce. Rather, they formed the Coordinating Commission of National Dialogue under the auspices of UDEL. Alfonso Robelo of INDE, Jorge Salazar, representing agricultural producers, Felix Guandique, a COSIP lawyer, Ramiro Sacasa and Rafael Córdova Rivas of UDEL, and Monsignor Miguel Obando y Bravo requested an audience with Somoza to discuss "the violent atmosphere in which the nation is living" and how to avoid "the desperate road of insurrection."

The proposed agenda included human rights abuses and amnesty for political prisoners, naming a new chief of the National Guard to ensure professionalism and objectivity in the military, the removal of official monitors on radio stations and newspapers, and free political association and participation. No economic issues were emphasized even though many businessmen influenced the list of negotiating points. The commission demanded "a process of political transformation that converts Nicaragua into an independent, democratic, pluralist society" (*La Prensa*, 19 October 1977, 1 and 18). However, American ambassador Mauricio Solaún, who arrived at his new post in September, asserted that the opposition had "little self-confidence in its power to negotiate with Somoza any plan to democratize Nicaragua" (quoted in Diederich 1981, 144).

The dialogue commenced while Pedro Joaquín Chamorro was in the United States receiving an award for journalism. On his return in early November, Chamorro made contact with the Sandinistas in Mexico. Chamorro told Miguel D'Escoto that he did not want UDEL to participate in any form of negotiation with Somoza and "for the first time showed that he was disposed to communicate with the FSLN" (Sergio Ramírez quoted in Arias 1980, 152–53). Upon arriving in Managua, Chamorro was angered by Monsignor Obando y Bravo's attempt to include the Zancudos, Agüero supporters, and his Social Christian associates in the dialogue. A faction of the PSCN, led by Chamorro's former UNAP colleague Reynaldo Antonio Téfel, had recently formed the People's Social Christian Party (PPSC) that "openly supported [the Sandinistas'] military actions against Somoza" (Eric Ramírez, a Social Christian leader, interviewed in *El Semanario* 1 [47]: 11). Therefore, the undercutting of his authority and the division of the PSCN prompted Chamorro's resignation from UDEL in the first week of December.

After leaving UDEL, Chamorro wrote in his diary: "It only remains for me to form another group separate from UDEL and struggle from there" (1990, 302). Just before Christmas, Chamorro sent a message to Sergio Ramírez in Costa Rica, through Edmundo Jarquín and a friend in the town of Rivas in southern Nicaragua, inquiring about a meeting for the second half of January 1978 (S. Ramírez, interview, 1991). Chamorro's novel, *El Enigma de las Alemanas,* accompanied the message and the dedication read: "To Sergio from the probable number thirteen" (Chamorro 1990, document 2). In a conversation with Ambassador Solaún in late December, Chamorro commented that "the FSLN gives the impression that . . . the Marxist-Leninist factions do not have hegemony but rather another faction" (a reference to the Terceristas to whom he spoke in Mexico) (1990, 320, 341). According to Arturo Cruz, Fernando Cardenal said that the Terceristas thought that "Pedro Joaquín Chamorro did not fit in with Los Doce at that point. . . . they would talk to him later" (Cruz, interview, 1991). Cruz insists that the Terceristas feared that Chamorro's general popularity with the Nicaraguan people would divert attention away from the goal of mass rebellion and civil war.

Pastor argues that Chamorro was the "undisputed leader of the Nicaraguan opposition" at the end of 1977 (1987, 59).[13] Yet, the facts suggest otherwise. By his own admission, Chamorro's leadership was resented by other prominent figures in UDEL: "All the action of [Conservatives] Emilio Alvarez and Luis Pasos [has been] to decapitate UDEL ... because they are not UDEL's leaders.... The Conservatives want to be visible.... [They] only feel equal to the liberalism of Ramiro [Sacasa of the MLC]" (Chamorro 1990, 300). Consequently, Chamorro was caught in political limbo when he resigned from UDEL. Even though he had spoken to the Terceristas, he was not prepared to commit himself to Los Doce and the FSLN. The National Guard and other state officials, including Somoza's attorney general Cornelio Hüeck, had been harassing Chamorro and employees of *La Prensa* in recent weeks (ibid., 318). Chamorro was one of the few elites who had demonstrated unbroken public defiance to the dynasty since the 1940s, always drawing praise from the working class. For thirty years, he was a part-time politician and plotter against the regime, but he enjoyed professional success only in journalism. By the end of 1977, his ability to tap wells of political discontent was in doubt.

The events of late 1977 set in motion a revolutionary situation whose trajectory would be shaped by the broadening of alliances between the Terceristas and nearly every sector of the Nicaraguan society in 1978 and 1979. Humberto Ortega concisely summarizes how the objective political conditions had changed.

> The policy of alliances that we pursued was not new.... it was something that we just could not develop [in the 1960s and early 1970s] even though Carlos Fonseca was truly trying.... From October 1977 the revolution came down from the mountains into the cities.... [but] not all of our comrades saw that. (Quoted in Invernizzi et al. 1986, 54–55)

The impetus for political change eluded political leaders of the centrist reform movement and businessmen mobilized within the UDEL framework. Moreover, the GPP and the TP factions of the FSLN were temporarily isolated from the growing revolutionary momentum in urban areas inspired by the Terceristas. This is not to suggest that the Terceristas suddenly commanded a mass following against a crumbling dictatorship at this juncture. On the contrary, the regime was showing no signs of vulnerability to disintegration. While "national dialogue" offered no hope for tangible change, the Terceristas recoiled from their defeat in October and assessed the possibility of further coalition-building.

7

The Alliance of Convenience and Necessity, 1978–1980

The goal of this chapter is to evaluate the process by which elites failed to remove Somoza peacefully before the Sandinistas could engage the National Guard in full-scale civil war in 1978 and destroy the regime in 1979. As the political and fiscal crises consistently worsened in this period, Somoza and the National Guard lashed out at elite and popular challenges. While elites pressured the dictatorship with nonviolent measures, for example, work stoppages and international mediation, individuals from business, professional, and labor groups and moderate political parties gravitated to the violent option of the FSLN. The analysis will show that though Somoza's corruption and intransigence sustained political mobilization among the wealthy, the inability of elite leaders to achieve his resignation and preempt armed insurrection was the fundamental cause of a cross-class alliance. The last section of this chapter will examine the almost immediate breakdown of cooperation between most business sectors and the FSLN in light of the subordination of private capital to the revolutionary leadership after Somoza fell.

"The Liquid That Burns"

The assassination of Pedro Joaquín Chamorro on 10 January 1978 is generally considered the catalyst for concerted action between a broad range of upper-class groups and the FSLN (Booth 1985; Goldstone et al. 1991, chaps. 5 and 14). Many observers have indicated conflicting reasons as to why Chamorro was killed at such a pivotal moment in the national crisis. One version suggests that Somoza got word of Chamorro's imminent move to join Los Doce and draw elements of UDEL into an alliance with revolutionaries.[1] Somocistas in Miami have argued that the FSLN murdered Chamorro in order to provide a "spark" for greater militancy and spontaneous rebellion.[2]

Most available evidence supports the scenario that Somoza was furious with Chamorro for publicizing the illegal export of blood by the "Plasmaferesis" company, owned by the dictator and his associates. Roberto Argüello Hurtado, the Chamorro family's lawyer, obtained an injunction against Plasmaferesis in late 1977. During subsequent hearings, Chamorro informed the United States Congress and the General Accounting Office about the activities of the "blood bank" (Chamorro 1990, 318). Thinking that they would be doing Somoza a favor, his son, Anastasio Somoza Portocarrero, and Silvio Peña Rivas ambushed Chamorro without actually receiving orders to do so (Booth 1985, 159–60).

In a recent interview, Argüello Hurtado reflected on his long association with Chamorro and said that, "The Plasmaferesis case had something to do with the murder. . . . Also, the lawyer for Plasmaferesis, who knew much about [the business], drowned mysteriously in Lake Nicaragua. . . . The truth about these murders was never known" (*El Semanario* 1 (45): 9). Undoubtedly, Chamorro's death ignited the highly flammable political atmosphere that hung over the country since the Sandinistas attacked at Masaya, San Carlos, and Ocotal in October. When *La Prensa* published a photograph of its editor's body in the morgue the next day, there was a collective gasp of disbelief. In the past, the wrath of the dictatorship was directed at peasants and workers and rarely touched the lives of elites. The grisly crime on a main thoroughfare in the early morning hours made the wealthy shiver.

Felipe Mántica resigned from Los Doce citing concerns about the potential for escalating violence in a letter to Carlos Andrés Pérez, president of Venezuela. He insisted that he did not want to feel responsible for the deaths of citizens who were advocating Los Doce's identification with the FSLN in Managua. From December 1977, Mántica was being pressured by his wife and mother-in-law, both of the Cuadra family of Granada, to disassociate himself from the Sandinistas. He began having second thoughts about his exposure to the national political spotlight as the most prominent businessman aligned with the Terceristas: "The situation was very explosive [after Chamorro's death], and we did not yet realize the future impact it would have" (Mántica, interview, 1991; background for the paragraph above was also drawn from interviews with Cuadra Chamorro, 1991; Cruz, 1991; and Edgard Parrales, 5 March 1991).

Consequently, elites intensified their quest to separate Somoza from power. The frenetic pace of political activity over the next year and a half would ultimately expose political divisions in the upper class and distinguish elites willing to participate in the Sandinista insurrection. Just after Mántica departed, Cuadra Chamorro and Arturo Cruz were implored by the Terceristas to recruit Alfonso Robelo into Los Doce. They considered Robelo the best replacement for Mántica because he represented "progressive" sectors of the business community (Cruz, interview, 1991). Robelo refused to join the group and, instead, prepared to commit the moderate opposition to a political and economic boycott of the regime. The Coordinating Commission of National Dialogue and UDEL abruptly withdrew from further talks with the government.

For the first time since the 1974 convention, representatives of the business community jointly announced their intentions to take action against the dictatorship. Capitalists from every chamber and guild of COSIP met to organize a business "lockout" and changed their title to the Superior Council of Private Enterprise (COSEP). COSEP issued a communique pledging to exact an economic price from Somoza (*La Prensa,* 18 January 1978, 1). This was significant because, from 1974 to Chamorro's death, "the majority of COSEP members were silent and divided.... Only INDE (under the leadership of William Baez, Alfonso Robelo, Enrique Dreyfus, and Manuel Torres) wrote openly against Somoza" (Gilberto Cuadra, interview, 1991).

Equally important was COSEP's attempt to court workers by paying them to stay home (Vargas 1990, 7). Despite 80 percent absenteeism beginning on 24 January, the immediate demands for civil liberties, better working conditions, and justice for Chamorro's death were predictably ignored by the regime. Somoza made a cynical offer to raise the minimum wage and social security payments; the National Assembly took no action to pass legislation. The Conservative Zancudos renounced their 1971 pact with Somoza and boycotted the upcoming municipal elections in February. Yet, they remained in the legislature while the National Guard brutalized striking employees (Booth 1985, 160). Idle workers soon became disgruntled with their employers as they waited in vain for concessions (Chavarría 1986, 153).

Enthusiasm for confrontation rapidly subsided as a heavy toll was taken on the same elites who inspired the economic standstill. Businessmen disagreed over continuing the lockout if Somoza was not going to compromise (Luis Carrión Montoya, interview by author, 2 June 1991). While ISA technicians and workers affiliated with the ATC continued to support the strike, ISA stockholders grappled with the contradiction between their anger with Somoza and the potential loss of the entire season's sugar harvest. The political will of the ISA sugar barons was eroded by their concerns for sustaining "the most profitable decade in the company's history" (Gould 1990, 281–82).

As described in chapter 6, private investment expanded in the mid-1970s as a result of abundant capital flowing through the commercial banks, BNN, INFONAC, BANIC, and BANAMER. In 1977, the Central Bank contracted $115 million from foreign private banks to lend to commercial and industrial sectors (Jarquín 1978, 7). Export production and imports increased in anticipation of higher consumer demand in the short term.

The increase in inventories and the expansion of credit to the private sector was based on a positive outlook toward the export sector. But, "the political struggles and the Sandinista presence [in late 1977 and early 1978] generated uncertainty which resulted in economic depression. . . . There was a mass withdrawal of deposits from the commercial banks. This situation, combined with the large credit exposure, created a problem of liquidity in the financial system. The commercial sector accumulated inventories because of the [sudden] drop in demand" (Jarquín 1978, 7).

Borrowers in the private sector delayed interest payments on lines of credit from commercial banks, ultimately affecting the Central Bank's capacity to service an external debt of more than $800 million. While the business community pondered economic stagnation, the guerrillas exploited the work stoppage to escalate combat with the National Guard. On 2 February, they attacked at Granada and Rivas and issued a threat to businessmen: "We are at war with the dictatorship.... All the participants in the strike must not regress in the face of pressures from the regime.... The FSLN warns that the most severe measures will be taken against all owners who want to negotiate with Somoza and open the doors of their stores and factories" (quoted in Carmona 1983, 199). On 6 February, the business community canceled the strike, nevertheless. After nearly two weeks of lost revenues estimated at between $50 and $100 million, capitalists were anxious to resume operations and move merchandise (Vargas 1991, 8). Socialist Domingo Sánchez of the CGTi, Social Christian Antonio Jarquín of the CTN, and José Espinoza of the Council of Union Unity (CUS), an independent affiliate of the AFL-CIO, wanted to prolong the strike, but were overruled by COSEP (ibid., 7). The hasty reversal repelled the labor force which many COSEP leaders hoped to attract. The newspaper of the Workers' Front, a group of former Socialist Party members who bolted in the early 1970s, doubted the courage of COSEP:

> According to the bourgeoisie, the strike was supposed to be one of folded arms, civic and pacific.... Since the first days of the strike, it became evident that the bourgeoisie's posture was limited to just closing factories [in contrast to] the posture of the masses who marched in the streets, organized hundreds of acts of protest, sabotage, and resistance against the National Guard and lost many lives.... The bourgeoisie made their strike and the people made another. (G. Gutiérrez 1988, 107)

Thus, it was not accurate to characterize UDEL's response to Chamorro's murder as "a demonstration of the organizational capacity of the workers [and] private initiative" (*La Prensa*, 11 February 1978, 2). Over the next few weeks, the FSLN maintained military pressure on the regime, using the aid of locals in a series of forays. Popular uprisings in the indigenous barrios of Monimbó, in Masaya, and Subtiava, in León, between 22 and 27 February have been described by eyewitnesses as "true insurrections." From this point, the National Guard indiscriminately targeted civilians which spurred a process of radicalization of urban and rural working classes (Vargas 1991, 8).

Meanwhile, coordination in UDEL collapsed. On 1 March, Rafael Córdova Rivas and Ramiro Sacasa, hoping to harness popular outrage, called for another strike without the endorsement of COSEP and Alfonso Robelo. Robelo had resigned from UDEL the previous day and gave an interview to *La Prensa* in which he "announced that he would enter fully into politics" (1 March 1978, 1). Only 20 percent of workers heeded UDEL's call (Vargas 1991, 8). Labor representatives lost confidence in the capacity of UDEL's leaders to effectively oppose the dictatorship through peaceful means. "We believed in Pedro Joaquín Chamorro. . . . he was always a leader of the workers. . . . we trusted him to speak for the workers. . . . After his death, the opposition lost its force and rhythm. . . . There was stagnation, so the workers looked for another option" (Castillo Fletes, interview, 1991). Disgruntlement among the unions provided the Terceristas an opportunity to open communication with CGTi and CTN leaders with whom they would cooperate in combat later in the year (G. Gutiérrez 1988, 98; Solórzano, interview, 1991).

On 16 March, Robelo formed the Nicaraguan Democratic Movement (MDN) with close BANIC associates in INDE and COSEP. Other founders were Ernesto Palazio, a corporate lawyer who wrote a book about Somoza's abuse of relief funds after the 1972 earthquake, Haroldo Montealegre Lacayo, a BANIC economist with degrees from the University of Chicago and Columbia University, his brother Jaime Montealegre, an MBA from the University of Chicago, and Reinaldo Hernández of the Chamber of Commerce (U.S. Department of State 1988, 42, 61, 79). The MDN consisted primarily of individuals from prominent families in León and Chinandega. It melded several capitalists and technocrats involved in the commercial and agro-industrial phases of cotton production in order to gain influence over economic policy making (Carrión Montoya, interview, 1991).[3]

The MDN also intended to garner support from labor and middle sectors to contain momentum toward open insurrection. Robelo and Palazio were two of the main strike organizers in January and February. But, working-class people were not likely to join the MDN which they identified closely with COSEP. The MDN's membership did not go beyond business and professional groups totaling about two hundred people (Vargas 1990, 133–35). The existence of the MDN contributed to a fractionalized moderate opposition at a time when it needed to present a coherent voice. Perhaps belatedly recognizing this situation, the MDN attached itself to UDEL and created the Broad Opposition Front (FAO) in May 1978. Initially, the FAO was not much broader than the original content of UDEL. The MDN constituted one more micropolitical segment trying to avert the ascendance of the Sandinistas while espousing a liberal agenda of reform.

While the MDN and other moderate factions grappled to build constituencies in the middle and working classes, the GPP and the TP were making substantial progress toward creating a revolutionary base in urban and rural areas. In March, cotton, coffee, and sugar laborers formed the Association of Rural Workers (ATC) under the guidance of Sandinista militants and progressive Catholics and invaded large estates in Chinandega (Booth 1985, 118–19; Paige 1985, 108–09). Most politically active teachers and professors became members of the National Association of Nicaraguan Educators (ANDEN) created by the Sandinistas. Radical university and secondary-level students started new organizations in the UCA and private high schools, complementing the long-established Revolutionary Students Front (FER) that dominated the UNAN. Public employees in strategic sectors like banking, health care, and transportation formed the Union of Nicaraguan Employees (UNE) under the banner of Sandino. The FSLN's call for the nationalization of the banking system in May to "guarantee that financial resources are channeled in favor of the popular sectors" was supported by these new organizations (quoted in García Márquez and Fajardo 1979, 174).

The revolutionary situation at this juncture was characterized by "polity members" in the FAO interested in preserving the basic institutional structure and "challenger groups" intent on complete economic and social renovation (see Tilly 1978, 213–14). Over the next few weeks, the FSLN would forge a popular revolutionary network while the FAO, which now included Agüero's Conservative faction, was beset by ideological debates similar to those that hampered the UDEL in past years. By mid-1978, the conditions were ripe for building a cross-class coalition between some "polity members" and "challenger groups." Goodwin and Skocpol correctly point out that such coalitions "are often . . . antirevolutionary in their consequences" (1989, 500–01), as in the cases of Haiti and the Philippines, for example. However, the remainder of this chapter will demonstrate that the Sandinistas were able to benefit from deteriorating political conditions and gain military superiority over the National Guard which inevitably made the alliance with "polity members" quite revolutionary, like in Mexico, Cuba, and Iran.

Reordering Elites and Masses

In June, the Carter administration brandished sanctions toward the dictatorship for human rights abuses. In response, Somoza lifted the state of emergency imposed after Chamorro's death and allowed Los Doce to return in a gesture to Carter's plea for moderation. On 30 June, Carter sent a "secret" letter to Somoza praising the "sensible" action and released $12 million in economic aid to Nicaragua. This gave the appearance of "normality" between the White House and the dictatorship (Blachman et al. 1986, 94; Booth 1985, 162–63; Pastor 1987, 65–67).

On 5 July 1978, Los Doce arrived in Managua from exile in Costa Rica on a flight provided by Panamanian president General Omar Torrijos. Los Doce was met at the airport by thousands of supporters. Yet, they were heckled by GPP and TP youths demanding that the FSLN "not be bought by the bourgeoisie and reformism" (Tunnerman, interview, 1991). The GPP and the TP had seized an opportunity to penetrate poor neighborhoods and establish direct contact with workers and peasants. On 17 July, twenty popular and middle-class groups coalesced in the United People's Movement (MPU) led by Julio López and Bayardo Arce of the GPP and Jaime Wheelock, Luis Carrión Cruz, and Carlos Nuñez of the TP.

The skepticism of the GPP and the TP about the intentions of Los Doce emerged from their more radical disposition than that of the Terceristas. Yet, ideological divisions in the FSLN were not defined strictly along class lines. López and Nuñez were from poor families, but Wheelock is the son of a wealthy coffee grower from Carazo, and Arce's father was a journalist for *La Prensa* (U.S. Department of State 1988, 15, 21). Wheelock became a proponent of "proletarian revolution" while studying in Germany in the early 1970s. It was there that he wrote his controversial treatise predicting an eventual uprising of dislocated and underemployed rural labor (Wheelock 1985). Arce was recruited into the GPP by Tomás Borge in the late 1960s while Arce was working for *La Prensa* after graduating from the UNAN. Arce spent several years in the northern mountains in the first half of the 1970s, but, like other GPP members, came to Managua once the Terceristas prevailed in the struggle for the guerrilla leadership.

For the rest of July, the three Sandinista factions met to address internal disputes for the first time since 1975. The leaders of the MPU expressed interest in reunifying the FSLN and including Los Doce in the organization. But, they insisted on talking only to Sergio Ramírez, Ernesto Castillo, and Carlos Tunnerman, who defended Tomás Borge in his trial after the assassination of Somoza García in 1956; they refused direct discussions with Joaquín Cuadra Chamorro and Emilio Baltodano. Marxist-Leninist Sandinistas became acquainted with Tunnerman when he was rector of the UNAN in the 1960s. For example, Jaime Wheelock was the assistant to Tunnerman's secretary, Alejandro Serrano Caldera, now a leading Sandinista philosopher. Julio López, president of the MPU, was Tunnerman's student for two years. Tunnerman also spoke many times to Carlos Fonseca about state repression of student groups on campus (Tunnerman, interview, 1991).

The professional and religious figures in Los Doce attempted to facilitate the reunification of the FSLN. The Terceristas recorded a series of secret sessions with the other factions in documents revealed after the victory in 1979. They discussed how to preserve the mobilized masses in the MPU and to manipulate the FAO in favor of insurrection, simultaneously. The GPP and the TP seemed conciliatory in the following statement: "The reunification of the tendencies will fortify the cohesion of the political forces of the workers and peasants [in the MPU] and ensure their independence from the bourgeoisie. . . . We concede to Los Doce the role of representing the most positive sectors of the bourgeoisie" (quoted in García Márquez and Fajardo 1979, 216). Of equal importance was the identification of divisions in the FAO and the MDN as a possible ally: "The political parties and labor unions in UDEL are ignoring their respective ideologies. . . . Private-sector representatives have separated into different groups, some of which comprehend the necessity to link themselves to the popular struggle. . . . We refer specifically to the MDN" (ibid., 219–20).

Despite these signs of convergence, tension persisted between the factions. Given that Tomás Borge was still in jail and Henry Ruíz was pinned in the mountains, conditions were not yet conducive for formal rapprochement with the Terceristas. Because the MPU was dominated by the GPP and the TP, Sergio Ramírez and Los Doce chose to join the FAO at the end of July. Ramírez insisted that Los Doce's presence in the FAO would increase elite confidence in the motives of the FSLN (S. Ramírez, interview, 1991). By that time, FAO members knew that Ramírez was a Sandinista and that Los Doce was acting on behalf of the Terceristas. Before Los Doce returned from exile, a German reporter for the magazine *Ichtern* interviewed Ramírez who revealed his formal affiliation with the FSLN. The article circulated widely in Managua in July. *La Prensa* based its claim that "Los Doce [did] not try to hide its alliance with the guerrillas whom they represent in the FAO" on the *Ichtern* article (Baez, interview, 31 October 1988; S. Ramírez, interview, 1991; *La Prensa*, 2 August 1978, 30).

Subsequently, collaborators with all three Sandinista factions independently infiltrated the MDN. The Terceristas used Fernando Guzmán, who presented evidence of human rights abuses to the United States Congress in 1977, and Noel Rivas Gasteazoro and César Delgadillo, members of the Chamber of Commerce. The two latter men were expelled from the PSCN in 1977 over ideological disagreements with its president, Eduardo Rivas Gasteazoro, Noel Rivas's brother. Delgadillo had a son in the Sandinista army at the time, and both men supported dissident Social Christians in the PPSC who were advocating violence against the dictatorship (interview with Social Christian leader Eric Ramírez in *El Semanario* 1 (47): 10–12).

Xavier Argüello Hurtado, a Proletarian confidant and brother of Roberto Argüello Hurtado, became the MDN's National Coordinator and traveled internationally on behalf of the party (Hernández, interview, 1991). Samuel Santos was chosen by GPP leader Bayardo Arce to approach the MDN; Santos soon became a member of the Executive Committee. But, neither the GPP nor the TP pursued an explicit alliance with capitalists. "For the GPP and the TP, the bourgeoisie as a class was not accepted as a partner, but rather the task was to capture the trust of bourgeois individuals that professed an ideology more or less of the left. . . . We did not have direct contact with Robelo like the Terceristas" (Samuel Santos, interview by author, 6 May 1991).

The objective of Marxist-Leninists in the MDN was to monitor the "strategies of the bourgeoisie" which produced more conflict with the Terceristas. According to Arce,

> The debate [between the factions] was basically about how to take power. . . . But the conspiratorial political structure of the FSLN impeded [progress toward unification at that time]. . . . A typical example is that of

the MDN where the three tendencies had infiltrated without previous agreement. . . . One of the Proletarios, for example, mistrusted the Terceristas who had been employed with the same task. (Quoted in Invernizzi 1986, 57)

Arce carried out a separate project of courting elites in the latter half of 1978. He was the first Sandinista to contact Leonel Argüello of INDE and FUNDE who would become one of COSEP's representatives to the Sandinista National Directorate in July 1979 (Leonel Argüello, interview by author, 6 March 1991).[4] Robelo knew that Guzmán, Delgadillo, and Rivas were Terceristas, but did not reveal this to other businessmen and professionals in the party. However, he did not know that Santos and Argüello were working for the other factions (background for the previous two paragraphs is drawn from interviews with Cuadra Chamorro, 1991; Hernández, 1991; Santos, 1991).

Under the auspices of the FAO, Robelo, Córdova Rivas, and Ramírez conferred about coordinating a strategy to oust Somoza. Robelo and Córdova Rivas supported neither a plan for violently overthrowing the dictatorship, nor the idea of dismantling the PLN and the National Guard put forth by Los Doce (Arias 1980, 159; S. Ramírez, interview, 1991). After much deliberation, Ramírez, Robelo, and Córdova Rivas formed a committee to orchestrate another national lockout planned for the end of August. Before it was executed, the Sandinistas shocked the government and the public with a dramatic assault on the National Palace. On 22 August, a team of Terceristas, led by Edén Pastora, captured 1,500 legislators and bureaucrats, including the president of the National Assembly Luis Pallais.

Several points need to be made here. For the first time since their split in 1975, the Sandinista factions cooperated in a guerrilla action. Henry Ruíz (GPP) brought weapons from the northern mountains for the Tercerista squad, and one of the demands for the release of the hostages was the freedom of Tomás Borge. Once out of jail, Borge went to Cuba and opened a dialogue with the Terceristas through Arce regarding a September military campaign. Moreover, Robelo was informed about the raid through Sandinista elements in the MDN (Baez, interview, 31 October 1991; Santos, interview, 1991). Pastora, Robelo's schoolmate and friend, would facilitate linkages between the MDN and the Terceristas over the next several months that led up to the "final offensive" financed by many economic elites in June and July 1979 (U.S. Department of State 1988, 83).

On 26 August 1978, the Executive Committee of the MDN announced a lockout on behalf of the entire business community in order to maintain pressure on the regime in the wake of the disconcerting hostage situation. Even though 90 percent of all enterprises closed, only merchants and industrialists associated with the MDN through Robelo, and INDE, led by William Baez, Enrique Dreyfus, and Manuel Torres, publicly endorsed the action (*La Prensa*, 27 August 1978, 1). This is partially reflected in the fact that the nexus of the lockout was the Centro Comercial and two industrial parks controlled by businessmen in the BANIC group (*La Prensa*, 1 September 1978, 1 and 8). "The dynamic of the national work stoppage was [different from the one earlier in the year].... All the chambers and guilds did not participate through public pronouncements.... There was a lack of concerted political expression that the private sector displayed previously" (IHCA 1978, 11).

Somoza placed responsibility for the lockout squarely on the shoulders of the Chamber of Commerce and INDE rather than blame the entire business community. The government immediately suspended the legality of the Chamber of Commerce and INDE, invoking the "prohibition" on the private sector from engaging in politics to punish those businessmen it considered personally responsible for the strike (Baez, interview, 7 December 1988). Somoza felt confident that he could withstand the strike by exploiting the financial vulnerability of his wealthy opponents: "They'll get tired or go broke.... It's a bourgeois strike. When they begin to hurt they'll return to work" (quoted in Diederich 1981, 188, 195). The dictator began a game of political brinkmanship with businessmen.

On 28 August 1978, the president of the Central Bank, Roberto Incer, wrote a letter to the National Planning Council evaluating the deteriorating condition of the financial system in light of conflict between government and business:

> Foreign banks have observed the weakening of Nicaraguan private enterprise and consider another business stoppage unwise.... Consequently foreign banks have proceeded with certain care about granting further lines of credit to the private sector.... The weakness has been most evi-

dent in the financial sector where political and economic uncertainty has meant a considerable drainage of resources at the moment when it needs to expand internal credit in order to substitute for direct external financing which is disappearing. The present internal "crunch" is due to the overexpansion of credit to commerce and industry [in recent years]. As a result, the Central Bank cannot support the commercial banks that are now going to have to make drastic credit cuts to commerce and industry. The private sector must demonstrate its autonomy from all political groups. . . . The strike will bring only further restrictions on internal and external credit. (Incer 1978)

The pronounced political belligerence of some merchants and industrialists can be explained partially in the context of direct economic conflict with the Somoza clique. Since early 1978, the government was searching for ways to reduce the external debt exceeding $800 million (Jarquín 1978, 6). The National Assembly, controlled by the PLN, passed new tax laws that were imposed selectively on merchants and manufacturers (*La Prensa*, 5 August 1978, 22). Elites in these sectors complained bitterly about the subsequent increase of consumer imports, like food and beverages, hardware, household appliances, stereos, televisions, automobiles, and spare parts, entering the country through Somocista agencies not subject to legal restrictions (Ramírez 1981a, 72). The Casa Pellas, Casa Dreyfus, SOVIPE Comercial, and the "Ferretaria Hernández," among others, were adversely affected by these state "policies." But, it is important to remember that the leaders of the private sector in 1978 were, in general, the same people who organized the 1974 convention. Though concerned about their personal economic situation, they were acting on the same basic political interests that inspired elite mobilization against the dictatorship in the first half of the decade. Questions of democratization, liberalization, and decentralization pervaded the political discourse.

Reinaldo Hernández describes concisely the motivation behind some members of the chambers of commerce and industry and the lack of total agreement in business community: "Most of us were not bridled by economic interests. . . . Our businesses were independent from Somoza. . . . The economic interests of young entrepreneurs were not developed like an oligarchy. . . . However, there were businessmen in other sectors who were compromised [with the state, like in agriculture and finance]" (Hernández, interview, 1991). Communication between the INDE directors, the MDN, and Los Doce assuaged the fears that the political leadership of the business community harbored toward the Sandinistas up to September. Men like Robelo, Hernández, Dreyfus, Manuel Torres, and Leonel Argüello were prepared to confront Somoza alongside the FSLN (Cuadra Chamorro, interview, 1991; Mántica, interview, 1991). However, even though these personalities represented an array of capitalist interests, "the majority of businessmen were silent. . . . the political situation in COSEP was driven only by a few people" (G. Cuadra, interview, 1991).

Many economic elites were timid. A close look at the situation of cotton growers bears this out. Before the planting season began in June, growers encountered reluctance from the BNN to lend due to the financial contraction since the death of Pedro Joaquín Chamorro. A large portion of the early plantings were abandoned because of insufficient capital to renew the cotton cycle (Booth 1985, 166). In early August, landowners of the Occident formed the León Cotton Growers' Association, the Chinandega Cotton Growers' Association, and the Western Cotton Growers' Association. The traditional families of cotton, Montealegre, Callejas, Deshon, Argüello, Dubon, and Gurdián, dominated these associations (Ramiro Gurdián, interview by author, 20 June 1991). They demanded an infusion of capital before optimum planting conditions vanished in early September. Growers also intended to wrest legal control of commercialization from the Central Bank so they could arrange independent export contracts for after the harvest between December and March. The National Cotton Commission (CONAL) and two foreign companies controlled nearly 70 percent of cotton exports by 1978. The Gurdián family of León established a cooperative and export house in the early 1970s, but it accounted for only 7 percent of the export business (Baumeister and Neira, 1983, 67–68; Gurdián, interview, 1991).

The cotton elite looked to the MDN for political efficacy and assumed "militant postures" (Baumeister and Neira 1983, 68). Paige interprets the presence of cotton business interests in the MDN as potential for a modern capitalist fraction with designs on political power (1985, 104; 1989, 115). Since BANIC's formation in the early 1950s, the elite structure in the cotton sector was graduated by those involved in the agro-industrial and commercial processing phases, for example, cooking oil, and landowners and renters who profited only from selling their harvests (Vilas 1985, 139). Robelo and other MDN members from commercial and professional sectors, like Hernández, Palazio, and Montealegre Lacayo, were involved in the business stoppage and coordination with the guerrilla military plan for September. Yet, many producers were restrained by immediate credit needs and the seasonal imperatives of export agriculture. The leaders of the elite opposition tied to the dynamic cotton cannot really be considered a "class fraction" whose political action stemmed solely from its relation to production. As already emphasized earlier in this study, Paige's interview data (1989, 119–21) convey a clash of political and moral values between Somoza and the cotton elite, not one over export markets and profits.

In early September, the Central Bank severed lines of credit to all closed businesses, including the large commercial and industrial centers mentioned earlier. This elicited bickering among capitalists who were following the INDE-recommended policy of paying employees. Eduardo Montealegre and other large financiers, like Jaime Morales of INDESA (of BANIC, see figure 4, p. 000) and Ernesto Fernández Holmann of the Financiera de Inversiones Agropecuaria (FIA of BANAMER, see figure 3, p. 000) opposed the continuation of the lockout (Carrión Montoya, interview, 1991). They were financing many of the idle commercial and industrial enterprises with foreign capital and state resources and, thus, were indebted to the BNN, INFONAC, and North American banks. Generalized political polarization and lost revenues endangered the stability of corporate finance and the possibility of replenishing liquidity with new loans from internal and external sources.

In early August, Eduardo Montealegre was suspected of negotiating a secret deal with Somoza to assure protection of BANIC capital. He flatly denied the accusation in an interview with *La Prensa* (4 August 1978, 1, 12). In a speech to commemorate the twenty-fifth anniversary of BANIC around that time, Montealegre emphasized the crucial role that the bank played in attracting foreign finance capital, promoting new industries, and establishing savings and loan institutions to generate more investment (cited in Ramírez 1981a, 69). But, the Central Bank's measures broke the crucial ties that bound the state and private enterprise together for two decades. Frightened citizens withdrew $30 million in savings from private banks, diminishing capitalists' ability to hold out (Diederich 1981, 194). "The economic damage sustained by businessmen cannot be minimized. Such damage, combined with the growing recognition of the structural barriers erected by the regime, [was making] any truly satisfactory arrangement by the FAO with the dictatorship even more unlikely" (IHCA 1978, 16). Therefore, rather than bringing economic pressure to bear on the regime, the lockout strategy drove a wedge between economic elites hoping to strengthen the hand of the FAO in potential negotiations.

The First Wave of Insurrection

Just before the Sandinistas began their September military campaign, interviews with FAO leaders Robelo and Ramírez revealed contradictory visions of a new government if Somoza were to fall.

> About the integration of the national government, FAO director [Robelo] expressed that "all of the political sectors must be represented in the [possible] new government." (*La Prensa*, 7 September 1978, 8)

> About the position of Los Doce [Ramírez said that] "we believe that in the formation of the new democratic government all the forces which are participating in the struggle must agree." (*La Prensa*, 9 September 1978, 8)

Los Doce refused to accept proposals for the participation of the PLN and the National Guard in overhauling the political system, whereas Robelo, Córdova Rivas, and Conservative and moderate factions in the FAO did not rule this out.

On 9 September, guerrilla bands attacked military installations in Managua, León, Chinandega, Masaya, Matagalpa, and Estelí, gaining control of several neighborhoods. As the fighting intensified, Social Christian labor leaders Antonio Jarquín and Adolfo Bonilla, Socialist labor leader Domingo Sánchez, and the ATC in Chinandega provided combatants for the Sandinista commanders. Because the strike failed once again to extract tangible concessions from Somoza, idle workers embraced the FSLN which had escalated the national crisis to open urban combat. Thus, the CGTi and the

PSN broke from UDEL and joined the MPU. "The increasing momentum of the Sandinista militias [in urban areas] led labor leaders to support the insurrectional movement."[5] Businessmen leading the lockout qualified their support for armed action in tactical terms: "The young ones shot at the Guard and the private sector stopped all business . . . because we wanted to show total unity against Somoza, not because we supported the Terceristas" (Dreyfus, interview, 1991). The military success of the FSLN surprised the FAO. According to William Baez, "We didn't expect that the FSLN would be so strong against the Guard" (Baez, interview, 31 October 1988). The Guard struck back fiercely at civilians, killing five thousand, injuring ten thousand, and leaving sixty thousand homeless. This forced the Sandinistas to pull back from densely populated areas on 20 September (Chavarría 1986, 155).

After the flow of credit congealed, some labor deserted to the FSLN, and more blood was spilled, business leaders had a change of heart. They lifted the lockout, showing the impotence of their methods once again (Vargas 1990, 10). This time, however, they did not return to business as usual. INDESA and FIA ceased operations and massive capital flight began. Pellas, Dreyfus, Mántica, and other BANAMER members activated a legal and financial shield under the guidance of Joaquín Cuadra Chamorro. BANAMER cash assets were protected outside Nicaragua in the International Bank of Central America with headquarters in Panama, a Mastercard and Visa financial service with offices in Guatemala, Costa Rica, El Salvador, and Honduras, the Financiera Centroamericana in Honduras, and a savings and loan company in Guatemala (*La Prensa,* 18 May 1990, 11). Then, BANAMER members with investments in these companies concentrated their stocks in a trust registered with the Cambridge Overseas Corporation in Panama. Ernesto Fernández Holmann was executive director and Alfredo Pellas was president of the trust (*Barricada,* 25 May 1990).[6]

The BANAMER group perceived a need to defend themselves against Somoza and the Central Bank, not necessarily against revolution. But, individual magnates expressed different attitudes about the ascendance of the Sandinistas. According to Felipe Mántica, the ineffective results of the second lockout and the onset of civil war marked the beginning of the "real permanent crisis" which broadened "the coincidence of interests on both sides [business and the FSLN]" (Mántica, interview, 1991). Yet, in early August just after the MPU and the FAO emerged, Pellas said that, "Somoza has to go, but in an orderly fashion without bullets.... Sandinismo has arrived in the precise moment of deteriorating political conditions" (*La Prensa*, 5 August 1978, 1, 22). By the end of September, the guerrillas had demonstrated their military maturity and capacity to capture popular sentiment.

BANIC members independently deposited cash assets in major private banks in the United States, Mexico, and Costa Rica. The dispersion of BANIC capital has been attributed to the group's heavy dependence on state resources for cotton-related operations and less financial coordination between the dominant investors like that practiced by the BANAMER "patrons" since the 1950s. Alfonso Callejas Deshon, Eduardo Montealegre, Roberto Argüello Téfel, all BANIC members, owed large debts to the BNN and INFONAC when they fled. It is estimated that $400 million was taken out of the country around this time. INDESA and FIA together were holding $86 million in outstanding loans, and private borrowers owed $30 million to INFONAC.[7]

The irreparable rupture between the dictatorship and economic elites in 1978 seems to indicate a contradiction between a dominant class fraction attempting to preserve its control over the state while simultaneously ensuring commercial, industrial, and financial interests. Poulantzas (1973) and other Marxist theorists would argue that the behavior of Nicaraguan elites can be predicted by their economic relationships with the state and how Somoza's attempt to address fiscal pressures affected their livelihoods. But, neither the wealthy men in Los Doce nor the leaders of the explicit business opposition were acting concertedly as a modernizing capitalist class to change relations of production. The Somoza clique was not a hegemonic landed oligarchy that hampered the development of new capitalist enterprises; the dynasty encouraged agro-industrialization that benefited the entire business community for nearly thirty years.

Furthermore, the linkages between the dictatorship and politically active members of BANIC and BANAMER in agriculture, industry, commerce, and finance make it difficult to identify a strict dichotomy between the interests of an autonomous neopatrimonial state and the dominant capitalist class. So, too much emphasis on the effect of state autonomy (Goodwin and Skocpol 1989; Skocpol 1979) on the political responses of sectors of the Nicaraguan upper-class yields a distorted picture of the revolutionary crisis. Confrontation between Somoza and businessmen was the consequence of an erosion of elite political relations established after 1950. These relations were characterized by an uneven distribution of political power among distinct elite social groups whose interests constituted the essence of the "modern" state and the "modern" economy (Domhoff 1990; Higley and Burton 1989; Lachmann 1989, 1990).

The Terceristas noted divisions between capitalist groups in a document entitled "Class Alliances and the Revolutionary Situation."

> We are seeing two forces of capital moving in different directions. The large finance capital, on one hand, and industrialists and merchants opposed to Somoza, on the other hand. . . . This implies a new social and political dynamic that the finance capitalists fear. (Quoted in Carmona 1983, 239)

This statement clearly borrows from Marx's (1984) and Lenin's (1968) analyses of the political behavior of separate capital fragments. However, the Terceristas continued to consider actual and potential elite allies in political terms. From their perspective, there was not one particular capital fragment more likely to support the revolution. Victor Tirado, a Tercerista commander, explained this important point:

> We did not categorize every capitalist into a group. . . . We looked at them as individuals. . . . Cuadra Chamorro was a coffee grower, but he did not represent coffee interests in Los Doce. . . . Robelo was an industrialist but he was acting alone. . . . We did identify a financial bourgeoisie more aligned with Somoza even though [the financiers] were not openly pro-Somoza. . . . Any businessman had to have links with Somoza because of the nature of the system of production. (Victor Tirado, interview by author, 28 August 1991)

Tirado's outlook offers a clear understanding of the actions and effectiveness of nonruling elites in the context of their broader conceptions of political change and the capacity of business interests to separate Somoza from power. Despite the "radicalization" of some elites, an explicit alliance between the FSLN and INDE/COSEP leaders did not emerge immediately. The next two sections will evaluate how the FAO continued to search for a peaceful mechanism to resolve the crisis without the participation of the Sandinistas.

Mediation

Over the objections of Los Doce, an FAO majority sought mediation by the United States and the Organization of American States. On 5 October, the FAO issued a statement explaining to the public its intention to invite foreign negotiators. In careful language, Ramírez, Robelo, and Córdova Rivas qualified their agreement to allow international intervention:

> In the first place, all of us know the history of Nicaragua, a victim of political and military intervention by the United States, and we know that the United States has made possible the existence of the dictatorship with military aid. . . . The United States must demonstrate a change of attitude. . . . In the second place, allowing the international commission to mediate does not mean to begin a dialogue or enter into pacts with Somocismo. For us, it is very clear that any attempt at a national solution has to separate the Somoza family from power in Nicaragua and dismantle the dictatorship because the transition to democracy is incompatible with any remnant of Somocismo. (FAO 1978)[8]

This statement is inconsistent with the positions taken by Robelo and Córdova Rivas in August and September and during subsequent efforts to arrange a graceful departure for Somoza. Political and economic elites in the FAO expected the Carter administration to succeed in removing Somoza and isolate the Sandinistas. According to Jaime Bengochea, "We drank a toast to [special envoy William] Bowdler when the United States' negotiating team arrived. . . . But there were too many people deliberating and we could not reach a consensus on how to get rid of Somoza. . . . On the other hand, the Sandinistas won a big political victory after the successful attacks on the National Guard posts [in September]" (Bengochea, interview, 1991).

The White House proceeded in incremental fashion. National Security advisor Zbigniew Brzezinski held "the preference to press [Somoza] gradually in a way that ensured that the [FAO members] would learn to organize themselves so that when they assumed power, they could govern" (Pastor 1987, 104). Yet, James Fitzgerald, an official for the United States Information Agency in Managua between 1976 and 1979, asserts that, "The moderates were in and out of the embassy asking what to do next. . . . They looked to United States foreign policy makers as their mentors" (James Fitzgerald, interview by author, 10 November 1987). The leaders of the FAO were not "learning" to be governors; they were following the instructions of North American officials. Carter's Policy Review Committee "recognized that a post-Somoza government that lacked a firm military could be overrun by the FSLN" (Pastor 1987, 107). According to Carlos Tunnerman, "[The United States] maintained the thesis that the National Guard was a powerful professional military organization that should remain intact if Somoza were to go. . . . I insisted that the Guard was praetorian . . . an internal organ of Somocismo. . . . The Carter policy was to look for a brake on the FSLN" (Tunnerman, interview, 1991).

Emilio Baltodano reflects on the divisions between elites following the United States' lead and Los Doce members: "We all in the private sector wanted change, but the question for [Los Doce] was to eliminate Somocismo. . . . We did not want to lose the opportunity to destroy the dictatorship completely" (Emilio Baltodano, interview by author, 26 July 1989). Los Doce definitely did not entertain the notion that there were allies for them in the National Guard as North American officials were suggesting. The guard did not contain independent junior officers who stood to gain politically by leading a coup against Somoza like the one against Romero in El Salvador. On 25 October, the FAO submitted a proposal demanding Somoza's resignation. However, it should have come as no surprise to the FAO or the United States government that Los Doce as a whole, and not just Ramírez, objected to the advocacy of Liberal Nationalists and National Guardsmen in a "transitional junta" and a "Government of National Unity" that excluded the FSLN. Los Doce resigned on the same day and called for mass insurrection.

On 12 November, the PLN counterproposed a plebiscite on the legitimacy of the party. The United States wanted to redefine the question in terms of whether Somoza should stay in power until the end of his term in 1981. Negotiations on this point plodded along through the end of the year with no tangible progress toward a mutually acceptable solution. Inevitably, several elements of the FAO became exhausted and explored a more radical alternative. On 3 January, Rafael Córdova Rivas, the PLI, the CTN, and radical Social Christians in the PPSC began talks with the MPU and Los Doce about developing "an alliance of all . . . forces willing to overthrow the dictatorship" (*La Prensa*, 4 January 1979, 1). This signaled the further disintegration of the FAO after it lost most of its labor support in September.

In mid-January, Robelo committed the MDN to full cooperation with the Terceristas in a secret meeting with Los Doce in Costa Rica. Concurrently, Los Doce expanded beyond the original twelve men to include Ernesto Cardenal, a priest and brother of Fernando Cardenal; Edgard Parrales, a priest; Roberto Argüello Hurtado, former lawyer for UDEL; and Reynaldo Antonio Téfel, leader of the PPSC and friend of Pedro Joaquín Chamorro (Parrales, interview, 1991; Cuadra Chamorro, interview, 1991). These prominent figures constructed a complex network of religious, professional, and middle-class support for the Terceristas, complementing the groups already organized in the MPU.

After Somoza requested political asylum and guaranteed protection of his assets by the United States if he were to lose a plebiscite, Brzezinski and Secretary of State Cyrus Vance held out for an agreement. Bowdler and Viron Vaky, assistant secretary for Inter-American Affairs, opposed further delays. The exhausting process lasted through late January. Finally, on 26 January, "Bowdler summarized the mediation and concluded that the impasse could not be broken without making concessions to Somoza that were unacceptable to the FAO" (Pastor 1987, 115). Pastor's explanation for the ineffectiveness of the mediation points to the "surreptitious" behavior of Ramírez and the FSLN:

> The FAO was fragile not just because of decades of Nicaraguan factionalism but because . . . Sergio Ramírez was playing a double role, trying to lead the group and undermine it simultaneously. Though technically representing the Group of Twelve [Los Doce], Ramírez was actually representing the FSLN. . . . The departure of Ramírez did not destroy the FAO, but it increased the pressure on it to quit if Somoza did not resign (1987, 102).

Yet, as indicated earlier, the fact that Ramírez was a Sandinista was common knowledge to most Nicaraguans since July 1978. The FAO did not fall apart because Ramírez and Los Doce clandestinely sabotaged the mediation. The United States' insistence on retaining the National Guard and the PLN directly contradicted the statement made by Ramírez, Robelo, and Córdova Rivas on 5 October 1978. Therefore, Los Doce did not even participate in the mediation between late October and late January. Furthermore, Robelo, not Ramírez, was playing a dual role, casting himself between the mediation and the Tercerista option until the eleventh hour. The FAO kept up the appearance of a viable governing body for "international consumption . . . to show the United States and the OAS that [it] was still prepared to take power if Somoza was removed" (Baez, interview, 7 December 1988). The futility of the mediation depleted the patience of many groups of the moderate opposition. They sought an alliance with the Sandinistas after the United States could not convince Somoza to go peacefully or even submit to a referendum. The United States' policy faltered, and the resolve of elite leaders and their supporters dwindled in the face of stalemate. Lake's study (1989) of the United States' ineffectiveness against Somoza Nicaragua complements Pastor's notion that the relevant foreign-policy agencies could not act decisively. The failure of the FAO to achieve real political leverage against the dictatorship allowed the FSLN time to fortify alliances and muster tremendous military momentum that carried the revolution to fruition.

The Lone Path: Making Revolution

> In revolutions . . . there comes a crucial point when people suddenly realize that they have irrevocably broken with the world they have known and accepted all their lives. For different classes and individuals this momentary flash of a new and frightening truth will come at successive points in the collapse of the prevailing system. (Moore 1966, 100)

The formation of the National Patriotic Front (FPN) on 1 February 1979 undercut the purpose of the FAO. The PLI, the CTN, the PPSC, and the independent Marxist Workers' Front joined Los Doce and the twenty constituent groups of the MPU in preparing an urban-based insurrection (Booth 1985, 316). The Conservative factions, the MLC, and the PSCN remained in the FAO with the backing of COSEP. Clearly, the FAO's claim to "broad" representation of civic opposition was weakened by attrition and the MPU's dominance over the popular movement (Black 1981, 122). The Carter administration's hope for avoiding radical revolution by bolstering centrist politicians evaporated in the next three months (Blachman et al. 1986, 307).

The main obstacle for the Sandinistas was still the reunification of the three factions in order to guide the offensive on the National Guard. The FPN had already achieved mass organization and added 2,500 combatants to the existing Sandinista force. Humberto Ortega linked military success directly to the existence of the FPN: "From my point of view, the fundamental factor [that facilitated unity] was the crisis of the dictatorship created by the ascendence of the insurgent popular movement. The necessity to unify forces was evident to all the tendencies because no one alone could provoke the fatal crack in the dictatorship" (quoted in Invernizzi et al. 1986, 52–53). The formal rapprochement between the Sandinista leaders in early March consolidated the guerrilla command with the FPN.

Like the FAO, the FPN represented a collective rejection of the political legitimacy of the dictatorship. But, unlike the FAO, the FPN was the axis of revolutionary coalition that could be considered what Tilly (1978) calls an "alternative polity." Gramsci (1971) would argue that the FPN, not the FAO, established the only viable "counter-hegemonic" force to the Somoza regime. Yet, the FPN was not the manifestation of any one class fraction, but of an amalgam of social groups pressing for wholesale change. At that point, actual revolution depended on how well the FSLN would utilize its diverse support network, not on any particular weakness of the Somoza regime. FAO members and other elites could not or would not acknowledge that the FPN embodied a regime in the making (Przeworski 1986). By the end of March, the Sandinistas held a distinct advantage in the competition to topple the Somoza dynasty that began with Pedro Joaquín Chamorro and Carlos Fonseca in the late 1950s. This rest of this section will evaluate how and why the FSLN attracted the political, financial, and logistical assistance from a broad range of economic elites to land the fatal blow.

From an economic standpoint, the Somoza regime lost all credibility with COSEP. The complete absence of liquidity and forthcoming capital from foreign lenders made it imperative for businessmen to wrest the banking system from the state. Central Bank president Roberto Incer openly expressed the government's policy of resurrecting Nicaragua's credit rating with the IMF, the World Bank, and the IDB: "The main objective... for 1979 is to maintain fiscal equilibrium.... so we have to sacrifice other objectives like economic growth, the expansion of public and private investment, and employment" (*La Prensa*, 6 January 1979, 1). An INCAE report indicated that the short-term external debt had increased from $220 million in 1972 to $824 million by the start of 1979 (cited in *La Prensa*, 5 May 1979, 1). While Somocista bureaucrats were concerned about shoring up fiscal imbalances, international forces were making this objective unattainable. Through an OAS resolution, officials in Washington, and Venezuela and Costa Rica, blocked further loans to Nicaragua proposed by the EXIMBANK. The White House also vetoed a $20 million structural adjustment loan advocated by the IMF (Booth 1985, 169–72). In February, the government defaulted on $65 million of external debt. Then, the Central Bank raised interest rates on outstanding loans in agriculture and sped up amortization on short- and medium-term credit (*La Prensa*, 18 February 1979, 1).

The bank's actions sparked the political convergence of agro-export producers. The Union of Agricultural Producers of Nicaragua (UPANIC) was created, with INDE's assistance, to combine coffee, sugar, cotton, and rice growers, and the Federation of Nicaraguan Cattle Ranchers (FAGANIC), a group of ranchers not affiliated with the Somocista ASGANIC. UPANIC became another interest group under the COSEP umbrella (Vilas 1985, 139). Of special significance is that most growers and ranchers in UPANIC proceeded as though the regime could be reformed and export operations could be rescued with a fresh flow of credit (Gurdián, interview, 1991).

The nascent cotton associations, founded in August 1978, were incensed about the Central Bank's refusal to continue financing cotton exports on the futures market in the United States and demanded guaranteed amounts of fertilizer, pesticides, and seed at costs calibrated to export value (*La Prensa*, 3 February 1979, 1). The traditional family names of the largest growers in the Occident were registered with CONAL to be eligible for credit and inputs from the government for the 1979 season; they fully expected to plant and harvest the crop (CONAL 1979; *La Prensa*, 10 May 1979, 8). FAGANIC demanded that the government establish exchange rate parity with countries importing Nicaraguan beef and liberalize export policies so ranchers could sell to any country they wished. FAGANIC also appealed to INFONAC to replace several of its officials for unprofessional management of the largest slaughterhouses owned by Somocistas (G. Ramírez, interview, 1991).

In early April, the Central Bank was forced by the IMF to devalue the Córdoba by 40 percent which was intended to make exports more attractive. But, the coffee, cotton, and sugar harvests between December and March were low compared to previous years due to insufficient investment in planting and labor boycotts inspired by the ATC. Furthermore, the devaluation destroyed merchants and industrialists who continued to operate their businesses in the midst of political chaos. Interest payments on short-term loans were pegged to dollar values. That is, $1 of debt that was worth seven Córdobas before April was now worth ten Córdobas. Remaining capital left the country after the devaluation, and COSEP was reduced to the political representatives of the private sector (Cruz, interview, 1991; Argüello, interview, 1991).

Moderate political leaders, including Robelo, continued to act within the boundaries of the FAO. In early May, Robelo, Córdova Rivas, and several labor leaders were arrested for participating in an FAO demonstration. The political nucleus of INDE visited Somoza in his offices and successfully obtained the release of the prisoners (*La Prensa*, 9 May 1979, 1, 12). By that time, INDE's leadership consisted of Leonel Argüello (FUNDE, Sandinista contact), William Baez, Enrique Dreyfus (president of COSEP), Francisco Cardenal (Chamber of Construction), Manuel Torres (UP-ANIC), and Noel Rivas and Juan Ignacio Gutiérrez (members of the Chamber of Commerce, the MDN, and Tercerista contacts). These men simultaneously pressured for Somoza's resignation and communicated with the FSLN through the FPN (Argüello, interview, 1991).

The FPN's Moises Hassan, Julio López, and Fernando Cardenal had discussions with the FAO for most of May to reach an agreement on a plan for a new government. An anonymous editorial in *La Prensa* claimed that "the two large blocs of civic opposition [FAO and FPN] [were] searching for points of convergence so, together with the FSLN, the National Guard, and the National Liberal Party can agree on a new political alternative to the dictatorship.... We must understand it is time for country not sectarianism" (3 May 1979, 2). In reality, the FPN was trying to winnow "patriotic" elites from the FAO, while buying time for the Sandinistas to design a revolutionary program and coordinate the insurrection planned for the end of the month (Tunnerman, interview, 1991).

The framework for economic and social transformation developed out of negotiations among the Sandinistas, Los Doce, and MDN associates in Costa Rica. A team of economists and intellectuals, including Alejandro Martínez Cuenca (INCAE), Roberto Mayorga (INCAE), Joaquín Cuadra Chamorro, Reynaldo Antonio Téfel, Carlos Tunnerman, and Alfredo César, a former ISA manager, designed a revolutionary guide based on a mixed economy, political pluralism, and a nonaligned foreign policy (Martínez Cuenca 1990, 59). Robelo was also present, representing the MDN. In late May, a five-person executive junta was selected to head the Governing Junta of National Reconstruction (JRN). The first four members chosen were Moises Hassan of the FPN, Sergio Ramírez, Daniel Ortega of the Sandinista command, and Violeta de Chamorro. The participants deemed it necessary to select a representative from the private sector. The position was offered to Robelo, but he vacillated. Then, the Sandinistas and the junta members considered Mario Amador Kühl, a well-respected doctor whose son had been killed by the National Guard. Amador Kühl was living in New York at the time and a message was left at his residence. While waiting for the return call, Robelo insisted on taking the fifth position on the junta (based on interview with Cuadra Chamorro, 1991).

On 30 May, the FSLN announced that the "final offensive" was ready, and the "Program of National Reconstruction" was revealed by the FPN to the FAO negotiators. But, only MDN representatives accepted its contents that included confiscation of Somocista property, agrarian reform, free unionization, and the nationalization of natural resources and foreign commerce (Booth 1985, 148). The FAO suspended further deliberations and published a counterproposal in *La Prensa* that recommended an "Executive Committee" made up of one representative from the "insurgent" sector, FAO, PLN, National Guard, COSEP, labor, and professions (*La Prensa*, 1 and 2 June 1979). Again, the FAO was acting on the guidance of the Carter administration which was still maneuvering for a new government that did not include the FSLN (Pastor 1987, 166).

The Conservative factions, the MLC, the PSCN, and some sectors of COSEP were angered by the MDN's immediate support for the "Program"

(Juan López, interview by author, 16 May 1991; Cuadra, interview, 9 April 1991). The INDE nucleus and the MDN were already committed to the JRN by virtue of Robelo's presence on the junta. This became clear when INDE and COSEP formally ceased intermittent communications with Somoza on 4 June. Two days later, COSEP, under the direction of Enrique Dreyfus, responded to the Sandinistas' call for a national strike (INDE 1979, 8).[9]

On 9 June, the Battle of Managua and other urban operations began involving citizens from nearly every social sector. The combatants in Managua were mainly traders, vendors, artisans, carpenters, bricklayers, mechanics, and students, making up over 60 percent of the civilian forces (Vilas 1985, 112). Rural workers organized by the FSLN in the ATC fought under Sandinista commanders in surrounding areas (Paige 1985, 107–08). After heavy casualties on both sides, the FSLN abruptly retreated from Managua to Masaya on 25 June to confuse the Guard and, in the Maoist spirit, give the appearance of "invisibility of forces" (Chavarría 1986, 158). The FSLN resumed the insurrection bolstered by nearly total popular mobilization in every strategic city.

Many economic elites realized that Somoza's days were numbered and provided political, financial, and logistical support. Some examples are as follows: Alfredo Pellas purchased $2 million worth of communications equipment so commanders could coordinate multiple urban attacks; Luis Carrión Montoya, who had three children in the Sandinista army, stockpiled food and weapons during the struggle for Managua; Julio Castillo, a rancher from León, provided safe houses in the Occident; FAGANIC members Rafael Martínez, Odell Incer, and Juan Tijerino assisted soldiers in Boaco and Chontales; Jaime Cuadra, a coffee grower from Matagalpa, ran guns, medicine, food and provided vehicles in mountainous areas (Spalding 1991, 4; Carrión Montoya, interview, 1991).

On 27 June, COSEP recognized the Junta as the legitimate government: "Nicaraguan businessmen consider that the free enterprise system is the best way to sustain economic and social development. . . . We express our patriotic determination to participate in the reconstruction of the republic that must be directed by the Junta of National Reconstruction" (INDE 1979, 9). In the same statement, COSEP urged "the solidarity of [all Latin American] countries . . . in this time of inevitable change in Nicaragua" and the implementation of an OAS resolution passed on 23 June calling for Somoza's immediate departure.[10]

In early July, COSEP and INDE sent Leonel Argüello and the UPANIC leader Gilberto Serrano to Costa Rica to discuss the meaning of a "mixed economy," especially with regard to the banking system. Serrano objected to the nationalization of private banks, while Argüello acceded. According to Argüello, "Serrano was not following the instructions of our leaders [in Managua], so we sent him back. . . . The Junta turned to me as the formal representative of COSEP" (Argüello, interview, 1991). In the "Declaration of Costa Rica" on 17 July, COSEP declared unconditional support for a mixed economy in exchange for full representation in the Council of State, the legislative body to be formed after the victory:

> The private sector will be present in the Council of State. . . . We are broadly represented by INDE, the Chamber of Industry, the Chamber of Commerce, UPANIC, the Chamber of Construction, and the Association of Nicaraguan Professionals. . . . We support the process of economic transformation to establish a mixed economy within which the private sector will coordinate itself with the public sector. (INDE 1979, 19–20)

Nevertheless, many politically reticent COSEP members received the information from Costa Rica with disgust. Gilberto Cuadra lamented that "[Robelo and Argüello] were my representatives [in Costa Rica] but I did not agree with them" (Cuadra, interview, 1991). Rational choice theorists would identify Cuadra's position as an accurate reflection of the interests of individual capitalists, who would not act collectively without the clear expectation of personal gain (Olson 1965). Elites hardly stood to benefit financially in the short term by supporting the FSLN. The group of businessmen that negotiated with the Sandinistas made a politically inspired choice to align with revolutionaries which would have significant political consequences (Eckstein 1989; Gourevitch 1986). An alliance with Sandinismo opened the possibility of assuming a role in building the new Nicaraguan state and society. Based on their positions on the Junta and the Council of State, they believed that they would be the governors and the Sandinistas would be the soldiers of the new Nicaragua (Gilbert 1988, 109; Paige 1989, 117). When the Junta arrived in Managua on 20 July, Francisco

Cardenal, new president of the Chamber of Construction, honored the dignitaries in a long speech:

> Progressive elements of the private sector have openly advocated the replacement of the Somoza regime with a new alternative of freedom, justice, and democracy.... When the valiant comrades of the FSLN decided to carry out their heroic final act, the organized private sector did not hesitate to offer them its broad support.... Nicaraguan businessmen will adopt adequate measures with the workers to constitute the human element responsible for the successful functioning of the economy.... Nicaragua requires a policy of rational stimuli for investment and production to restore lost confidence and to offer an image of stability to the international community.... We are united with the members of the Junta in the desire to rebuild our liberated country. (INDE 1979, 23–26)[11]

The Somoza government was undoubtedly narrow and patrimonial. Mobilized elites were vulnerable to retaliation when they challenged the dictatorship's dominance over financial and political institutions. However, there was no direct correlation between the exclusionary nature of the dictatorship and the immediate formation of a revolutionary coalition, including large numbers of elites advocating violent overthrow (Goodwin and Skocpol 1989, 505; Huntington 1968, 277). In other words, the advent of an alliance between some business interests and the FSLN was not a direct function of the degree of elite alienation from the regime (Tilly 1973, 431, 447). Przeworski argues convincingly,

> A common feature of dictatorships ... is that they cannot and do not tolerate independent organizations. The reason is that as long as no collective alternatives are available, individual attitudes matter little for its stability. ... Only when collective alternatives are available does political choice become available to isolated individuals. (1990, 54–55)

The Sandinistas' shrewd manipulation of deteriorating political conditions and widespread discontent served to divide the FAO and fortify the FPN. Especially after the return of Los Doce in July 1978, the Terceristas were extremely successful in attracting elite and middle-class supporters who were crucial to the survival and effectiveness of the FAO. Sandinismo won a decisive victory not only over Somocismo, but also over the centrist, liberal reform movement that so weakly responded to the national crisis after 1972 and failed to construct a solid social base.

Breakdown of the Revolutionary Coalition

> The private sector supported a national insurrection, not a social revolution.
>
> —*Enrique Dreyfus*

The divergence of major objectives and the disparity of political power between businessmen and the FSLN became immediately apparent in the postinsurrectionary period. Naturally, the imperatives of genuine social revolution clashed with the moderate vision of change that developed within elite circles since about 1974.

In August 1979, the Junta nationalized the banks, insurance, foreign commerce, and mining. Alfonso Robelo promulgated the bank nationalization in a public ceremony. Later, he would comment that, "I was one of the proponents of the nationalization [because] I knew that the banks were centers of power and that we had to eradicate them from Nicaragua to achieve a truly just society" (Robelo 1980, 7). Leonel Argüello was in charge of the BNN during the first month of the new government. After the nationalization, the BNN became the National Development Bank (BND) under the control of the Central Bank and Arturo Cruz. Finance minister Joaquín Cuadra Chamorro, and Luis Carrión Montoya provided assistance in turning over BANIC and BANAMER buildings and equipment to the Junta. The Industry and Commerce minister, Noel Rivas Gasteazoro, the Agricultural Development minister, Manuel Torres, and the Planning minister, Roberto Mayorga, all Tercerista confidants from COSEP, endorsed this action. Of course, the commercial banks possessed no liquid assets due to massive capital flight orchestrated by Somocistas and the two private financial groups. The revolutionary government could only nationalize the stock of BANAMER and FIA, BANIC and INDESA,

Somoza's Bank of Central America, and the Bank of Caley Dagnall in Matagalpa. No law or decree was passed that prohibited private banks (Cuadra Chamorro, interview, 1991). But, the Sandinistas and their elite partners had taken control of all existing conduits of credit to capitalists remaining in the country.

Robelo's behavior after the Junta took power confounded many businessmen, even his close associates in the MDN. Despite the fact that many capitalists flocked to the MDN as a realistic political option, the party did not forge a consensus around a specific economic platform. "Robelo acted for Robelo, not for the MDN.... The bank nationalization was his personal conception" (Hernández, interview, 1991). Other capitalists not belonging to the MDN maintained their mistrust of Robelo's motives established before Somoza was overthrown: "Robelo was totally taken in by the revolution.... He appeared in fatigues on the 26th of July, the anniversary of Castro's attack on the Moncada barracks [in 1953]" (G. Cuadra, interview, 1991). Even elites who became Sandinistas were astonished by Robelo's enthusiasm for wholesale change. The former minister of foreign commerce and economic planning, Alejandro Martínez Cuenca, asserted, "I explain the radicalism of Robelo to myself as the typical euphoria of a capitalist who [joins a] revolution and [acts] more Catholic than the Pope" (Martínez Cuenca 1990, 59).

The attitude of Pedro Joaquín Chamorro toward the centralization of economic resources has been a subject of great debate and speculation. Rafael Córdova Rivas, in his political autobiography, insists that Chamorro "would have been in agreement with [the confiscation] of the property of Somocista thieves ... and the nationalization of the ... entire financial system" [1983, 68–69].[12] This statement reflects the fact that Chamorro was neither a large investor in the banking groups, nor was he financially compromised with Somoza.

Decrees three and thirty-eight confiscated over three hundred properties of the Somoza family and hundreds more properties of known Somocista associates. The Area of People's Property (APP) was created from these farms and enterprises, constituting 1,200 State Production Units in agro-export, industrial, and commercial sectors (*Barricada*, 28 August 1991, 1, 7). Also, the "Public Utility" law was passed to provide a mechanism to confiscate businesses that were drained of capital or left idle by their owners during the insurrectionary period in 1978 and 1979. But,

> Nationalization decrees affecting the big financial groups during the initial months of the revolutionary regime did not involve a corresponding political alienation of their representatives and officials. . . . many of them moved from the administration of those groups and their main firms to the economic and financial offices of the new government. . . . The loss of legal ownership did not necessarily imply loss of . . . the ability to make decisions on the firms' operations, investments, labor force and the like, through access to state control of previously private, now public, assets. (Vilas 1992, 330)

With the exception of Somocista-owned properties, coffee, cotton, and sugar plantations and cattle ranches remained in private hands. But, commercial export houses were the domain of state. Officials of FAGANIC and several technocrats employed at ISA complexes in central and southern Nicaragua assumed high positions in the BND and the Ministry of Agricultural Development and Agrarian Reform (MIDINRA) and influenced policy making toward the key agro-export sectors (Spalding 1991; Vilas 1992, 328). It should also be noted that members of the INDE nucleus or other elites with close ties to the Sandinistas were not affected by Decrees three and thirty-eight or Public Utility in 1979.[13] Furthermore, the Chamorro family maintained control of *La Prensa,* although the FSLN would restrict its publication for criticizing the government on several occasions in subsequent years.

Nevertheless, Robelo was unable to accomplish the task of "pacifying the commercial and industrial bourgeoisie" from León, Chinandega, and Managua given him by the Sandinista National Directorate (Cuadra Chamorro, interview, 1991). Tensions developed between the objective of building an institutional base for fundamental economic and social change and the expectations of the truncated business community. The Sandinistas recognized that they needed to move quickly so the "business groups could not impede the revolution . . . and claim a power quota" (S. Ramírez, interview, 1991). Ramírez insisted that the "second level" of capitalists who replaced those who fled the country could not objectively achieve political hegemony.

In the first months after the victory, the bourgeoisie tried to penetrate the structures of the new state and establish an implicit parity in the spectrum of the alliance. "They hoped that [we would be incapable of governing] and hand over decision-making power in the economic arena to them. . . . They seemed to think that the private sector could exercise sufficient pressure to claim a voice and vote in everything based on their so-called 'participation in the struggle'" (Ramírez 1981a, 74).

The Terceristas' strategy of alliances with elites and middle-classes helped bring Marxist-Leninist elements in the FSLN into political prominence, too (Gorman 1981, 139). In September 1979, the GPP and the TP met with the Terceristas in a secret session to discuss short-term tactics for consolidating their power and isolating the "principal enemies" of the revolution.

> We realized more clearly that the true enemy we would have to confront was the imperialist power of the United States and, to a lesser degree, the treachery of the local reactionary bourgeoisie. . . . The conduct of the bourgeoisie in the last weeks . . . gives us an important clue about how to determine, if not the character of our revolution in the global sense, at least a frame of reference for formulating a political strategy for the current phase. (FSLN 1979)[14]

After this meeting, the Sandinista leadership, including the Terceristas, began to assume a more belligerent attitude toward business groups and developed "defensive instincts" toward the possibility of intervention by the United States. Victor Tirado has written and spoken candidly about the internal dynamics of the Sandinista National Directorate in the immediate postinsurrectionary period:

> Tercerismo, as a tendency of the FSLN, was overshadowed as a genuine project of the revolution. . . . Many phenomena were mixed together. . . . socialist doctrine was one of those. We had a strategy designed to reinforce ourselves in the socialist camp. . . . [We] developed another project detached from the one that helped us triumph. . . . We let ourselves be guided, perhaps for comfort, by Cuban and Soviet ideas. (*El Semanario*, 1 [47]: 9)

However, the phenomenon of collegial rule by the Sandinista commanders did not signify "the disappearance of factional tendencies within the FSLN" (Gorman 1981, 139). The Terceristas continued to advance the idea of creating socialism in the context of political pluralism and a mixed economy (Martínez Cuenca 1992, 33–34). However, "the [imminent] alliances with Cuba and the Soviet Union alienated the leaders of moderate political parties and the bourgeoisie.... We lost the chance to implement our original plan of revolutionary pragmatism that included [a role] for the private sector" (Tirado, interview, 1991). By late 1979, COSEP and INDE leaders began to emphasize "an absence of confidence" toward the Junta and the FSLN before the promulgation of the Council of State (Ramírez 1981a, 74–78). In December, the economic cabinet was reshuffled: the Sandinista commander Henry Ruíz replaced Roberto Mayorga as planning minister; the Sandinista commander Jaime Wheelock, became head of the agricultural ministry over Manuel Torres; the Tercerista Fernando Guzmán became the minister of industry, ousting Noel Rivas Gasteazoro. Also, Alejandro Martínez Cuenca, the former INCAE professor who joined the FSLN in 1978, became chief of the new ministry of foreign trade. The once-open lines of communication between the Sandinistas and elites deteriorated into a series of bitter accusations between COSEP and the National Directorate (Hernández, interview, 1991).

The FSLN was clearly the best equipped political force to sustain the mobilization of the middle- and lower-classes organized in the MPU. The Confederation of Sandinista Workers (CST) became the predominant labor institution, far outnumbering the CGTi, CTN, and CUS. The Federation of Health Workers (FETSALUD), ANDEN, UNE, the Sandinista Youth Organization (JS-19), and the Association of Professionals-Heroes and Martyrs fortified the revolutionary network. Moreover, the Sandinista Defense Committees (CDS) gave the common citizen a role in local decision making for the first time (Black 1981, 240–50; T. Walker 1982, 95–113). The progressive clergy broadened Ecclesial Base Communities (CEB) which sensitized the urban poor to national problems and broke down the notion that poverty was ordained by God (Berryman 1984, 1987; Dodson 1988). Sandinista militants initiated a Literacy Crusade under the guidance of Fernando Cardenal and Carlos Tunnerman in the Ministry of Education. The literacy program was the means by which to imbed revolutionary ideology in poor rural and urban communities.

The balance of power in the Junta inevitably tilted in favor of Daniel Ortega and Sergio Ramírez. In April 1980, they proposed to expand the Council of State from the original thirty-three seats to forty-seven in order to accommodate more popular organizations and give the FSLN an absolute majority. Moises Hassán voted with Ortega and Ramírez, which brought the resignation of Alfonso Robelo and Violeta de Chamorro. Arturo Cruz and Rafael Córdova Rivas were selected as replacements. COSEP, though already assured representation, divided into those who recognized the legality of the Council of State and those who did not. Many capitalists, including UPANIC president Jorge Salazar, boycotted the inaugural ceremony in early May; Manuel Torres participated on UPANIC's behalf. The COSEP delegates were the same people who were politically active before Somoza fell: Enrique Dreyfus (president), Reinaldo Hernández (Chamber of Commerce), Francisco Cardenal (Chamber of Construction), Alfredo Montealegre Lacayo (Chamber of Industry). Haroldo Montealegre Lacayo of the MDN was appointed to a high post in the Ministry of Economic Planning under Henry Ruíz.

Once the Council was in place, the Junta and the FSLN introduced an avalanche of legislation that delineated economic and social objectives and completely reorganized the national economic system. The centralization of decision making toward banking, commerce, and agro-export operations evoked sharp criticism from COSEP, even though state control in these sectors was expected. While several elites close to the FSLN continued to occupy important decision-making posts in state economic institutions, COSEP complained about constraints on private initiative.

> The government has carried out macro-economic transformations that have completely changed the economic system. . . . The nationalization of the banks was not contemplated in the [original] Program of National Reconstruction [that was revealed in late May 1979]. . . . As a consequence of these changes, the State controls the keys to our economy, financial system, and foreign commerce and is responsible for 40 percent of national production. (COSEP 1980, 9)

Regardless of whether one considers the legislative majority of the Sandinistas legitimate or not, the revolutionary leadership harnessed the euphoria of the victory and translated popular support into comprehensive institutional changes without any significant countervailing pressure from business sectors opposed to such changes. Undoubtedly, the shaping and utilization of the Council of State exemplified the Sandinistas' superior capacity to manage mobilized resources in the first year of the revolution.

After his resignation from the Junta, Robelo commented,

> Within the MDN and in my personal actions I have always carried the banner of workers and peasants, knowing that they are the great majority of this country and that it is they who should benefit from government measures.... [The MDN] arrived at the conclusion that we could not continue in the political posts that we occupied ... and become like "zancudos" ... servile to the government. (Robelo 1980, 8)

Though the intention here is not to berate Robelo, as of mid-1980, the MDN did not contain members of working-class origin. Moreover, despite the presence of INDE and COSEP in the Council of State from its inception, these organizations did not advocate any "government measures" proposed by the Junta and the FSLN regarding the plight of the popular sectors. COSEP complained about restrictions on "independent" labor unions, that is, those not affiliated with the CST and the ATC, and accused CDS leaders of intimidating private citizens (COSEP 1980, 6–7).

The rise and fall of Robelo in the Junta had a significant impact on COSEP's willingness to defend capitalist interests over the long run. Even though most businessmen did not consider Robelo their formal representative, they sought to benefit from his position. William Baez asserts that, "We wanted to influence Robelo on the Junta, but if he blew it, we were not responsible.... That's the kind of game we were playing then" (Baez, interview, 7 December 1988). With little sway over the Council of State, COSEP members rapidly lost their resolve to weather the effects of economic reconstruction and social renovation. The former assistant secretary for Inter-American Affairs Viron Vaky put it succinctly: "Robelo and COSEP didn't want to stay and fight" (Viron Vaky, interview by author, 8 October 1987).

When Humberto Ortega declared on 23 August 1980 that national elections would be postponed until 1985, COSEP concluded that the FSLN intended to stay in power indefinitely (COSEP 1980, 4). From this point, sectors of the business community contacted National Guardsmen in Honduras to overthrow the Sandinista National Directorate (Booth 1985, 206–07). Jorge Salazar, a coffee grower, and Mario Hanón, a rice baron, both of UPANIC, first communicated with exiled National Guardsmen in October and recruited other large landowners. Suspicious of increasing anti-Sandinista political activity by elites, police and army officers broke up an MDN rally in Nandaime and arrested Robelo on 9 November. Robelo would later claim that at least sixty thousand MDN members would have protested the government (*Latin American Regional Report: Mexico and Central America*, 21 March 1981, 1). COSEP resigned from the Council of State on 12 November. On 17 November, Jorge Salazar was killed by Sandinista security officers when "he was surprised while transporting weapons in order to effect a counterrevolutionary conspiracy" (Martínez Cuenca 1992, 118). The FSLN arrested several COSEP leaders and closed *La Prensa*. According to Reinaldo Hernández, "We saw that there was no interest in achieving democracy. . . . We became disillusioned because there was nothing more we could do. . . . The FSLN was totally Marxist-Leninist" (Hernández, interview, 1991; see also Paige 1989, 117). We will return to this claim in the conclusion.

This chapter has related the business community's subordination to the Somoza dynasty and dependence on state resources to its weak response to the revolutionary situation in 1978 and 1979. When Anastasio Somoza Debayle jeopardized established elite relations and, eventually, the health of the economy, business leaders could not remove the dictator by themselves. The Sandinistas, for the most part, hastened the fall of the regime by rapidly accumulating civilian support and gaining tactical advantage over the National Guard in combat. The broad social alliance was ultimately more convenient for the FSLN and more necessary for those businessmen who were advocating moderate political change in the short run.

> Businessmen rarely take to the streets, because they generally can rely on effective behind-the-scenes informal political channels of influence to which the "popular" classes have no access. However, when elite groups are unable to defend their interests through either formal or informal means, they too have taken to the streets. (Eckstein 1989, 28–29)

Most businessmen did not really take to the streets in Nicaragua. They opted for accommodation with the Sandinistas that lasted only briefly. They made a political decision based on the circumstances confronting them. The inevitability of the overthrow of Somoza by June 1979 dictated limited options for elites who had tried to achieve a peaceful solution in the Broad Opposition Front (FAO).

8

Conclusions and Reflections

A revolutionary coalition may not have been the original intention of the FSLN or economic elites when the earthquake leveled Managua in 1972 and Anastasio Somoza Debayle proceeded to ruthlessly betray the Nicaraguan people. One could interpret the events that led to revolution in 1979 as a conjuncture of "separately determined and not consciously coordinated processes" (Skocpol 1979, 298). However, as this study has demonstrated, and as Wickham-Crowley asserts in his comparative work (1992, 318), elites and the Sandinistas explicitly and deliberately cooperated to violently destroy the Somoza dictatorship. The politics and political strategies of groups and individuals engaged in coalition-building are at least as influential on the path of political change as state structures and the relationships between the state and classes.

Important insights can be drawn from this critical point to sharpen the theoretical perspective on revolutionary patterns in Central America established in chapter 2. First, the transformation of agricultural production processes often destroys the traditional institutions and social structure of peasant communities. Rural tensions exacerbated by rapid change increase the potential for class conflict over land and threaten political stability. Whether we are concerned with the global impact of the Russian or Chinese experiences, or with insurrection and civil war in Central America, mobilization in the countryside has played a central role in challenging anachronistic dictatorships. Economic dislocation of the peasantry in El Salvador and Nicaragua was caused by a similar process of agro-export expansion driven by repressive states especially after 1950. Rural conditions in both cases by the end of the 1960s could be construed as ripe for peasant uprisings. The data cited on land tenure and availability reveals that the security of peasant farmers and rural labor was jeopardized by agro-export crops in both countries.

However, differences of magnitude do not account for why some Nicaraguan economic elites advocated insurrection, while the Salvadoran upper class cosponsored a war against the FMLN in the 1980s. Demographic trends and poor timing and preparation hindered the FSLN's efforts to establish a strong campesino following in the 1960s. The guerrilla groups that preceded the FMLN exploited the return of thousands of Salvadoran migrants from Honduras and gained the support of rural inhabitants through popular organizations. While the FSLN was revising its strategy toward the city and potential elite collaborators in the 1970s, Salvadoran guerrillas were preparing for a war on the oligarchy that erupted in the early 1980s.

It is a common assertion in the theoretical literature on revolution that as the bureaucratic machine of the neopatrimonial dictatorship becomes more complex, the state takes on a life of its own and is "tempted" to monopolize resources in pursuit of its autonomous interests. Many studies have attributed the participation of some landowners and businessmen in the Nicaraguan revolution to the nature of the Somoza regime (Dix 1984; Goldstone 1986; Goodwin and Skocpol 1989; Midlarsky and Roberts 1985; Wickham-Crowley 1989b, 1992). No one can deny the mobilizing effects of the egregious behavior of the Somoza family, the PLN, and the National Guard. But, Somoza's personal control of decision making had little to do with some economic elites deserting to the FSLN. The problem with this conventional notion vis-à-vis the Nicaraguan case is that it conceives a separation between the interests of the state and those of private enterprise, when in fact none existed by the 1960s.

The development of the agro-industrial economy and the national banking system after 1950 made it difficult, if not impossible, to discern the state apparatus from the constellation of capitalist interests. This study has presented clear evidence for the circulation of elites between private- and public-sector positions and the convergence of bureaucracy and business from 1950 to the early 1970s (see chaps. 3–5). Most bureaucrats were drawn from the same wealthy families that dominated the upper social strata. Elites employed in state financial and administrative institutions maintained close ties with business, professional, and elite social circles while influencing economic policies. This interpretation has not only been made here but by several other scholars of Nicaraguan and Central American politics (Biderman 1982; Gould 1990; Stone 1990; T. Walker 1986). The Somoza clique and peripheral elites would eventually engage in an intraelite feud over the distribution and exercise of political power, not because there was an inherent contradiction between an expanding autonomous bureaucracy and the parochial interests of capitalist fragments (Domhoff 1990, 7).

Despots often use state privileges in a manner that violates long-standing elite protocol. Such a "regime type" certainly encourages elite discontent when it ruthlessly excludes much of the dominant class from political power and economic patronage. Yet, as the advocates of the "state centric" theory have acknowledged, autocracy in Latin America or other developing areas has not inevitably led to the formation of any sort of revolutionary alliance. At times, one-man rule has proven to be a very durable form of exclusionary government (Diederich 1969, 1978; Latin American Bureau 1985; Remmer 1989; Ropp 1992; Valenzuela 1989). In fact, the long tenure of a "caudillo" figure can assuage tensions among several economic elite groups. Thus, an explanation of conflict in the upper class and cross-class collective action that goes beyond the characteristics of the state is necessary.

The comparative historical analysis of national crises in Nicaragua and El Salvador employed in this study is essential here. Chapters 4 and 5 have shown how the upper class was organized differently in Nicaragua and El Salvador. Economic growth in Nicaragua facilitated the emergence of separate groups of businessmen and professionals who did not constitute elements of a cohesive, hegemonic oligarchy. Yet, the business community was not neatly divided into distinct class fragments whose competition for hegemony over the state was driven by relations to production. Capitalist modernization after 1950 did not produce an inherent contradiction between the plantation and the factory. Export agriculture was the engine of the main industrial and commercial firms. Despite Somoza's preeminence in state economic institutions, independent capitalist groups dominated key agro-industrial, commercial, and financial sectors of the economy. The dependence of BANIC and BANAMER on external capital, the central banking system, and favorable state policies led to a convergence of the Somocista bureaucracy and private enterprise. Political tension and rupture in the upper social strata in the 1970s was not caused by "bourgeois factions" clamoring to control the state and impose a new hegemonic relationship with society based on a narrow set of economic interests (Gramsci 1971; Poulantzas 1973).

Marxist structuralist and state-centric approaches are insufficient to explain the outcome of elite conflict in Nicaragua. Consequently, theories of state autonomy cannot account for the participation of economic elites in a revolutionary alliance with a radical guerrilla movement.

> Before analyzing state autonomy, one has to be able to distinguish between state and society, between public and private. . . . [When] the distinction [has] evaporated . . . it should be more fruitful to employ other concepts in elite . . . politics . . . than to marshal analytic muscle in order to pry society out of the state or vice versa. (Schneider 1993, 345–46)

This study has evaluated theoretically the distribution of political power within the structure of elite relations (Domhoff 1990; Stone 1990) in order to predict why elite conflict may arise and when alienated elite groups may join a revolutionary movement. Anastasio Somoza Debayle exploited political power that had been ceded to his father and brother by Conservative and Liberal factions of the upper class in the 1950s and 1960s. The elite pact between capitalist interests during this period rested on the exclusion of middle and lower classes from decision making and the repression of labor (Higley and Burton 1989; Poulantzas 1974). Relations between business and government remained stable even though the Somozas were challenged periodically by the young Conservative and Social Christian movement. The dictatorship had been narrowly based on the PLN, the National Guard, and the national banking system to which economic elites willingly deferred much political discretion. The "Last Dictator" violated time-honored elite arrangements that encouraged a close relationship between government and business. Disputes erupted over "business protocol" and some peripheral elites' desire to realize more democratic decision-making processes. Elite conflict was possible because of the existence of multiple elite factions with unequal access to resources and political power (Goldstone 1991; Lachmann 1989, 1990; Stone 1990). Nevertheless, an alliance with the FSLN was not immediately forthcoming once the business community mobilized against the regime.

Here, we should consider the politics and political strategies of the moderate and revolutionary movements against Somoza to account for the outcome of the revolutionary situation in Nicaragua. In his analysis of non-revolutionary outcomes, Snyder states that, "we must examine the organizational capacities and strategic choices of both revolutionaries and moderate elites alienated by the dictator, [and] the coalition options available to moderates" to explain the breakdown of and transition from neopatrimonial dictatorship (1992, 384). However, Snyder relies on the degree to which the state excludes elites from patronage to evaluate these variables and explain the outcome of the collapse of patrimonial rule. Like Goodwin and Skocpol (1989), Dix (1984), Midlarsky and Roberts (1985), Goldstone (1986), and Wickham-Crowley (1989b, 1992), Snyder predicts a multiclass revolutionary alliance only if elites are completely denied the favors of the state and a coherent guerrilla movement exists. Unfortunately, potential for the "success" of reformist movements over revolutionary ones, or vice versa, is not historically linked to the development of elite political and economic organizations, competing elite interests, and the degree of affinity between business and labor. These variables are not put into the context of how interclass relations determine the effectiveness of elite efforts to remove the dictatorship peacefully and implement democratic civilian rule.

This study of the Nicaraguan case has demonstrated that some elites tried to advance a specific agenda of Western liberal reform and did not act for the sole purpose of removing Somoza. The leaders came primarily from new industrial and commercial sectors that depended to a large extent on the health of export agriculture. "Progressive" businessmen and professionals mobilized within the UDEL, the MDN, and the FAO in the second half of the 1970s. But, they failed to create a political mechanism capable of eliminating the dictatorship peacefully and isolate the Sandinista option. The lack of cohesion in the UDEL and FAO, weak coordination between employers and employees, and divisions between elite leaders representing diverse economic and political interests were obstacles to the development of a coherent reformist alternative. Prominent figures, who attempted to harness popular outrage in the wake of Pedro Joaquín Chamorro's death, lost the confidence of most working-class groups that they hoped to attract.

This afforded the FSLN ample time and space to escalate its war on the National Guard and recruit sympathizers from nearly every social level. The Tercerista strategy of bringing the war from the countryside to the city, and rejecting extreme ideological schemes that pervaded the FSLN since the 1960s, was as critical for building a multiclass revolutionary coalition as the weakness of the moderate opposition. When the United-States-sponsored mediation effort collapsed, the FSLN easily persuaded several elements of the FAO to align with the MPU and Los Doce in the FPN in early 1979. Consequently, the FPN constituted the only viable "alternative polity" to the Somoza regime. Recognizing this fact, several more landowners, businessmen, and professionals joined many of their colleagues and associates in backing the unified Sandinista command of a lower- and middle-class army. Social alliances emerge from the politically inspired choices of social groups (Eckstein 1989; Gourevitch 1986; Rogowski 1989). These choices are deliberate responses to changing political and economic conditions and the interaction between mobilized interests pursuing different levels of political change. The outcomes of protracted episodes of political instability in the developing world are not determined entirely by the relative strength or weakness of state structures; they depend heavily on political relationships between an array of social groups mobilized against the regime.

Coalitions of elites and revolutionaries are likely when neither possesses sufficient resources to eliminate the prevailing order. From the late 1950s to the mid-1970s, the Sandinista and moderate opposition consistently failed to mount an effective political or military challenge to the dictatorship. Clearly, the claims that the FSLN cynically manipulated their elite partners, and ultimately never intended to allow an open democratic process to take hold in Nicaragua, are subject to fierce debate. What can be said, at minimum, is that the Sandinistas provided education, health care, affordable housing, and jobs to thousands of Nicaraguans who had been completely neglected and abused by the Somoza dictatorship (Booth 1985; Spalding 1987; Vilas 1985; T. Walker 1982, 1985). Furthermore, in 1987, the FSLN cooperated with six other national political parties in the promulgation of Nicaragua's first constitution that explicitly guaranteed human rights to all citizens regardless of sex, ethnic background, or political affiliation. This constitution was not imbued with Marxist-Leninist dogma, but rather guided by the three tenets of Tercerismo: political pluralism, a mixed economy, and a nonaligned foreign policy (see Asamblea Nacional de Nicaragua 1987, esp. articles 23–91).

Also, it is important to mention that the Sandinistas willingly submitted to two free and fair elections in 1984 and 1990, winning the former with two-thirds of the popular vote and losing the latter to Violeta de Chamorro's Nicaraguan Opposition Union (UNO) (Booth 1985, 215–23; LASA 1984, 1990). The FSLN's failure to consolidate political power was caused in large part by the economic disaster wrought upon Nicaragua in the second half of the 1980s. The United-States-sponsored "Contra" war, trade embargo, and international lending moratorium, combined with Sandinista technical mismanagement and tensions between state directives and market incentives, led to a decline in living standards, leaving the FSLN vulnerable to electoral defeat (Martínez Cuenca 1990, 1992; Vargas 1990, 1991). The FSLN accepted its role as the largest organized opposition to the ruling UNO coalition and set its sights on regaining the presidency in the next scheduled election in 1996.

The trajectory of the national crisis was quite different in El Salvador. An opposition coalition did emerge by 1979, but it included neither economic elites nor guerrillas and their supporters. The historical unity and continuous hegemony of the oligarchy over the economy directly influenced the trajectory of political conflict in the 1970s and 1980s. The rise of independent capitalist groups that might have formed an alliance with middle and lower classes against the Somoza regime was virtually impossible. Thus, the absence of a cross-class revolutionary coalition is not completely explained by the fact that successive military dictatorships in El Salvador were less appalling, and thus more legitimate, than the Somoza dynasty. General Romero's regime was blatantly corrupt and resorted to brutal repression, in a manner not unlike Somoza and the National Guard. But, the Romero government was a political instrument of the unified oligarchy. It was not the result of explicit and implicit agreements between competing elite factions like those that allowed the Somoza dynasty to consolidate its power over the state after 1950.

Of course, the structure of the military was an important aspect of the state that influenced the pattern of the revolutionary situations in El Salvador and Nicaragua. The autonomous behavior of the military certainly affects regime stability and the nature and degree of political change (Snyder 1992, 380–82). In El Salvador, dissident officers acted to remove Romero through a coup, preserving political and economic stability. They generally supported the Christian Democratic program in the early 1980s. But, efforts toward agrarian reform originated in the PDC and the Foro Popular, not from military officers. The civilian junta was blocked by army conspirators who masterminded the coup in 1979. "The key problem was that [Generals] García [and Gutiérrez] refused to take the army out of politics" (Montgomery 1982, 20–21). Their aversion to fundamental institutional changes enabled the oligarchy to maintain a firm grip on the economy and eventually employ faithful army and paramilitary groups for its war of extermination against the guerrillas. The political environment for civilian government was maintained in the 1980s with direct aid from the United States and constant military pressure on the FMLN and its sympathizers.

In Nicaragua, the primary objective of the National Guard was not to protect class privileges, although constant repression certainly served this purpose. Still, the Guard was Somoza's dominion, rather than an instrument of a landed class. The FSLN eventually assembled a reliable guerrilla army and an extensive civilian militia that seized the military high ground after September 1978. The Guard performed poorly in urban battles with the FSLN even though it was equipped and trained by the United States (Diederich 1981; Millett 1977). While the Sandinistas executed the "final offensive" between May and July 1979, the Carter administration withdrew official support for the dictatorship, leaving Somoza without his principal foreign ally (Fahri 1988; Goldfrank 1979; Goldstone 1986; Snyder 1992, 384–85; Soberg-Shugart 1989, 259–60). Of course, elites who encouraged the overthrow of the dictatorship did not have the luxury of allies in the army. They found themselves subordinate to the political and military strength of the FSLN and could not counter momentum toward fundamental economic and social change on behalf of the poor.

Comparative research on the nature of the state has refined the study of revolution in the developed and the developing world. Upper-class structures and elite capacities do not displace state structures and regime type as variables in general analyses of how revolutionary situations arise and deepen. Nevertheless, the features of the neopatrimonial state do not dictate the relative organizational strengths and political strategies of elites

CONCLUSIONS AND REFLECTIONS

and revolutionaries. This study emphasizes differences in the organization of the upper class and elite relations to clarify the origin of a coalition of incompatible partners instigating collective violence in Nicaragua, and the basis for a civil war pitting the oligarchy and the extreme right wings of the military and civilian population against a predominantly rural-based uprising in El Salvador.

By separating major components of the cross-class alliance in Nicaragua and analyzing the conditions under which some elites mobilized against the Somoza regime, we have gained insight into how and why the FSLN benefited from wealthy supporters. Twenty-five years of agro-export growth administered by a progressively corrupt regime dislocated peasants, swelled the ranks of the urban poor, radicalized middle sectors, and alienated large portions of the business community. The scurrilous behavior of a despot exacerbated pressures toward mass mobilization. Clearly, coalitions form after a revolutionary situation begins. However, the primary independent variable of a revolutionary situation that culminates in a broad social alliance is not a narrowly based dictatorship. In Nicaragua, the coordinated political and military actions of mobilized social groups under Sandinista guidance hastened the collapse of the Somoza dynasty. Had the nonviolent strategies of political parties, labor unions, and business and professional groups in the UDEL and FAO been more coherent and sustained for a longer period of time, perhaps an alliance with the FSLN would have been unnecessary.

Goldstone argues that fiscal distress, elite conflict, and popular mobilization are necessary conditions for the breakdown of the state and the emergence of a broad opposition alliance (Goldstone et al. 1991, chap. 3). In Nicaragua, the revolutionary situation was initiated by Sandinista attacks in October 1977. Capitalists' own fears of the guerrilla threat precipitated economic decline more so than the behavior of the Somocista bureaucracy. Subsequently, elite relations deteriorated after the death of Pedro Joaquín Chamorro. The accelerated alienation of elites from Somoza in 1978 revealed the weakness of their political responses to the crisis and their incapacity to mobilize resources for reform (Tilly 1978). The guerrillas' mass appeal and two business lockouts in 1978 fueled the financial crisis and jeopardized Nicaragua's status with traditional sources of capital in the United States. For years, the business community was heavily dependent on foreign sources of capital to drive the agro-export economy. The "needs of the state," that is, securing the flow of international financing, was certainly a "need" of most economic elites through the 1970s. In this regard, the Somoza clique's interests were no different than those of BANIC and BANAMER. Mounting external debt was the result of Somoza and other economic elites incurring international financial obligations in the years after the earthquake that could not be sustained after businessmen lost confidence and the FSLN mobilized popular rural and urban backing in the MPU. By early 1979, more prominent figures began to view the FSLN as the lone path to change.

In the final months of the civil war, business leaders negotiated with the Sandinistas in Costa Rica and the FPN in Managua in pursuit of objectives that went far beyond immediate economic concerns. They perceived an opportunity to become governors of the new Nicaragua (Gilbert 1988; Paige 1989; Vilas 1992). The subordination of elites to the FSLN in the Council of State stemmed from their inability to galvanize a political constituency from which to inject an agenda of Western liberal reform into the process of reconstructing the state and society. The outcome of elite conflict and the revolutionary situation in the 1970s was shaped in crucial ways by the weak position of peripheral elite groups in the structure of political power. The consequence was "a close alliance between the [Sandinistas] and [some] traditional elite groups who had opposed the Somoza regime less for its dictatorial features than for its impact on business competition and family affairs [which defined elite relations since the 1950s]" (Vilas 1992, 324).

If the emergence of broad revolutionary coalitions in developing countries indicates a common phenomenon in the process of revolution, then comprehensive comparisons with other episodes of protracted social conflict and political instability that did not feature cross-class collective action are needed. If the formation of a broad social alliance depends on the existence of a neopatrimonial dictatorship, then comparative research only needs to describe when and how dictators become excessively greedy, corrupt, and repressive. Autocrats have ruled all over the world, yet genuine social revolution has been a rare occurrence.

Therefore, we should analyze the structure of the upper class and elite capacities in order to understand fully the circumstances that facilitate a partnership between businessmen and a guerrilla movement in overthrowing the prevailing order. The composition of a revolutionary coalition reflects an array of social interests opposed to the old regime, but whose specific objectives clash after successful insurrection. The politics of revolutionary alliances must not be neglected by focusing too much on the effect of the state on the potential for and scope of political change. Several analyses of the Mexican revolution within the last decade have emphasized deliberate group or class action at various social levels (Hart 1987; Knight 1986; Saragoza 1988; Wasserman 1984). More research is required on how the expansion of capitalist production under dictatorship affects overall class structures and elite relations and, in turn, how these variables influence the outcome of revolutionary situations in developing countries.

Elites' reactions to threatening political situations, especially those that are revolutionary, depend heavily on whether or not there are divisions within the dominant class and the nature of the actions of middle and lower classes (Roxborough 1984, 26). As Peter Smith asserts, "It may be, in some cases, that the dominant elite pursues a common purpose; it may also be, in other cases, that those possessing power do not have a sense of unity. That is a matter for empirical research, not for a priori definition" (1979, 6). Before we conclude that the characteristics of dictatorship encouraged or discouraged cross-class cooperation, we should recognize how agro-industrialization affected elite relations and capitalist interests in Nicaragua and El Salvador in the 1960s and 1970s (Paige 1987, 1989; Stone 1990).

Notes

References

Index

NOTES

Chapter 1. Introduction

1. Statement by Enrique Dreyfus, former president of the Superior Council of Private Enterprise (COSEP) of Nicaragua and former foreign minister of Violeta de Chamorro's government elected in 1990.

2. The Cuban and Iranian revolutions resemble that of Nicaragua insofar as insurrection occurred in urban areas and elites played pivotal roles in the fall of the old order. Detailed comparisons have been made by Goldstone et al. (1991), Fahri (1990), and Goodwin and Skocpol (1989).

3. All interviews were conducted in Managua, Nicaragua, unless otherwise indicated. Interviews lasted from one to two hours on average and were conducted in Spanish. All translations of interviews and documents from the Spanish are by the author, except where otherwise noted.

Chapter 2. Theories of Revolution and Revolutionary Coalitions

1. See Blasier's (1967) study of the Mexican, Bolivian, and Cuban revolutions. He concludes that revolution occurred in these cases because of "the vices of old elites" (57).

2. Other studies have examined the role of civilian bureaucrats and military officers in the process and outcome of revolution. Trimberger (1978) argues that bureaucrats can be revolutionary activists when they are not motivated by class interests and possess substantial autonomous control over state resources. Bureaucratic elites may even act on behalf of lower classes by destroying the institutions of upper-class domination and attempting to renovate relations between state and society. See McClintock (1981) on the 1968 military coup in Peru and the Velasco regime's subsequent effort at agrarian reform.

3. See O'Donnell (1973) for his original theoretical formulation of bureaucratic-authoritarianism (BA), and the political and economic conditions that gave

rise to this regime type in Latin America in the 1960s and 1970s. Collier (1979), Remmer and Merkx (1982), and Remmer (1989) have criticized and refined O'Donnell's conception to account for how variations in institutional arrangements had implications for policy, authority, legitimacy, and political change in the cases where BA occurred.

4. See Marx (1984) on why the French bourgeoisie supported the coup d'état of Louis Bonaparte in 1851 and surrendered direct political influence in exchange for order and commercial freedom.

Chapter 3. Defining the Dynasty and Changing Elite Relations, 1950–1962

1. Luis Carrión Montoya is one of several wealthy men who cooperated with the Sandinistas in the late 1970s. His son, Luis Carrion Cruz, is one of the nine members of the Sandinista National Directorate. Carrión Montoya was an intimate friend of Eduardo Montealegre Callejas until the Sandinistas took power in 1979. Carrión Montoya has firsthand knowledge of Nicaragua's banking system in its pre- and postrevolutionary forms.

2. Joaquín Cuadra Chamorro solicited the operating license for BANAMER from the Somoza government in 1952. He is the son of two of the most prominent families in Nicaraguan history (Stone 1990, 191–94). In the late 1970s, he helped finance the FSLN's war on the dictatorship. His son, Joaquín Cuadra Lacayo, is chief of the Sandinista Popular Army. Cuadra Chamorro is still the Pellas family's lawyer.

3. Edmundo Jarquín was a Sandinista deputy in the National Assembly. He was a founding member of the Nicaraguan Social Christian Party and a confidant of Pedro Joaquín Chamorro for twenty years, acting as Chamorro's liaison to the Sandinistas in the late 1970s. Jarquín married Chamorro's daughter, Claudia, several years after Chamorro was assassinated in 1978. He served as ambassador to Spain and Mexico under the Sandinista government in the 1980s.

4. A thorough discussion of the development of the Sandinista National Liberation Front (FSLN) in the 1960s and 1970s appears in chapters 5 and 6.

5. Alejandro Maltes was a journalist and PLN propagandist.

Chapter 4. Business, Politics, and Agro-Industrialization, 1963–1972

1. This statement is based on an interview with Carlos Tunnerman (5 August 1991), rector of the UNAN from 1964 to 1974. He joined the FSLN in 1975. He was minister of education and ambassador to the United States for the Sandinista government in the 1980s. He is now a delegate to the Executive Committee of the United Nations Education, Social, and Cultural Organization (UNESCO).

2. Biographical information was drawn from oral histories and curriculum vitae provided by these men, and from the United States Department of State (1988).

3. Alberto Chamorro is a cousin of Alfredo Pellas Chamorro, who helped found BANAMER. The overlap of economic interests of Nicaraguan families has been an important aspect of elite politics in the pre- and postrevolutionary period. See Vilas (1991, 1992) for a concise discussion.

4. César Grijalva was a lawyer for the Nicaraguan Meat Corporation (CNC) that was created by the Sandinista government in 1988 to run eight state-owned slaughterhouses. In 1991, the government of Violeta de Chamorro vowed to sell all meat processing plants to private investors by the end of 1992. Grijalva investigated whether some potential bidders on the slaughterhouses confiscated by the FSLN after 1979 had links to the Somoza regime.

5. Import substitution in Nicaragua was limited by the relatively small industrial capacity compared to El Salvador and Guatemala. Consumer and manufacture imports flooded Nicaragua during the 1960s and 1970s. BANIC and BANAMER capitalists owned several distribution houses, retail stores, and private custom services. See figures 3 and 4 (pp. 000, 000).

6. Sources for figures 2, 3, and 4 are Wheelock (1985, chap. 6); Strachan (1976, 8–12); CIERA (1989, 151–55); Williams (1986, 201); and numerous interviews with former BANIC and BANAMER members.

Chapter 5. Class Structure and Political Organization: Land, Labor, and Opposition

1. Williams (1986), Weeks (1985), Bulmer-Thomas (1987), and Brockett (1990) synthesize the political significance of land tenure trends in terms of the regional crisis in the 1980s. Development in Central America cannot be understood unless the connection between export agriculture, rapid economic change, and military dictatorship is made explicitly. The studies above have achieved much progress toward this end.

2. Quote from Anastasio Somoza Debayle cited in Biderman (1982, 129).

3. The Programa Sandinista was announced over a clandestine radio station in Nicaragua in May 1969. The program was reprinted in the Sandinista newspaper *Barricada* on 19 July 1991.

4. Sandinista disputes over strategy in the 1970s will be discussed in detail in chapter 6.

5. See Zapata's (1990) theoretical discussion of how political parties and state institutions have failed to protect Latin American working classes from capitalist interests and provide channels of direct and indirect participation in decision making.

Chapter 6. The Political Roots of Cross-Class Cooperation, 1973–1977

1. The *Diario Político* of Pedro Joaquín Chamorro is a collection of reflections on his experiences as a leader of UDEL from the beginning of 1975 to the end of 1977. The book was published by his son, Carlos Fernando Chamorro, and Edmundo Jarquín, both long-time members of the FSLN. This chapter relies frequently on information about Chamorro's perspective on this crucial period of political mobilization revealed twelve years after his death. Carlos Fernando Chamorro became a reporter for *La Prensa* shortly after his father's murder in January 1978. He gathered many of his father's documents and held them secretly until just before the February 1990 election that brought his mother, Violeta de Chamorro, to power. Some Nicaraguans speculate that the publication of the diary was a Sandinista propaganda ploy to portray Pedro Joaquín Chamorro as a supporter of the Tercerista tendency. The authenticity of the typed and handwritten entries has been confirmed by the Chamorro family, which is divided between the Nicaraguan Opposition Union (UNO) and the FSLN. Carlos Fernando commented in an interview that, "As a youth, I was impetuous and mistrusted older generations of politicians that could have changed Nicaragua. . . . From this point of view [my father and I] had different political visions . . . [but] there was a principle of mutual admiration between us" (*El Semanario* 1 (44): 9–11).

2. This general political disposition of the business community was reflected in interviews with Gilberto Cuadra (9 April 1991), a construction engineer who served as COSEP president in the late 1980s and early 1990s, and Enrique Bolaños (25 June 1989), a coffee and cotton grower, who holds the title of honorary president of COSEP after serving a term in the mid-1980s. Cuadra was involved in breaking SCAAS strikes in 1973 and 1974. He is now a shareholder in the Banco de Producción, a private bank based in León. Bolaños's SAIMSA cotton processing plant in the Occident was confiscated by the Sandinistas in the early 1980s. He competed against Violeta de Chamorro for the UNO nomination in the campaign before the February 1990 election which Chamorro won.

3. Alejandro Solórzano is one of many "socialists" whose politics is to the right of many social democratic and social christian elements of UNO that currently have seats in the National Assembly. Solórzano became a member of the Independent general Confederation of Workers when the CGT split in the early 1960s.

4. The responses of Dreyfus (interview, 1991), Mántica (interview, 1991), and Bengochea (interview, 1991) to the question about why they got involved in the convention were based on the reasoning that the time-honored arrangements between businessmen and the Somoza clique, who shared the basic interests, were eroding.

5. In late 1978, cotton growers in the Occident formed political associations which attempted to force the state to relinquish control over the commercialization

of cotton. The political consequences of this belated effort at organizing cotton capitalists will be discussed in chapter 7.

6. The current president of Nicaragua, Violeta de Chamorro, descends from the Barrios family of Rivas which owned and, as of early 1992, retrieved the IGOSA slaughter facility.

7. The Spanish word *política* can mean politics or policy depending on the context in which it is used. Businessmen were warned by Somoza to stay out of politics and address only macroeconomic policy when they invoked *política* in public statements.

8. Those elites most active in the opposition to Somoza expressed this idea, for example, Hernández, Baez, Dreyfus, Mántica, Bengochea, but others like Gilberto Cuadra and Enrique Bolaños did not place much importance on UDEL as a useful mechanism for change.

9. Herty Lewites is a Nicaraguan of Jewish parents who spent years traveling in the United States and Europe in the 1970s on behalf of the FSLN. He served as minister of tourism in the Sandinista regime in the 1980s. He is now a Sandinista deputy in the National Assembly and a self-described "millionaire revolutionary" (*El Semanario* 1 (27): 9–11).

10. See Victor Tirado's discussion of the internal dynamics of the Sandinista factions in *El Semanario* 1 (47): 8–9. Tirado was a member of the GPP faction until Humberto Ortega convinced him to join the Terceristas in 1977.

11. A comprehensive analysis of the influence of Liberation Theology on the Nicaraguan revolution is found in Dodson (1988) and Berryman (1984, 1987).

12. Sources for this paragraph are: Cuadra Chamorro, interview, 1991; *La Prensa*, 18 May 1990, 11; Chamorro (1990, 338 n. 156).

13. Robert Pastor was a policy-making official for Latin America on the Carter administration's National Security Council. He was one of the few high officials directly concerned with the situation in Nicaragua. The Iranian hostage crisis, peace in the Middle East, relations with China, and the Strategic Arms Limitation Treaty diverted the attention of executive advisors away from Central America in the late 1970s (see Garthoff 1985).

Chapter 7. The Alliance of Convenience and Necessity, 1978–1980

1. Edmundo Jarquín and Sergio Ramírez have maintained this thesis since Pedro Joaquín Chamorro's death.

2. See Nicolas López-Maltes. *Cómo y Porque Mataron a Pedro Joaquín Chamorro* (How and Why They Killed Pedro Joaquín Chamorro). In *La Estrella de Nicaragua*. 25 January 1991, a Miami-based newspaper.

3. Luis Carrión Montoya was a member of the MDN briefly in 1978, but left the party at the end of the year.

4. Leonel Argüello owned shares in Somoza's Bank of Central America in the mid-1970s.

5. Statement by Gastón Castillo Fletes, assistant secretary of the Autonomous Confederation of Nicaraguan Workers (CTNa) (interview, 1991). The changing perceptions of organized labor in the FAO during this pivotal period were gleaned from interviews with Castillo (1991) and Alejandro Solórzano (1991) of the PSN and CGTi. Both Solórzano and Castillo were labor organizers in the FAO who contributed to the Sandinista military operations in September 1978.

6. Carlos Pellas, son of Alfredo Pellas, assumed the executive directorship of the trust after Fernandez Holmann resigned in 1985.

7. See articles by Jaime Wheelock in *Barricada* 18 and 19 September 1991. Background for the previous three paragraphs was drawn from interviews with Carrión Montoya, 1991; Argüello, 1991; and Cuadra Chamorro, 1991.

8. The FAO statement can be found in the COSEP archive. The document clearly displays the signatures of Robelo, Cordova Rivas, and Ramírez.

9. *El Sector Privado en La Insurrección* is a collection of pronouncements made by COSEP and INDE between 6 June and 20 July 1979. The documents were compiled by Enrique Dreyfus and William Baez for publication.

10. The OAS resolution was sponsored by a group of Andean countries and passed by a 17–2 vote with the United States and Nicaragua dissenting.

11. Francisco Cardenal was arrested in the 1959 Olama/Mellojones attacks orchestrated by Pedro Joaquín Chamorro.

12. One should note that Cordova Rivas wrote his book while he was a member of the JRN after he replaced Violeta de Chamorro in 1980.

13. In 1981, the GRACSA cooking oil plant passed into state hands through Public Utility, and Decree 759 confiscated the Plaza España, Camino Oriente, Santa Mónica commercial complexes, the IGOSA and San Martín slaughterhouses, and BANAMER soap and milk factories (Spalding 1991, 5–6). The Ingenio San Antonio was "intervened" by the state in 1988, but was returned to its original owners in June 1992 (*Latin American Weekly Report*, 2 July 1992, 5).

14. This passage was translated by the United States Department of State.

REFERENCES

Abraham, David. 1981. *The Collapse of the Weimar Republic.* Princeton: Princeton University Press.

Almond, Gabriel, and James Coleman, eds. 1960. *The Politics of the Developing Areas.* Princeton: Princeton University Press.

Almond, Gabriel, and Sidney Verba. 1963. *The Civic Culture.* Princeton: Princeton University Press.

Alvarado, Enrique. 1985. "Los Partidos Liberal y Conservador en la Historia Nacional." *Encuentro* 23: 12–15.

Anderson, Perry. 1974. *Lineages of the Absolutist State.* London: New Left Books.

Anderson, Thomas. 1971. *Matanza: El Salvador's Communist Revolt of 1932.* Lincoln: University of Nebraska.

ANEP (Asociación Nacional de la Empresa Privada). 1976. *Estudios Centro Americanos* 31 (335/336): 611–15.

Argüello, Alvaro. 1979. "Posturas de los Cristianos Frente al Proceso Revolucionario Nicaragüense." In *Fe Cristiana y Revolución Sandinista en Nicaragua.* Managua: Instituto Histórico Centroamericano.

Arias, Pilar. 1980. *Nicaragua: Relatos de Combatientes del Frente Sandinista.* Mexico: Siglo Veintiuno Editores.

Asamblea Nacional de Nicaragua. 1987. *Constitución Política de la República de Nicaragua.* Managua: Asamblea Nacional.

Baez, William. 1970. "Cuánto daría para hacer una Revolución." *Revista Conservadora de Pensamiento* 25 (123): 45–47.

Baloyra, Enrique. 1982. *El Salvador in Transition.* Chapel Hill: University of North Carolina.

———. 1983. "Reactionary Despotism in Central America." *Journal of Latin American Studies* 15: 295–319.

BANAMER (Banco de América). 1979. "Inversión desde 1958." *Actividad Económica* 2 (3): 1–8.

Baumeister, Eduardo, and Oscar Neira. 1983. *El Subsistema de Algodón en Nicaragua*. Managua: INIES.

BCN (Banco Central de Nicaragua). 1970. *Productos de Exportación*. Managua: BCN.

———. (1977) 1979. *Anuario Estadístico de Nicaragua*. Managua: Instituto Nacional de Estadísticas y Censos.

———. 1979. *Indicadores Economicos* 5 (1–2): 1–30.

Becker, David. 1983. *The New Bourgeoisie and the Limits of Dependency*. Princeton: Princeton University Press.

———. 1990. "Business Associations in Latin America: The Venezuelan Case." *Comparative Politics* 23 (1): 114–38.

Bendaña, Alejandro. 1978. "Crisis in Nicaragua." *North American Congress on Latin America* 7 (6): 1–42.

Berejikian, Jeffrey. 1992. "Revolutionary Collective Action and the Agent Structure Problem." *American Political Science Review* 86 (3): 647–57.

Berryman, Philip. 1984. *The Religious Roots of Rebellion*. London: SCM.

———. 1987. *Liberation Theology*. New York: Pantheon.

Biderman, Jaime. 1982. "Class Structure, the State, and Capitalist Development in Nicaraguan Agriculture." Ph.D. diss., Berkeley and Los Angeles: University of California.

Blachman, Morris, William LeoGrande, and Kenneth Sharpe, eds. 1986. *Confronting Revolution: Security Through Diplomacy in Central America*. New York: Pantheon.

Black, George. 1981. *Triumph of the People*. London: Zed Press.

Blasier, Cole. 1967. "Studies in Social Revolution." *Latin American Research Review* 2 (3): 28–64.

BNN (Banco Nacional de Nicaragua). 1975, 1977. *Informe Anual*. Managua: BNN.

Booth, John. 1985. *The End and the Beginning*. 2nd ed. Boulder: Westview Press.

———. 1991. "Socioeconomic and Political Roots of National Revolts in Central America." *Latin American Research Review* 26 (1): 33–73.

Booth, John, and Thomas Walker. 1989. *Understanding Central America*. Boulder: Westview Press.

Bottomore, Thomas. 1964. *Elites and Society*. New York: Basic Books.

Brockett, Charles. 1989. "Cycles of Protest and the Impact of Repression in Central America." Paper presented at the XV International Congress of the Latin American Studies Association.

———. 1990. *Land, Power and Poverty: Agrarian Transformation and Political Conflict in Central America.* Boston: Allen and Unwin.

———. 1992. "Measuring Political Violence and Land Inequality in Central America." *American Political Science Review* 86 (1): 169–76.

Bulmer-Thomas, Victor. 1987. *The Political Economy of Central America Since 1920.* Cambridge: Cambridge University Press.

Camacho, Daniel, and Rafael Menjivar. 1985. *Movimientos Populares en Centroamérica.* San Jose: EDUCA.

Cámara de Comercio de Nicaragua. 1991. *Lista de Importadores.* Managua: Cámara de Comercio.

Cardoso, Fernando. 1967. "The Industrial Elite." In *Elites in Latin America,* ed. Seymour Martin Lipset and Aldo Solari. London: Oxford University.

———. 1968. *Cuestiones de Sociología del Desarrollo.* Santiago de Chile: Editorial Universitario.

———. 1986. "Entrepreneurs and the Transition: The Brazilian Case." In *Transitions from Authoritarian Rule: Prospects for Democracy,* ed. Guillermo O'Donnell, Philippe Schmitter, and Laurence Whitehead. Baltimore: Johns Hopkins University Press.

Cardoso, Fernando, and Enzo Faletto. 1979. *Dependency and Development in Latin America.* Berkeley and Los Angeles: University of California Press.

Carmona, Fernando, ed. 1983. *Nicaragua: La Estrategia de la Victoria.* 2nd. ed. Mexico: Editorial Nuestro Tiempo.

Castillo, Carlos. 1966. *Growth and Integration in Central America.* New York: Praeger.

Chamorro, Pedro Joaquín. 1948. "El Derecho del Trabajo." Thesis. Mexico: National Autonomous University.

———. 1990. *Diario Político.* Managua: Editorial Nueva Nicaragua.

Chavarría, Ricardo. 1986. "The Revolutionary Insurrection." In *Revolutions: Theoretical, Comparative, and Historical Studies,* ed. Jack Goldstone. Orlando: Harcourt Brace Jovanovich.

Christian, Shirley. 1985. *Nicaragua: Revolution in the Family.* New York: Random House.

CIERA (Centro de Investigaciones y Estudios de Reforma Agraria). 1989. *La Reforma Agraria en Nicaragua, 1979–1989: Sistema Alimentario.* Managua: CIERA.

Close, David. 1988. *Nicaragua: Politics, Economics, and Society.* New York: Pinter.

Colburn, Forest. 1986. *Post-Revolutionary Nicaragua: State, Class and the Dilemmas of Agrarian Policy.* Berkeley and Los Angeles: University of California Press.

Cole, Alejandro. 1967. *145 Años de Historia Política de Nicaragua.* Managua: Instituto Histórico Centroamericano.

Colindres, Eduardo. 1976. "La Tenencia de la Tierra en El Salvador." *Estudios Centro Americanos* 31 (335/336): 463–72.

Collier, David. 1979. *The New Authoritarianism in Latin America.* Princeton: Princeton University Press.

CONAL (Comisión Nacional de Algodón). 1973. *Estadísticas del Algodón, 1950–1972.* Managua: CONAL.

———. 1979. *Lista de Productores de Algodón Inscritos en El Ministerio de Agricultura y Ganadería.* Managua: CONAL.

Córdova Rivas, Rafael. 1983. *Contribución a la Revolución.* Managua: Centro de Publicaciones de Avanzada.

COSEP (Consejo Superior de la Empresa Privada). 1980. "Análisis Sobre La Ejecución del Programa de Gobierno de Reconstrucción Nacional." Managua: COSEP.

Cruz, Ernesto. 1974. *Estrategia de Desarrollo para los Años 70.* Managua: INCAE.

Cruz, Ernesto, and Kenneth Hoadley. 1975. *Necesidad de Una Política Oficial Sobre Comercialización del Algodón de Nicaragua.* Managua: INCAE.

Davidheiser, Evelyn. 1992. "Strong States, Weak States: The Role of the State in Revolution." *Comparative Politics* 24 (4): 463–75.

Departamento de Ciencias Sociales. 1982. *Apuntes de Historia de Nicaragua.* Managua: Universidad Nacional Autonoma de Nicaragua (UNAN).

Deutsch, Karl. 1971. "Social Mobilization and Political Development." In *Political Development and Social Change,* ed. Jason Finkle and Richard Gable. 2nd ed. New York: John Wilks and Sons.

Diederich, Bernard. 1969. *Papa Doc: The Truth About Haiti Today.* New York: Mcgraw Hill.

———. 1978. *Trujillo: Death of the Goat.* New York: Markus Weiner.

———. 1981. *Somoza and the Legacy of U.S. Involvement in Central America.* New York: Dutton.

Dix, Robert. 1983. "The Varieties of Revolution." *Comparative Politics* 15 (3): 281–94.

———. 1984. "Why Revolutions Succeed and Fail." *Polity* 16 (3): 423–47.

Dodd, Thomas. 1992. *Managing Democracy in Central America, A Case Study: The United States Election Supervision in Nicaragua, 1927–1933.* New Brunswick: Transaction Books.

Dodson, Michael. 1988. "The Church and Political Struggle: Faith and Action in Central America." *Latin American Research Review* 23 (1): 230–43.

REFERENCES

Domhoff, G. William. 1990. *The Power Elite and the State.* New York: Aldine de Gruyter.

Doyle, William. 1988. *Origins of the French Revolution.* London: Oxford University Press.

Dunkerley, James. 1988. *Power in the Isthmus.* New York: Verso.

Durham, William. 1979. *Scarcity and Choice in Central America.* Palo Alto: Stanford University Press.

Easton, David. 1965. *A Systems Analysis of Political Life.* New York: Wiley.

Eckstein, Susan. 1989. "Power and Popular Protest in Latin America." In *Power and Popular Protest: Latin American Social Movements,* ed. Susan Eckstein. Berkeley and Los Angeles: University of California Press.

Evans, Peter. 1979. *Dependent Development: The Alliance of Multinational, State, and Capital in Brazil.* Princeton: Princeton University Press.

Evans, Peter, Dietrich Reuschemeyer, and Theda Skocpol, eds. 1985. *Bringing the State Back In.* New York: Cambridge University Press.

Fahri, Farideh. 1988. "State Disintegration and Urban-Based Revolutionary Crisis." *Comparative Political Studies* 21 (2): 231–56.

———. 1990. *States and Urban-Based Revolutions.* Chicago: University of Illinois Press.

FAO (Frente Amplio Opositor). 1978. "Al Heróico Pueblo de Nicaragua." Managua: FAO.

FER (Frente Estudiantil Revolucionario). 1975. *Historial del FSLN.* Managua: INIES archive.

Fernandez Holmann, Ernesto. 1975. *Nicaragua y las Compañías Transnacionales.* Managua: BCN.

Foro Popular. 1979. *Estudios Centro Americanos* 34 (371): 843–45.

Frank, Andre Gunder. 1967. *Capitalism and Underdevelopment in Latin America.* New York: Monthly Review Press.

FSLN (Frente Sandinista de Liberación Nacional). 1979. "Analysis of the Situation and Tasks of the Sandinista People's Revolution." Translated by the United States Department of State, Washington, D.C.

García Márquez, Gabriel and Jose Fajardo, eds. 1979. *Los Sandinistas.* Bogotá: Editorial La Oveja Negra.

Garthoff, Raymond. 1985. *Detente and Confrontation: American-Soviet Relations from Nixon to Reagan.* Washington: Brookings Institution.

Gerrity, Martin. 1965. *Beef Export Trade in Central America.* Washington: USDA.

Gerschenkron, Alexander. 1962. *Economic Backwardness in Historical Perspective.* Cambridge: Harvard University Press.

Gibson, Bill. 1987. "An Overview of the Nicaraguan Economy." In *The Political Economy of Revolutionary Nicaragua,* ed. Rose Spalding. Boston: Allen and Unwin.

Giddens, Anthony. 1973. *The Class Structure of the Advanced Societies.* New York: Harper and Row.

Gilbert, Dennis. 1988. *Sandinistas: The Party and the Revolution.* New York: Basil Blackwell.

Goff, Fred. 1970. "The Latin American Agribusiness Development Corporation." *North American Congress on Latin America* 4 (5): 1–15.

Goldfrank, Walter. 1979. "Theories of Revolution and Revolution Without Theory: The Case of Mexico." *Theory and Society* 7: 97–134.

Goldstone, Jack. 1980. "Theories of Revolution: The Third Generation." *World Politics* 32 (3): 425–53.

———. 1986. "Revolutions and Superpowers." In *Superpowers and Revolution,* ed. J. R. Adelman. New York: Praeger.

Goldstone, Jack, ed. 1991. "Ideology, Cultural Frameworks, and the Process of Revolution." *Theory and Society* 20 (4): 405–53.

Goldstone, Jack, Ted Gurr, Farrokh Moshiri, eds. 1991. *Revolutions of the Late Twentieth Century.* Boulder: Westview Press.

Goodwin, Jeff, and Theda Skocpol. 1989. "Explaining Revolutions in the Contemporary Third World." *Politics and Society* 17 (4): 489–509.

Gorman, Stephen. 1981. "Power and Consolidation in the Nicaraguan Revolution." *Journal of Latin American Studies* 13: 133–49.

Gould, Jeffery. 1987. "'For an Organized Nicaragua': Somoza and the Labor Movement, 1944–48." *Journal of Latin American Studies* 19: 353–87.

———. 1990. *To Lead as Equals: Rural Protest and Political Consciousness in Chinandega, Nicaragua, 1912–1979.* Chapel Hill: University of North Carolina Press.

Gourevitch, Peter. 1986. *Politics in Hard Times: Comparative Responses to International Economic Crisis.* Ithaca: Cornell University Press.

Gramsci, Antonio. 1971. *Selections from the Prison Notebooks.* New York: International Publishers.

Grijalva, César. 1991. *Los Mataderos de ENAMARA.* Document series. Managua: author.

Gurr, Ted. 1970. *Why Men Rebel.* Princeton: Princeton University Press.

Gutiérrez, Gustavo. 1988. "Historia del Movimiento Obrero en Nicaragua." *Cuadernos Centroamericanos de Historia* 2: 61–110.

REFERENCES

Gutiérrez, Pedro. 1978. *Breve Historia de la Cámara de Comercio.* Managua: Cámara de Comercio de Nicaragua.

Hart, John. 1987. *Revolutionary Mexico: The Coming and Process of the Mexican Revolution.* Berkeley and Los Angeles: University of California Press.

Higley, John, and Michael Burton. 1989. "The Elite Variable in Democratic Transitions and Breakdowns." *American Sociological Review* 54 (1): 17–32.

Hodges, Donald. 1986. *Intellectual Foundations of the Nicaraguan Revolution.* Austin: University of Texas Press.

Huntington, Samuel. 1968. *Political Order in Changing Societies.* New Haven: Yale University Press.

IBRD (International Bank of Reconstruction and Development). 1953. *The Economic Development of Nicaragua.* Baltimore: Johns Hopkins University Press.

IDB (Interamerican Development Bank). 1969. *Activities, 1961–68.* Washington: IDB.

———. 1975. *Fifteen Years of Activities, 1961–75.* Washington: IDB.

———. 1977, 1978. *Economic and Social Progress in Latin America.* Washington: IDB.

IHCA (Instituto Histórico Centroamericano). 1978. *Nicaragua: Analisis Interpretativa Provisional.* Managua: IHCA.

INCAE (Instituto Centroamericano de Administración de la Empresa). 1975. *Primera Encuesta Sobre El Empleo en las Zonas Urbanas de Nicaragua.* Managua: INCAE.

———. 1976. *Segunda Encuesta Sobre El Empleo en las Zonas Urbanas de Nicaragua.* Managua: INCAE.

Incer, Roberto. 1978. "Memorandum a Consejo Nacional de Planificación." Managua: Banco Central de Nicaragua.

INDE (Instituto Nicaragüense de Desarrollo). 1979. *El Sector Privado en La Insurección.* Managua: INDE.

Institute for the Comparative Study of Political Systems. 1967. *Nicaragua Election Factbook.* Washington: author.

Invernizzi, Gabriele, Francis Pissari, Jesus Ceberio, eds. 1986. *Sandinistas: Entrevistas a Humberto Ortega, Jaime Wheelock, y Bayardo Arce.* Managua: Editorial Nueva Nicaragua.

Jarquín, Edmundo. 1977. *Nicaragua: Notas Sobre Su Desarrollo Económico, Social, y Político.* Managua: Instituto Histórico Centroamericano.

———. 1978. *Análisis de la Situación Económica de Nicaragua.* León: Cámara de Indústria de León.

Johnson, John. 1958. *Political Change in Latin America: The Emergence of the Middle Sectors.* Palo Alto: Stanford University Press.

Jonas, Susanne. 1974. "La Ayuda Externa no Ayuda a la Integración Centroamericana." *Estudios Sociales Centroamericanos* 3: 35–74.

Klarén, Peter, and Thomas Bossert, eds. *Promise of Development: Theories of Change in Latin America.* Boulder: Westview Press.

Knight, Alan. 1986. *The Mexican Revolution.* 2 vols. Cambridge: Cambridge University Press.

Lachmann, Richard. 1989. "Elite Conflict and State Formation in 16th and 17th-Century England and France." *American Sociological Review* 54: 141–62.

———. 1990. "Class Formation Without Class Conflict: An Elite Conflict Theory of the Transition to Capitalism." *American Sociological Review* 55: 398–414.

Lake, Anthony. 1989. *Somoza Falling.* Boston: Houghton Mifflin.

LASA (Latin American Studies Association). 1984. *The Electoral Process in Nicaragua.* Pittsburgh: LASA.

———. 1990. *Electoral Democracy Under International Pressure.* Pittsburgh: LASA.

Latin American Bureau. 1985. *Haiti: Family Business.* London: Latin American Bureau.

LATINOCONSULT. 1975. *Mercadeo de Ganado y Carne Bovina en Nicaragua.* Managua: BNN and INFONAC.

Lenin, V. I. 1968. *Imperialism: The Highest Stage of Capitalism.* Moscow: Progress Publishers.

LeoGrande, William. 1979. "The Revolution in Nicaragua: Another Cuba?" *Foreign Affairs* 58 (1): 28–50.

Leonard, Thomas. 1984. *The United States and Central America, 1944–1949.* Montgomery: University of Alabama Press.

Lewis, Paul. 1980. *Paraguay Under Stroessner.* Chapel Hill: University of North Carolina Press.

Lindblom, Charles. 1977. *Politics and Markets: The World's Political-Economic Systems.* New York: Basic Books.

Lipset, Seymour Martin. 1967. "Values, Education, and Entrepreneurship." In *Elites in Latin America,* ed. Seymour Martin Lipset and Aldo Solari. London: Oxford University Press.

Maltes, Alejandro. 1960. *Evolución Histórica de la Doctrina Liberal.* Managua: Partido Liberal Nacional.

Martínez Cuenca, Alejandro. 1990. *Nicaragua: Una Década de Retos.* Managua: Editorial Nueva Nicaragua.

———. 1992. *Sandinista Economics in Practice: An Insider's Critical Reflections.* Boston: South End Press.

Martz, John. 1959. *Central America: The Crisis and the Challenge.* Chapel Hill: University of North Carolina Press.

Marx, Karl. 1984. *The 18th Brumaire of Louis Bonaparte.* New York: International Publishers.

Maxfield, Sylvia. 1990. *Governing Capital: International Finance and Mexican Politics.* Ithaca: Cornell University Press.

———. 1992. "The International Political Economy of Bank Nationalization: Mexico in Comparative Perspective." *Latin American Research Review* 27 (1): 75–103.

McCamant, John. 1968. *Development Assistance in Central America.* New York: Praeger.

McClintock, Cynthia. 1981. *Peasant Cooperatives and Political Change in Peru.* Princeton: Princeton University Press.

———. 1984. "Why Peasants Rebel." *World Politics* 37 (1): 48–84.

———. 1989. "Peru's Sendero Luminoso: Origins and Trajectory." In *Power and Popular Protest,* ed. Susan Eckstein. Berkeley and Los Angeles: University of California Press.

Menjívar, Rafael. 1974. "La Inversión no Directa en El Mercado Común Centroamericano." *Estudios Sociales Centroamericanos* 3: 75–123.

Midlarsky, Manus. 1988. "Rulers and Ruled: Patterned Inequality and the Onset of Mass Political Violence." *American Political Science Review* 82 (2): 491–509.

Midlarsky, Manus, and Kenneth Roberts. 1985. "Class, State, and Revolution in Central America." *Journal of Conflict Resolution* 29 (2): 163–93.

Migdal, Joel. 1974. *Peasants, Politics and Revolution.* Princeton: Princeton University Press.

Millett, Richard. 1977. *Guardians of the Dynasty.* Maryknoll, N.Y.: Orbis.

———. 1988. "Patria Libre." *Wilson Quarterly* 12 (1): 98–118.

Miranda, Carlos. 1990. *The Stroessner Era: Authoritarian Rule in Paraguay.* Boulder: Westview Press.

Montgomery, Tommie Sue. 1982. *Revolution in El Salvador.* Boulder: Westview Press.

Moore, Barrington. 1966. *Social Origins of Dictatorship and Democracy.* Boston: Beacon.

Mosca, Gaetano. 1939. *The Ruling Class.* New York: McGraw Hill.

Munro, Dana. 1918. *The Five Republics of Central America.* London: Oxford University Press.

———. 1964. *Intervention and Dollar Diplomacy in the Caribbean, 1900–1921*. Princeton: Princeton University Press.

North, Liisa. 1986. "Bitter Grounds: Roots of Revolt in El Salvador." In *Revolutions: Theoretical, Comparative, and Historical Studies*, ed. Jack Goldstone. Orlando: Harcourt Brace Jovanovich.

O'Donnell, Guillermo. 1973. *Modernization and Bureaucratic-Authoritarianism: Studies in South American Politics*. Berkeley and Los Angeles: University of California Press.

OEA (Organización de Estados Americanos). 1976. *Cuadros Estadísticos del Financimiento Externo*. Washington: OEA.

Ogliastri, Enrique. 1986. "Estado, Empresarios, Sindicatos, Trabajadores, y Administradores: Experiencias sobre Gerencia y Revolución en Nicaragua." Paper presented at the XIII Congress of the Latin American Studies Association, Boston, Mass.

Olson, Mancur. 1963. "Rapid Growth as a Destabilizing Force." *Journal of Economic History* 23 (4): 529–52.

———. 1965. *The Logic of Collective Action*. Cambridge: Harvard University Press.

Ortega, Alejandro. 1990. "Alimentos, Desarrollo, y Democrácia." *Cuadernos Empresariales* 25: 4–16.

Ortega, Humberto. 1979. *Cincuenta Años de Lucha Sandinista*. Mexico: Editorial Diogenes.

———. 1980. *La Estrategia de la Victoria*. Managua: Junta de Gobierno de Reconstrucción Nacional.

Paige, Jeffery. 1975. *Agrarian Revolution: Social Movements and Export-Agriculture in the Underdeveloped World*. New York: Free Press.

———. 1985. "Cotton and Revolution in Nicaragua." In *States Versus Markets in the World System*, ed. Peter Evans et al. Beverly Hills: Sage.

———. 1987. "Coffee and Politics in Central America." In *Crises in the Caribbean Basin*, ed. Richard Tardanico. Beverly Hills: Sage.

———. 1989. "Revolution and the Agrarian Bourgeoisie in Nicaragua." In *Revolution in the World System*, ed. Terry Boswell. New York: Greenwood Press.

Palmer, Steven. 1988. "Carlos Fonseca and the Construction of Sandinismo in Nicaragua." *Latin American Research Review* 23 (1): 91–109.

Pareto, Vilfredo. 1979. *The Rise and Fall of Elites: An Application of Theoretical Sociology*. New York: Arno.

Pastor, Robert. 1987. *Condemned to Repetition: The United States and Nicaragua*. Princeton: Princeton University Press.

PCN (Partido Conservador Nacional). 1958. *Primer Año de Acción Cívica y Lucha Parlementaria.* Managua: PCN.

Pearce, Jenny. 1986. *Promised Land: Peasant Rebellion in Chalatenango El Salvador.* London: Latin American Bureau.

Popkin, Samuel. 1979. *The Rational Peasant.* Berkeley and Los Angeles: University of California Press.

Portes, Alejandro. 1985. "Latin American Class Structures." *Latin American Research Review* 20 (3): 7–9.

Poulantzas, Nicos. 1973. *Political Power and Social Classes.* London: New Left Books.

———. 1974. *Fascism and Dictatorship.* London: New Left Books.

Powell, G. Bingham. 1982. *Contemporary Democracies: Participation, Stability, and Violence.* Cambridge: Harvard University Press.

Przeworski, Adam. 1986. "Some Problems in the Study of the Transition to Democracy." In *Transitions from Authoritarian Rule: Comparative Perspectives,* ed. Guillermo O'Donnell, Phillippe Schmitter, and Laurence Whitehead. Baltimore: Johns Hopkins University Press.

———. 1990. *Democracy and the Market: Political and Economic Reforms in Eastern Europe and Latin America.* London: Cambridge University Press.

Ramírez, Sergio. 1979. *El Pensamiento Vivo de Sandino.* 5th ed. San José: EDUCA.

———. 1981a. "Sobrevivientes del Náufragio." In *Estado y Clases Sociales en Nicaragua.* Managua: Asociación Nicaragüense de Ciencias Sociales.

———. 1981b. "Sandinismo, Hegemony, and Revolution." In *Revolution and Intervention in Nicaragua,* ed. Marlene Dixon and Susanne Jonas. San Francisco: Synthesis.

Remmer, Karen. 1989. *Military Rule in Latin America.* Boston: Unwin Hyman.

Remmer, Karen, and Gilbert Merkx. 1982. "Bureaucratic-Authoritarianism Revisited." *Latin American Research Review* 17 (2): 3–40.

Robelo, Alfonso. 1980. "Robelo Interviewed on Differences with Junta." *Foreign Broadcasting Information Service.* 30 April 1980: P6–P13.

Rogowski, Ronald. 1989. *Commerce and Coalitions: How Trade Affects Domestic Political Alignments.* Princeton: Princeton University Press.

Ropp, Steve. 1992. "Explaining the Long-Term Maintenance of a Military Regime: Panama before the U.S. Invasion." *World Politics* 44 (2): 210–34.

Rostow, Walt. 1960. *The Stages of Economic Growth.* New York: Cambridge University Press.

Roxborough, Ian. 1984. "Unity and Diversity in Latin American History." *Journal of Latin American Studies* 16: 126.

Ruíz, Henry. 1980. "La Montaña Era Como un Crisol Dónde se Forjaban los Mejores Cuadros." *Nicarauac* 1: 12–18.

Santos, Theotonio dos. 1970. "The Structure of Dependence." *American Economic Review* 60 (2):231–36.

Saragoza, Alex. 1988. *The Monterrey Elite and the Mexican State, 1880–1940.* Austin: University of Texas Press.

Schick, Rene. 1963. *Nicaragua y La Alianza para El Progreso.* Managua: BCN.

Schmitter, Philippe. 1972. *Autonomy or Dependence as Regional Outcome: Central America.* Berkeley and Los Angeles: University of California Press.

Schneider, Ben Ross. 1993. "The Career Connection: A Comparative Analysis of Bureaucratic Preferences and Insulation." *Comparative Politics* 25 (3): 331–50.

Scott, James. 1976. *The Moral Economy of the Peasant.* New Haven: Yale University Press.

———. 1977. "Hegemony and the Peasantry." *Politics and Society* 7 (3): 267–96.

Selser, Gregorio. 1979. *Sandino: General de Hombres Libres.* San José: EDUCA.

SIECA (Secretaría Permanente del Tratado General de Integración Económica Centroamericana). 1972. *Estadísticas sobre Alimentación y la Agricultura en Centroamérica.* Guatemala.

———. 1973a. *El Desarrollo Integrado de Centroamérica en la Presente Década.* BID: Washington.

———. 1973b. *Series Estadísticas Seleccionadas de Centroamerica.* Guatemala.

———. 1981a. *Estadísticas Macroecónmicas de Centroamérica.* Guatemala.

———. 1981b. *VII Compendio Estadistico Centroamericano.* Guatemala.

Skocpol, Theda. 1973. "A Critique of Barrington Moore's Social Origins of Democracy and Dictatorship." *Politics and Society* 4 (1): 1–34.

———. 1979. *States and Social Revolutions: A Comparative Analysis of France, Russia and China.* New York: Cambridge University Press.

———. 1982. "What Makes Peasants Revolutionary?" *Comparative Politics* 14 (3): 351–75.

Smith, Peter. 1979. *Labyrinths of Power: Political Recruitment in Twentieth Century Mexico.* Princeton: Princeton University Press.

Snyder, Richard. 1992. "Explaining Transitions from Neopatrimonial Dictatorships." *Comparative Politics* 24 (4): 379–99.

Soberg-Shugart, Matthew. 1989. "Patterns of Revolution." *Theory and Society* 18: 249–71.

Spalding, Rose, ed. 1987. *The Political Economy of Revolutionary Nicaragua.* Boston: Allen and Unwin.

———. 1991. "Capitalists and Revolution: State-Private Sector Relations in Revolutionary Nicaragua." Paper presented at the XVI Congress of the Latin American Studies Association, Washington, D.C.

Stahler-Sholk, Richard. 1984. "The National Bourgeoisie in Post-Revolutionary Nicaragua." *Comparative Politics* 16 (3): 253–76.

Stepan, Alfred. 1985. "State Power and the Strength of Civil Society in the Southern Cone of Latin America." In *Bringing the State Back In*, ed. Peter Evans, Deitrich Reuschemeyer, and Theda Skocpol. New York: Cambridge University Press.

Stevenson, Joseph. 1964. *Cotton Production in Central America*. Washington: USDA.

Stone, Samuel. 1982. *La Dinastía de Los Conquistadores*. 3rd ed. San Jose: EDUCA.

———. 1990. *The Heritage of the Conquistadors: Ruling Classes in Central America from the Conquest to the Sandinistas*. Lincoln: University of Nebraska Press.

Strachan, Harry. 1976. *Family and Other Business Groups in Economic Development: The Case of Nicaragua*. New York: Praeger.

Taylor, Charles, and David Jodice, eds. 1983. *World Handbook of Political and Social Indicators*. 3rd ed. New Haven: Yale University Press.

Tilly, Charles. 1973. "Does Modernization Breed Revolution?" *Comparative Politics* 5 (3): 425–47.

———. 1978. *From Mobilization to Revolution*. London: Addison-Wesley.

Tilly, Louise, and Charles Tilly. 1981. *Class Conflict and Collective Action*. London: Sage.

Tirado, Victor, Humberto Ortega, and Tomás Borge. 1982. *Carlos Fonseca Siempre*. Managua: Departamento de Propaganda y Educación Política del FSLN.

Torres-Rivas, Edelberto. 1981. *Interpretación del Desarrollo Social Centroamericano*. 7th ed. San José: EDUCA.

———. 1983. *Crisis del Poder en Centroamérica*. San José: EDUCA.

Trimberger, Ellen Kay. 1978. *Revolution from Above*. New Brunswick, N.J.: Transaction.

United States Department of State. 1988. *Nicaraguan Biographies: A Resource Book*. Washington: Department of State.

Valenzuela, Arturo. 1989. "Chile: Origins, Consolidation, and Breakdown of a Democratic Regime." In *Democracy in Developing Countries: Latin America*, ed. Larry Diamond, Juan Linz, and Seymour Martin Lipset. New York: Lynne Reiner.

Valenzuela, J. Samuel, and Arturo Valenzuela. 1978. "Modernization and Dependency: Alternative Perspectives in the Study of Latin American Underdevelopment." *Comparative Politics* 10 (4): 535–57.

———. 1986. *Military Rule in Chile: Dictatorship and Oppositions.* Baltimore: Johns Hopkins University Press.

Vargas, Oscar René. 1990. *Nicaragua: Los Partidos Políticos y La Búsqueda de un Nuevo Modelo.* Managua: ECOTEXTURA.

———. 1991. *A Dónde Va Nicaragua.* Managua: Nicarao.

Vilas, Carlos. 1985. *The Sandinista Revolution.* New York: Monthly Review Press.

———. 1991. "Clase, Linaje y Política." *Crítica* 2 (1): 14–25.

———. 1992. "Family Affairs: Class, Lineage, and Politics in Contemporary Nicaragua." *Journal of Latin American Studies* 24: 309–41.

Walker, David. 1986. *Kinship, Business, and Politics: The Martinez del Rio Family in Mexico, 1824–1867.* Austin: University of Texas Press.

Walker, Thomas. 1970. *The Christian Democratic Movement in Nicaragua.* Tucson: University of Arizona Press.

———. 1986. *Nicaragua: The Land of Sandino.* 2nd ed. Boulder: Westview Press.

Walker, Thomas, ed. 1982. *Nicaragua in Revolution.* New York: Praeger.

———. 1985. *Nicaragua: The First Five Years.* New York: Praeger.

Wallerstein, Immanuel. 1982. *World-Systems Analysis: Theory and Methodology.* Beverly Hills: Sage.

Warnken, Philip. 1974. *An Analysis of Agricultural Production in Nicaragua.* Washington: Agency for International Development.

Wasserman, Mark. 1984. *Capitalists, Caciques, and Revolution.* Chapel Hill: University of North Carolina Press.

Weber, Max. 1964. "Bureaucracy." In *From Max Weber: Essays in Sociology,* ed. Hans Gerth and C. W. Mills. New York: Oxford University Press.

———. 1985. *The Protestant Ethic and the Spirit of Capitalism.* London: Unwin.

Webre, Stephen. 1979. *José Napoleon Duarte and the Christian Democratic Party in Salvadoran Politics, 1960–1972.* Baton Rouge: Louisiana State University Press.

Weeks, John. 1985. *The Economies of Central America.* New York: Holmes and Meier.

———. 1986. "An Interpretation of the Central American Crisis." *Latin American Research Review* 21 (3): 31–54.

Wheelock, Jaime. 1985. *Imperialismo y Dictadura.* Managua: Editorial Nueva Nicaragua.

Wiarda, Howard. 1982. *Political and Social Change in Latin America: The Distinct Tradition.* Amherst: University of Massachusetts Press.

Wickham-Crowley, Timothy. 1989a. "Understanding Failed Revolution in El Salvador." *Politics and Society* 17 (4): 511–37.

———. 1989b. "Winners, Losers, and Also-Rans: Toward a Comparative Sociology of Latin American Guerrilla Movements." in *Power and Popular Protest*, ed. Susan Eckstein. Berkeley and Los Angeles: University of California Press.

———. 1992. *Guerrillas and Revolution in Latin America*. Princeton: Princeton University Press.

Wilkie, James. 1974. *Statistics and National Policy*. Berkeley and Los Angeles: University of California Press.

Wilkie, James, and Adam Perkal, eds. 1984. *Statistical Abstract of Latin America*. Berkeley and Los Angeles: University of California Press.

Williams, Robert. 1986. *Export Agriculture and the Crisis in Central America*. Chapel Hill: University of North Carolina Press.

Wionczek, Michael. 1972. "The Central American Common Market." In *International Economic Integration*, ed. Peter Robson. Harmondsworth: Penguin.

Wolf, Eric. 1969. *Peasant Wars of the Twentieth Century*. New York: Harper and Row.

Woodward, Ralph Lee, Jr. 1984. "The Rise and Decline of Liberalism in Central America." *Journal of Interamerican Studies and World Affairs* 26 (3): 291–312.

———. 1985. *Central America: A Nation Divided*. 2nd ed. London: Oxford University.

Wynia, Gary. 1972. *Politics and Planners: Economic Development Policy in Central America*. Madison: University of Wisconsin.

Zapata, Francisco. 1990. "Towards a Latin American Sociology of Labour." *Journal of Latin American Studies* 22 (2): 375–402.

Zeitlin, Maurice, and Richard Ratcliff. 1975. "Research Methods for the Analysis of the Internal Structure of Dominant Classes: The Case of Landlords and Capitalists in Chile." *Latin American Research Review* 10 (3): 561.

———. 1988. *Landlords and Capitalists: The Dominant Class in Chile*. Princeton: Princeton University Press.

Zuvekas, Clarence. 1992. "Alternative Perspectives on Central American Economic Recovery and Development." *Latin American Research Review* 27 (1): 125–50.

Interviews

Leonel Argüello, 6 March 1991.

William Baez, cofounder of INDE, 31 October and 7 December 1988.

Emilio Baltodano, 26 July 1989.

REFERENCES

Jaime Bengochea, cofounder of INDE and former president of the Nicaraguan Chamber of Industry, 22 April 1991.

Enrique Bolaños, 25 June 1989.

Luis Carrión Montoya, 2 June 1991.

Gastón Castillo Fletes, secretary of the Autonomous Confederation of Nicaraguan Workers (CTNa), 17 September 1991.

Arturo Cruz, 31 October 1991, Washington, D.C.

Gilberto Cuadra, member of the Chamber of Construction and current president of COSEP, 9 April 1991.

Joaquín Cuadra Chamorro, corporate lawyer of the BANAMER group and coffee grower, 28 July 1991.

Enrique Dreyfus, former BANAMER member, 30 July 1991.

James Fitzgerald, 10 November 1987, Washington, D.C.

Ramiro Gurdián, former cotton grower and current COSEP president, 20 June 1991.

Reinaldo Hernández, former president of the Chamber of Commerce of Nicaragua, 27 August 1991.

Edmundo Jarquín, 7 May 1991.

Juan López, former president of the Chamber of Commerce, 16 May 1991.

Felipe Mántica Abaunza, 19 February 1991.

Edgard Parrales, 5 March 1991.

Gastón Ramírez, former Vice-President of Industry, Meat Corporation of Nicaragua, 22 July 1991.

Sergio Ramírez, 25 April 1991.

Samuel Santos, 6 May 1991.

Alejandro Solórzano, Socialist labor leader in the 1970s and at present, 28 May 1991.

Victor Tirado, 28 August 1991.

Carlos Tunnerman, 5 August 1991.

Viron Vaky, former assistant secretary for Inter-American Affairs, 8 October 1987, Washington, D.C.

Newspapers

Barricada

New York Times

La Prensa

El Semanario

INDEX

Actividades Bursatiles de Fomento, 124
Agency for International Development (USAID), 56, 63, 65, 79, 92, 111, 122
Agro-industry, 51–52, 54–55, 66–75, 81–85
Agüero, Fernando, 57, 105, 107–08, 110, 115, 135; and 1967 UNO campaign, 62; and rivalry with Chamorro, 107; and transitional junta, 108; and withdrawal from 1963 presidential race, 58
Alliance for Progress, 4, 16–17, 59, 72, 88, 106
Alvarez, Emilio, 127, 136
Amador Kühl, Mario, 164
Anderson, Jack, 128–29
Arce, Bayardo, 145–48
Area of People's Property (APP), 169
Argentina, 38
Argüello, Leonel, 163, 166, 168
Argüello, Uriel, 115
Argüello Cardenal, José, 121
Argüello Hurtado, Roberto, 139, 157
Argüello Hurtado, Xavier, 147–48
Argüello Téfel, Roberto, 155
Association of Professionals-Heroes and Martyrs, 172
Association of Rural Workers (ATC), 130, 141, 144, 153, 165, 174
Authentic Conservative Party, 111, 116

Baez Sacasa, William, 61, 79, 112, 126, 140, 149, 154, 163, 174
Baltodano, Alvaro, 131
Baltodano, Emilio, 130–31, 134, 146, 158

Banco Central de Nicaragua (BCN), 63, 141, 149
Banco de América (BANAMER), 48–50, 59–60, 64–65, 71, 76–77, 80, 118–19, 122, 124, 132, 141, 152, 154–55, 168; Financiera de Inversiones Agropecuaria (FIA) of, 152, 154–55; founding families of, 48–49; SOVIPE construction company of, 49, 58, 112–13, 124
Benard, Adolfo, 48
Banco Nacional de Nicaragua (BNN), 48, 52, 54, 60, 65–66, 111, 120, 122, 141, 151; and cotton, 52, 66–67, 151
Banco Nicaragüense (BANIC), 49–50, 59–60, 64–65, 76–77, 80, 91, 118–19, 122, 124, 132, 141, 151–52, 155, 168; CONTECSA of, 112; Financiera de Vivienda of, 49; founding families of, 49
Bank of Caley-Dagnall, 71, 169
Batista, Fulgencio, 27
beef, 68–70; and Amerrisque slaughterhouse, 121; and CARNIC slaughterhouse, 69–70, 78, 121, 123, 125; effect on peasants, 93; and EMPANICSA slaughterhouse, 69–70, 94, 121; and Federation of Nicaraguan Ranchers' Associations (FAGANIC), 120, 162–63, 170; and IGOSA slaughterhouse, 70, 121; and Institute of Cattle Development (IFAGAN), 68–69, 78, 94, 121; and Nicaraguan Association of Cattle Ranchers (ASGANIC), 68, 121, 162; and San Martín slaughterhouse, 121
Bengochea, Jaime, 61, 114, 157

INDEX

Bonilla, Adolfo, 153
Borge, Tomás, 53, 93, 104, 129, 145–46
Brazil, 38, 77
Broad Opposition Front (FAO), 143–44, 146, 153, 157–60, 164, 167, 176

Callejas Deshon, Alfonso, 92, 116–18, 155
Cardenal, Ernesto, 159
Cardenal, Fernando, 132–35, 159, 163, 172
Cardenal, Francisco, 163, 167, 173
Carrión Cruz, Luis, 129, 145
Carrión Montoya, Luis, 49, 80, 165, 168
Castillo, Chema, 115
Castillo, Ernesto, 130–31, 134
Castillo, Julio, 165
Castro, Fidel, 55–56, 70
Centeno, Carlos, 130
Central American Bank of Economic Integration (CABEI), 65
Central American Common Market (CACM), 4, 16, 36, 59, 72, 77, 79, 88
Central American Institute of Business Administration (INCAE), 61–63, 79, 105, 112–14, 120; and minifaldas, 63
César, Alfredo, 130, 164
Chamorro, Alberto, 68
Chamorro, Edmundo, 127
Chamorro, Filadelfo, 115
Chamorro, Pedro Joaquín, 9, 12, 107–10, 118–19, 129, 161, 169; assassination of, 138–39; and Conservative Party, 62; and Democratic Liberation Union (UDEL), 116, 135–36; and Document of the, 27, 115; and *La Prensa*, 51–52; and Los Doce, 135–36; and National Union of Popular Action (UNAP), 53; and Nicaraguan Opposition Union (FAO), 55; and opposition to Somoza, 62; and popular struggles, 91; and rivalry with Fernando Agüero, 107–08
Chamorro, Violeta de, 164, 173
Chamorro, Xavier, 118
China, 25–26
Chinandega Cotton Growers' Association. *See* cotton

Christian Democratic Party (PDC). *See* El Salvador
Christian Democratic Popular Movement (MPDC), 54–55, 57–58, 91, 105, 107–08; and coffee growers, 71–72; and Molinos de Nicaragua, 71
Confederation of Nicaraguan Workers (CTN). *See* Labor unions
Conservative Democratic Party. *See* National Conservative Party
Conservative National Action (ANC). *See* National Conservative Party
Contreras, Eduardo, 129
Coordinating Commission of National Dialogue. *See* Democratic Liberation Union
Córdova Rivas, Rafael, 53, 55, 111, 115, 134, 148, 157, 163, 169, 173
Coronel Kautz, Ricardo, 130, 133–34
Corporación de Finanzas Transmundiales, 124
Corrales, General Humberto, 123
cotton, 51–52, 66–68; and Chinandega Cotton Growers' Association, 151; and effect on peasants, 90–91; and León Cotton Growers' Association, 151; and Western Cotton Growers' Association, 151
Council of Union Unity (CUS). *See* Labor unions
Cruz, Arturo, 53, 112, 119, 133–35, 140, 168, 173
Cruz, Ernesto, 62, 112
Cuadra, Gilberto, 168
Cuadra, Jaime, 165
Cuadra Chamorro, Joaquín, 130–32, 134, 140, 146, 154, 164, 168
Cuadra Lacayo, Joaquín, 131
Cuba, 24, 27, 29, 42

Delgadillo, César, 147
Democratic Liberation Union (UDEL), 116, 118–19, 125–27, 132, 134–36, 139–40, 142–44, 154; Coordinating Commission of National Dialogue of, 134–35
D'Escoto, Miguel, 128, 130–31, 133
Díaz, Porfirio, 33
Dominican Republic, 29

INDEX

Dreyfus, Enrique, 49, 61, 79, 112, 114, 118, 124, 126, 133, 140, 149–50, 154, 163, 173
Duvalier, "Baby Doc," 29

earthquake of 1972, 108–12
Ecclesial Base Communities (CEB), 172, 268
El Chaparral, 55–56, 104
El Salvador, 6, 8, 23, 27–28, 88; agroexports of, 74–76; Christian Democratic Party (PDC) of, 98, 100; death squads of, 99, 101; economic elites of, 73–76; and effect of agro-industry on peasantry, 95–97; guerrilla armies of, 100; and land reform, 99–100, 102; military of, 102–03; National Democratic Union (UDN) of, 98, 100, 107; National Revolutionary Movement (MNR) of, 98, 100, 107; Popular Forum of, 98; and Soccer War, 97; United Confederation of Salvadoran Workers (CUTS), 98–99
Espinoza, José, 142

Farabundo Martí National Liberation Front (FMLN), 8, 88, 102
Federation of Health Workers (FETSALUD). *See* Sandinista National Liberation Front
Federation of Nicaraguan Ranchers' Associations (FAGANIC). *See* beef
Federation of Workers of Managua (FTM). *See* Labor unions
Fernández-Holmann, Ernesto, 49, 119, 124, 152, 154
Financiera de Inversiones Agropecuraria (FIA). *See* Banco de América
Fonseca, Carlos, 53, 93, 95, 104, 110, 127, 129, 161

García, Edgar, 130
García, General Arnoldo, 69
General Confederation of Workers (CGT). *See* Labor unions
General Treaty of Central American Integration, 56
Governing Junta of National Reconstruction (JRN), 164–66, 168–69

Guandique, Felix, 134
Guerrero Montalvan, Salvador, 60
Gutierrez, Carlos, 132, 134
Gutierrez, Juan Ignacio, 163
Guzmán, Fernando, 132, 147–48, 172

Haiti, 29–30
Hanon, Mario, 175
Hassan, Moises, 163–64, 173
Hernández, Reinaldo, 124–26, 143, 150–51, 173, 175
Holmann, Carlos, 49
Hueck, Cornelio, 190, 211

Incer, Odell, 165
Independent Liberal Party (PLI), 45–46, 60, 103, 159–60
Industrial Association of Nicaragua, 60
Ingenio San Antonio (ISA). *See* sugar
Institute of Cattle Development (IFAGAN). *See* beef
Interamerican Development Bank (IDB), 64–65, 122, 162
International Bank for Reconstruction and Development (IBRD), 47, 50, 122, 162
Iran, 29

Jarquín, Antonio, 142, 153

Labor unions, 103–05, 172; and Confederation of Nicaraguan Workers (CTN), 127, 142, 159–60, 172; and Council of Union Unity (CUS), 172; and Federation of Workers of Managua (FTM), 103; and General Confederation of Workers (CGT), 103–05; and Independent General Confederation of Workers (CGTi), 105, 113, 116, 127, 142, 153, 172; and Sandinista Confederation of Workers (CST), 172, 174; and Syndicate of Carpenters, Bricklayers, and Masons (SCAAS), 105, 113; and Union of Nicaraguan Employees (UNE), 144, 172; and Workers' Front, 142
Lacayo, Danilo, 115
Lacayo Farfán, Enrique, 55
Lainéz, Francisco, 63, 116–18

INDEX

Lang, Guillermo, 115
Latin American Agribusiness Development Corporation (LAAD), 78, 91
León Cotton Growers' Association. *See* cotton
Lewites, Herty, 127, 130
Liberal Constitutionalist Movement (MLC), 80, 107, 115, 160, 164
López, Julio, 145–46, 163
López Pérez, Rigoberto, 53
Los Doce, 134, 139–40, 145–47, 157–60, 167
Lovo Cordero, Adolfo, 108

Mántica, Felipe, 49, 79, 112, 114, 124, 126, 130, 132–34, 139–40, 154
Mántica Abaunza, Felipe, 60, 62
Marenco, Dionisio, 130, 132
Marin, Wilfredo, 121
Martínez, Juan, 181
Martínez, Rafael, 165
Martínez Cuenca, Alejandro, 164, 169, 172
Martínez Lacayo, General Roberto, 108
Mayorga, Roberto, 164, 168, 172
Mayorga, Silvio, 53, 93–94, 104
Mexico, 29, 33
Ministry of Agricultural Development and Agrarian Reform (MIDINRA), 170
Miranda, Enrique, 121
Montealegre, Horacio, 92
Montealegre, Jaime, 143
Montealegre, Tomás, 92
Montealegre Callejas, Eduardo, 47–50, 60–61, 115, 131–32, 152, 155
Montealegre Lacayo, Alfredo, 173
Montealegre Lacayo, Haroldo, 143, 173
Montiel, William, 69
Montiel Argüello, Alejandro, 63, 115
Morales, Jaime, 118, 152
Morales, Nicolas, 127

National Autonomous University of Nicaragua (UNAN), 53, 61, 93, 104, 144
National Conservative Party (PCN), 44–46, 62, 103, 132; and Authentic Conservative Party, 111, 116; and Conservative Democratic Party, 111, 116; and Conservative National Action (ANC), 111, 115; General Emiliano Chamorro of, 46; and Pact of the Generals, 46, 54, 103; split of, 111; Zacundos of, 111, 115, 127, 135, 140
National Cotton Commission (CONAL), 66–68, 151, 162
National Democratic Union (UDN). *See* El Salvador
National Development Bank (BND), 168, 170
National Development Institute (INFONAC), 48, 63, 68, 80, 111, 120–23, 129, 141, 151
National Guard, 45–46, 62, 64, 90, 93–94, 105, 111, 132–33, 138, 148, 158; offensive against Sandinistas of, 129
National Liberal Party (PLN), 44–45, 57–58, 103, 107, 148–50, 153, 158; René Schick of, 59–60, 62; and transitional junta, 108
National Opposition Union (UNO), 55, 62
National Patriotic Front (FPN), 160–64, 167; Program of National Reconstruction of, 163–64
National Revolutionary Movement (MNR). *See* El Salvador
National Sugar Company (CANSA), 71, 91, 122
National Union of Popular Action (UNAP), 53, 119
Nicaraguan Agricultural Institute (IAN), 92
Nicaraguan Association of Cattle Ranchers (ASGANIC). *See* beef
Nicaraguan Association of Educators (ANDEN). *See* Sandinista National Liberation Front
Nicaraguan Democratic Movement (MDN), 143–44, 146–49, 151–52, 159, 164–65, 169, 174–75
Nicaraguan Development Foundation (FUNDE), 79, 108, 163
Nicaraguan Institute of Development (INDE), 60–63, 79–80, 112–14, 134, 143, 149, 151, 156, 163, 165, 172, 174; and First Convention of the Private Sector, 112
Nicaraguan Social Christian Party (PSCN), 54, 57–58, 62, 107, 147, 160, 164

INDEX

Nicaraguan Socialist Party (PSN), 53, 103–05, 107, 142, 154
Noriega, Manuel, 30, 33
Nuñez, Carlos, 145

Obando y Bravo, Monsignor Miguel, 134–35
Olama/Mellojones, 55–56, 60
Ortega, Daniel, 115, 129, 164, 172
Ortega, Humberto, 127–30, 174

Paguaga, Edmundo, 111
Palazio, Ernesto, 143
Pallais Debayle, Luis, 123
Pallais Debayle, Noel, 63, 115
Panamerican Development Fund (PADF), 61–62, 79
Parrales, Edgard, 159
Pasos, Carlos, 127
Pasos, Luis, 127, 136
Pastora, Eden, 148
Pellas Chamorro, Alfredo, 48, 115, 130–32, 150, 154–55, 165
Peñas Rivas, Silvio, 139
People's Social Christian Party (PPSC), 135, 147, 159
Pereira, Enrique, 49, 119, 132
Pérez, Carlos Andres, 133
Peru, 24, 39
Pinochet, Augusto, 30–32
Popular Forum. *See* El Salvador
Porras, Adonis, 123
Proletarian Tendency (TP), 129–31, 136, 144–47, 171
Prolonged Popular War (GPP), 129–31, 136, 144–47, 171

Ramírez, Sergio, 127–28, 130–32, 146–47, 153, 157, 159–60, 164, 170–72
revolution, 14–43, 177–87; and dependency theory, 35–36; and modernization, 15–21; and multiple sovereignty, 20; and rational choice, 18–19; and role of elites, 34–42; and role of peasantry, 21–25, 86–88; and state autonomy, 25–34
Revolutionary Students' Front (FER), 144
Ríos, Abner, 69
Rivas Gasteazoro, Eduardo, 147, 168
Rivas Gasteazoro, Noel, 147–48, 168
Robelo, Alfonso, 62, 79, 111, 124, 126, 134, 140, 143, 147–48, 151, 153, 157, 159–60, 163–64, 168–69, 173–75; and Governing Junta of National Reconstruction (JRN), 164; and Nicaraguan Democratic Movement (MDN), 143
Robelo, Mauricio, 60
Robelo, Rodolfo, 115
Ruíz, Henry, 129, 146, 172–73

Sacasa Guerrero, Alfredo, 80
Sacasa Guerrero, Ramiro, 80, 108, 115, 134, 136
Salazar, Jorge, 134, 173, 175
Sánchez, Domingo, 142, 153
Sandinista Confederation of Workers (CST). *See* Labor unions
Sandinista Defense Committees (CDS). *See* Sandinista National Liberation Front
Sandinista National Liberation Front (FSLN), 88, 138–42, 153–54, 163, 165, 170–76; Association of Professionals-Heroes and Martyrs of, 172; and economic elites, 3–4, 8–11, 128–137; Federation of Health Workers (FETSALUD) of, 172; Nicaraguan Association of Educators (ANDEN) of, 144, 172; offensive of 1963, 93; offensive of 1967, 94; Programa Sandinista of, 94; raid on National Palace by, 148; reunification of, 161–62; Sandinista Defense Committees (CDS) of, 172–74; Sandinista Youth Organization (JS-19) of, 172; Tercerista faction of, 129–33, 140, 145–48, 154, 159–60, 171–72
Sandino, Augusto César, 3, 45, 96, 68, 159
Santos, Samuel, 147–48
Secretariat of Central American Economic Integration (SIECA), 63, 65
Sendero Luminoso, 24
Serrano, Gilberto, 166
Serrano Caldera, Alejandro, 146
Sevilla Sacasa, Guillermo, 63, 65, 129
Schick, René, 59–60, 62. *See also* National Liberal Party

Smith, Adán, 69
Solórzano, Alfredo, 49
Somoza Debayle, Anastasio, 3, 11, 62–63; and assassination of Chamorro, 139–40; and business lockout, 149; and Carter administration, 145; and cattle ranching, 69; corruption of, 110–12; and economic elites, 64, 76–77, 114, 118–19, 149–50; election of, 115; and First Convention of the Private Sector, 114; investments of, 80, 108, 123–24; and Kupia Kumi, 108; and minifaldas, 63–64; and Plasmaferesis, 139; and sugar production, 70; War Council of, 116
Somoza Debayle, Luis, 53–56; and agrarian reform, 91; and cattle ranching, 69; death of, 62; election of, 62
Somoza García, General Anastasio, 44–47, 50–52, 93, 103–04, 110
Somoza Portocarrero, Anastasio, 139
Sotelo, Casmiro, 131, 134
SOVIPE construction company. *See* Banco de América
Spencer, Donald, 123
Stroessner, Alfredo, 30, 32
sugar, 64, 70–71; and effect on peasants, 91; and Ingenio San Antonio (ISA), 45, 70, 122, 125, 141, 170; structure of ownership of, 70–71
Superior Council of Private Enterprise (COSEP), 140, 142–43, 156, 161–62, 164–66, 172–74
Superior Council of Private Initiative (COSIP), 60–63, 79, 112, 114, 126, 134
Syndicate of Carpenters, Bricklayers and Masons (SCAAS). *See* Labor unions

Téfel, Reynaldo Antonio, 53, 55, 107, 135, 159, 160, 164
Tercerista faction. *See* Sandinista Front for National Liberation
Tijerino, Juan, 165
Tirado, Victor, 156
Torres, Manuel, 140, 149, 151, 168, 172–73
Torrijos, General Omar, 32–33, 145
Trujillo, Rafael, 29
Tunnerman, Carlos, 53, 128, 134, 146, 158, 164, 172

Union of Agricultural Producers of Nicaragua (UPANIC), 162, 166, 173, 175
Union of Nicaraguan Employees (UNE). *See* Labor unions
United People's Movement (MPU), 145–46, 154, 159, 172
United States of America, 44–45, 56, 63, 65, 102–03, 157–60, 162
University of Central America (UCA), 61, 79, 105, 144

Vaky, Viron, 159
Valle, Pablo, 69
Vance, Cyrus, 159
Venezuela, 39–40
Vietnam, 24
Villa, Julio, 49

Western Cotton Growers' Association. *See* cotton
Wheelock, Jaime, 118, 129, 145–46, 172
Workers' Front. *See* Labor unions
World Bank. *See* International Bank for Reconstruction and Development

Zancudos. *See* National Conservative Party

Augsburg College
Lindell Library
Minneapolis, MN 55454

Augsburg College
Lindell Library
Minneapolis, MN 55454